New York
2010

WHAT'S NEW | WHAT'S ON | WHAT'S BEST

www.timeout.com/newyork

Contents

Published by Time Out Guides Ltd
Universal House
251 Tottenham Court Road
London W1T 7AB
Tel: + 44 (0)20 7813 3000
Fax: + 44 (0)20 7813 6001
Email: guides@timeout.com
www.timeout.com

Managing Director Peter Fiennes
Editorial Director Ruth Jarvis
Business Manager Daniel Allen
Editorial Manager Holly Pick
Assistant Management Accountant Ija Krasnikova

Time Out Guides is a wholly owned subsidiary of Time Out Group Ltd.

© **Time Out Group Ltd**
Chairman Tony Elliott
Chief Executive Officer David King
Group General Manager/Director Nichola Coulthard
Time Out Communications Ltd MD David Pepper
Time Out International Ltd MD Cathy Runciman
Time Out Magazine Ltd Publisher/Managing Director Mark Elliott
Production Director Mark Lamond
Group IT Director Simon Chappell
Marketing & Circulation Director Catherine Demajo

Time Out and the Time Out logo are trademarks of Time Out Group Ltd.

This edition first published in Great Britain in 2009 by Ebury Publishing
A Random House Group Company
Company information can be found on www.randomhouse.co.uk
Random House UK Limited Reg. No. 954009
10 9 8 7 6 5 4 3 2 1

Distributed in the US by Publishers Group West
Distributed in Canada by Publishers Group Canada

For further distribution details, see www.timeout.com

ISBN: 978-1-84670-136-8

A CIP catalogue record for this book is available from the British Library.

Printed and bound in Germany by Appl.

The Random House Group Limited supports The Forest Stewardship Council (FSC), the leading international forest certification organisation. All our titles that are printed on Greenpeace approved FSC certified paper carry the FSC logo. Our paper procurement policy can be found at www.rbooks.co.uk/environment.

Time Out carbon-offsets all its flights with Trees for Cities (www.treesforcities.org).

New York Shortlist

The **Time Out New York Shortlist 2010** is one of a series of annual guides that draws on Time Out's background as a magazine publisher to keep you current with everything that's going on in town. As well as New York's key sights and the best of its eating, drinking and leisure options, it picks out the most exciting venues to have opened in the last year and gives a full calendar of annual events from September 2009 to December 2010. It also includes features on the important news, trends and openings, all compiled by locally based editors and writers. Whether you're visiting for the first time in your life or the first time this year, you'll find the *Time Out New York Shortlist* contains all you need to know, in a portable and easy-to-use format.

The guide divides central New York into four areas, each containing listings for Sights & Museums, Eating & Drinking, Shopping, Nightlife and Arts & Leisure, and maps pinpointing their locations. At the front of the book are chapters rounding up these scenes city-wide, and giving a shortlist of our overall picks. We also include itineraries for days out, plus essentials such as transport information and hotels.

Our listings give phone numbers as dialled within the US. Within New York you need to use the initial 1 and the three-digit area code even if you're calling from within that area code. From abroad, use your country's exit code followed by the number (the initial 1 is the US's country code).

We have noted price categories by using one to four $$$ signs ($-$$$$), representing budget, moderate, expensive and luxury. Major credit cards are accepted unless otherwise stated. We also indicate when a venue is `NEW`, and give **Event highlights**.

All our listings are double-checked, but places do sometimes close or change their hours or prices, so it's a good idea to call a venue before visiting. While every effort has been made to ensure accuracy, the publishers cannot accept responsibility for any errors that this guide may contain.

Venues are marked on the maps using symbols numbered according to their order within the chapter and colour-coded as follows:

❶ Sights & Museums
❶ Eating & Drinking
❶ Shopping
❶ Nightlife
❶ Arts & Leisure

Map key	
Major sight or landmark	
Hospital or college	
Railway station	
Park	
River	
Freeway	
Main road	
Main road tunnel	
Pedestrian road	
Airport	✈
Church	✚
Subway station	Ⓜ
Area name	SOHO

Time Out **New York** Shortlist 2010

EDITORIAL
Editor Lisa Ritchie
Deputy Editor Anna Norman
Proofreader Tamsin Shelton
Indexer Rob Norman

DESIGN
Art Director Scott Moore
Art Editor Pinelope Kourmouzoglou
Senior Designer Henry Elphick
Graphic Designers Kei Ishimaru,
  Nicola Wilson
Advertising Designer Jodi Sher

Picture Editor Jael Marschner
Deputy Picture Editor Lynn Chambers
Picture Researcher Gemma Walters
Picture Desk Assistant Marzena Zoladz
Picture Librarian Christina Theisen

ADVERTISING
Commercial Director Mark Phillips
International Advertising Manager
  Kasimir Berger
International Sales Executive Charlie Sokol
Advertising Sales (New York) Julia Keefe-
  Chamberlain **(Time Out New York)**;
  Siobhan Shea-Rossi

MARKETING
Marketing Manager Yvonne Poon
**Sales & Marketing Director, North America
  & Latin America** Lisa Levinson
Senior Publishing Brand Manager
  Luthfa Begum
Art Director Anthony Huggins

PRODUCTION
Production Manager Brendan McKeown
Production Controller Damian Bennett
Production Co-ordinator Kelly Fenlon

CONTRIBUTORS
This guide was researched and written by Gabriella Gershenson, Beth Greenfield,
Howard Halle, Richard Koss, Gia Kourlas, Amy Plitt, Lisa Ritchie, Jay Ruttenberg, Colin
St John, Steve Smith, Bruce Tantum and the writers of *Time Out New York* and the *Time
Out New York Guide*. The editor would like to thank Elizabeth Barr and Cinzia Reale-
Castello.

PHOTOGRAPHY
All photography by Michael Kirby except pages 7, 42 Carl Saytor; page 9 David M
Heald, © SRGF, New York; page 15 Roxana Marroquin; pages 20, 91 Jeff Gurwin; page
21 courtesy of Topshop; page 32 Joan Marcus; pages 53, 67, 137 Alys Tomlinson;
page 66 Jonathan Perugia; page 73 Carl Fowler Matt Peyton Photography LLC; page
153 Daio Acosta/Metropolitan Opera; page 179 Jeremy Pelley.

The following images were provided by the featured establishments/artists: pages 41,
127, 176.

Cover photograph: Brooklyn Bridge. Credit: © Photolibrary.com

MAPS
JS Graphics (john@jsgraphics.co.uk).

About **Time Out**

Founded in 1968, Time Out has expanded from humble London beginnings into
the leading resource for those wanting to know what's happening in the world's
greatest cities. As well as our influential what's-on weeklies in London, New York
and Chicago, we publish nearly 30 other listings magazines in cities as varied as
Beijing and Mumbai. The magazines established Time Out's trademark style: sharp
writing, informed reviewing and bang up-to-date inside knowledge of every scene.
  Time Out made the natural leap into travel guides in the 1980s with the City Guide
series, which now extends to over 50 destinations around the world. Written and
researched by expert local writers and generously illustrated with original photography,
the full-size guides cover a larger area than our Shortlist guides and include many
more venue reviews, along with additional background features and a full set of maps.
  Throughout this rapid growth, the company has remained proudly independent,
still owned by Tony Elliott four decades after he started Time Out London as a single
fold-out sheet of A5 paper. This independence extends to the editorial content of all
our publications, this Shortlist included. No establishment has been featured because
it has advertised, and no payment has influenced any of our reviews. And, for our critics,
there's definitely no such thing as a free lunch: all restaurants and bars are visited
and reviewed anonymously, and Time Out always picks up the bill.
For more about the company, see www.timeout.com.

Don't Miss 2010

TOP OF THE ROCK™
OBSERVATION DECK
at Rockefeller Center'

HELLO
skyline
THIS IS YOUR NEW YORK™

SEE OUR LISTING ON PAGE 131

TOP OF THE ROCK OBSERVATION DECK
50th Street between 5th and 6th Avenues
Open daily from 8am to midnight
For tickets call 212-698-2000
topoftherocknyc.com

Solomon R Guggenheim Museum p147

WHAT'S BEST

Sights & Museums

In a city that's always been about change, the cultural landscape can shift in a New York minute. These days, things are especially unpredictable. Of the bumper crop of new attractions due to open in the past few years, at press time at least three had been delayed and one – the Sports Museum of America – had come and gone in under a year. Those that have opened and remain so, however, have proved to be welcome additions for both residents and visitors, joining a growing number outside traditional museum enclaves. In autumn 2008 the Museum of Arts & Design re-opened in a (controversially) renovated landmark building – not on the Upper East Side's crowded Museum Mile or in the cultural cluster off the Midtown stretch of Fifth Avenue, but adjacent to the Time Warner Center mall on Columbus Circle.

Downtown has long been the must-go-to area for dining, shopping and nightlife, but, aside from small performance spaces and art galleries, it hasn't been known for cultural institutions. That changed with the opening of the New Museum of Contemporary Art (p79) on the Bowery in late 2007. The first art museum built from the ground up in lower Manhattan, the striking stacked structure kicked off a gallery boom in the Lower East Side and has been drawing those with an interest in mould-breaking architecture as well as challenging contemporary art. Downtown Manhattan is known for its rock 'n' roll legacy, but it took an out-of-towner to give it a collection devoted to the history of the genre.

Airline flights are one of the biggest producers of the global warming gas CO_2. But with **The CarbonNeutral Company** you can make your travel a little greener.

Go to **www.carbonneutral.com** to calculate your flight emissions then 'neutralise' them through international projects which save exactly the same amount of carbon dioxide.

Contact us at **shop@carbonneutral.com** or call into the office on **0870 199 99 88** for more details.

CarbonNeutral®flights

Cleveland's Rock & Roll Hall of Fame opened its Annex NYC in Soho (p69) in late 2008, and we've been groupies ever since. Another relative newcomer, the Museum of American Finance, on Wall Street, has responded to the global financial predicament by launching a timeline exhibit tracking the evolution of the credit crisis.

Of course, the main priority for first-time visitors will be to visit some of the world-class collections for which the city is famous. The Metropolitan Museum of Art (p144) has been undergoing a rolling modernisation programme for several years. Having unveiled its $220 million remodelled Greek & Roman wing in 2007, which allowed many objects languishing in storage for decades to be displayed, it has turned its attention to the American wing, much of which has been closed since spring 2007. The centrepiece, the lovely Engelhard Court, was poised to re-open at press time (see box p145).

The Guggenheim, whose landmark building is gleaming from a spruce-up for its big 5-0 in 2009, is another New York essential. If you want a bit of background, the Museum of the City of New York provides fascinating insight into this multi-faceted town. Other, more specialised, institutions are equally illuminating. The Lower East Side Tenement Museum (p78) brings New York's immigrant history to vivid life, and a pair of institutions devoted to two key ethnic groups re-open in 2009: the Museum of Chinese in America (p76), in a new building designed by high-profile architect Maya Lin, and El Museo del Barrio (p146), devoted to Latin American art. Spring 2010 brings a bumper crop of new visual art: as well as the controversial Whitney Biennial, P.S.1's Greater New York,

SHORTLIST

Best new
- High Line (p121)
- Museum of Arts & Design (p150)
- Museum of Chinese in America (p76)
- Rock & Roll Hall of Fame Annex NYC (p69)

Best for local insights
- Lower East Side Tenement Museum (p78)
- Museum of the City of New York (p146)
- New-York Historical Society (p151)

Best free
- Brooklyn Bridge (p162)
- Governors Island (p59)
- Staten Island Ferry (p66)

Best urban oases
- Central Park (p137)
- The Cloisters (p158)
- Madison Square Park (p115)
- New York Botanical Garden (p160)

Must-see collections
- Metropolitan Museum of Art (p144)
- Museum of Modern Art (MoMA) (p130)

New York icons
- Chrysler Building (p134)
- Empire State Building (p129)
- Statue of Liberty (p67)
- Times Square (p123)

Best museum buildings
- Cooper-Hewitt, National Design Museum (p144)
- Frick Collection (p144)
- New Museum of Contemporary Art (p79)
- Solomon R Guggenheim Museum (p147)

held every five years, surveys the work from artists across all five boroughs (see box p41).

At press time, New Yorkers were gearing up for one of the most highly anticipated public works projects in the city's recent history: the High Line (see box p121), a 1.5-mile defunct elevated train track on the west side, is being converted into a verdant urban walkway and, despite previous delays, will be ready for visitors before publication of this guide. Ground Zero is still an essential stop on many visitors' itineraries, but at the time of writing there was not much to see; there is still no completion date for the planned museum and memorial and the 1,776-foot Freedom Tower, but the massively over-budget project is unlikely to meet the original 2011 deadline.

Until the Freedom Tower's completion, the Empire State Building remains New York's tallest building. Although there can be long lines to ascend to the observation deck, it's now open until 2am and late-night viewings are usually less crowded (and the illuminated cityscape is spectacular). Another option is the Top of the Rock observation deck, which debuted five years ago, perched above Midtown's Rockefeller Center (p131). The art deco tower gets one up on the Empire State by allowing a view of that iconic structure.

Slicing up the Apple

This book is divided by area. Downtown is the oldest part of Manhattan and also the most happening. At the tip of the island is the seat of local government and the epicentre of capitalism in the Financial District, but to the north-east, trendy bars, boutiques and galleries have moved into the tenement buildings of erstwhile immigrant neighbourhood the Lower East Side. Former bohemian stomping ground Greenwich Village still resounds with cultural associations; to the west, leafy, winding streets give way to the Meatpacking District's warehouses, now colonised by designer stores and clubs. The once-radical East Village brims with bars and

Museum of the City of New York p146

restaurants. Former art enclave Soho is now a prime shopping and dining destination, along with well-heeled neighbour Tribeca. Meanwhile, Little Italy is being squeezed out by ever-expanding Chinatown and, to the north, Nolita.

In Midtown, Chelsea contains New York's main gallery district and also the city's most prominent gay enclave. Once mainly commercial, the Flatiron District has evolved into a fine-dining destination and nearby Union Square attracts foodies four days a week to New York's biggest farmers' market. Among the skyscrapers of Midtown's prime commercial stretch are some of NYC's most iconic attractions. Here, Fifth Avenue is home to some of the city's poshest retail, while Broadway is the world's most famous theatreland. Love it or loathe it, garish Times Square is a must-gawp spectacle.

Uptown, bucolic Central Park, with its picturesque lakes, expansive lawns and famous zoo, is the green divider between the patrician Upper East Side and the less conservative but equally well-heeled Upper West Side. Between them, these wealthy locales contain the lion's share of the city's cultural institutions: most museums are on the UES – the Metropolitan Museum of Art and others on Fifth Avenue's Museum Mile, in the stately former mansions of the 20th-century elite – but the UWS has the Metropolitan Opera, the New York Philharmonic and the New York City Ballet at Lincoln Center. Further north, regenerated Harlem offers vibrant nightlife, great soul food and plenty of history.

Making the most of it

First, accept that you can never see it all. The typical week's visit to the city will involve some tough choices: the Upper East Side alone is home to a dozen world-class institutions and there are must-sees in every area. Similarly, it's self-defeating to attempt to hit all the major collections in one visit to an institution as large as the Met or the American Museum of Natural History. So plan, pace yourself and take time to enjoy aimless wandering in picturesque areas like the West Village or Central Park.

Because the city's museums are privately funded and receive little or no government support, admission prices can be steep. However, these usually include entry to temporary shows as well as the permanent collections, and many institutions, including MoMA, the Whitney and the Guggenheim, offer at least one evening a week when admission fees are either waived or switched to a voluntary donation. And bear in mind that 'suggested donation' prices are just that. If your stay includes a Monday, be warned that many museums are closed – except on some holidays, such as Columbus Day and Presidents' Day. Otherwise, most are closed on major holidays.

The subway (p185) is no longer a no-go zone after dark and is generally well populated, reasonably clean and relatively easy to navigate. It will often get you from one end of the city to another far quicker (not to mention more cheaply) than a cab. Charge up a MetroCard and you can travel seamlessly by subway and bus. Of course, as in any city, you should keep your wits about you and take basic precautions, but New York of the noughties is a pretty safe place. The best way to get to know New York, however, is by pounding the pavements. Manhattan is relatively small – a mere 13.4 miles long and 2.3 miles across at its widest point – and once you've mastered the grid, it's easy to find your way (although it gets a little trickier Downtown).

Raines Law Room p116

Eating & Drinking

The prevalent New York dining theme seems to be 'old is new again'. One trend that has hit a crescendo in 2009 is the revival of neglected classics into of-the-moment hotspots. *Vanity Fair* editor-in-chief Graydon Carter, who revamped old West Village mainstay the Waverly Inn in 2007, transforming it from a public house into a VIP haunt, has now taken over Midtown institution the Monkey Bar in the Hotel Elysée (p181). A comfort-food menu, Edward Sorel mural and deco-style dining room with a definite table-placement pecking order are some of the elements that have renewed its cachet as something of a power-brokering centre.

Legendary restaurateur Keith McNally (Pastis, Balthazar, Schiller's Liquor Bar), meanwhile,

has taken on a similar project with the Minetta Tavern (p94) in Greenwich Village. The one-time beat hangout has been restored to a heyday that it probably never knew, thanks to McNally's talents. The interior, with its long wooden bar and vintage murals, attracts a crowd largely for the scene. The food – classics like steak, pasta and seafood – isn't outstanding, but that's not really the point.

Two more dusted-off institutions include La Fonda del Sol (200 Park Avenue, at 44th Street & Vanderbilt Avenue, 1-212 867 6767), the *Mad Men*-era design classic, and the Plaza's majestically restored Oak Room and Oak Bar (p132). For more relaunches, look to Daniel (p147), Daniel Boulud's fine-dining spot off Park Avenue; after its redesign by Adam Tihany, the formal decor

1000 ways to spend your weekends

1000 things to do in **Britain**

1000 things to do in **New York**

1000 things to do in London for under £10

1000 **things for kids to do in the holidays**

From £12.99/ $19.95

looks a little less Versailles and a little more Gotham. The refined modern French cuisine is still top-notch, garnering six out of six stars from *Time Out New York*'s food critic. Another haute comeback came courtesy of chef and restaurateur David Bouley. He recently reshuffled his collection of Tribeca eateries and food store-cum-bakery-café Bouley Market (p68), relocating his flagship to new, plusher-than-ever digs – recession be damned.

There are other recent additions that also look awfully familiar. The Flatiron District's favourite Spanish tapas bar, Boqueria, saw the emergence of a larger clone in Soho (p69); the same goes for Madison Square Park's Shake Shack (p116), which launched an indoor location across from the Museum of Natural History on the Upper West Side; and Zak Pelaccio opened a roomier, sleeker outpost of his celebrated Malaysian eaterie Fatty Crab, also Uptown (p152).

As much as we love recycling, there is plenty of new blood. Among the most exciting recent additions are Corton (p70), the culinary temple that replaced Tribeca's Montrachet. Restaurateur Drew Nieporent teamed up with avant-garde chef Paul Liebrandt to create one of the city's most memorable dining experiences, featuring imaginative dishes like squab with bacon, chestnut cream and pain d'épices foam. The title of most buzzed-about opening in recent memory, meanwhile, belongs to Momofuku Ko. The fine-dining entry from chef David Chang has got to be the toughest reservation to get in the city, and can only be made online (www.momofuku.com). But if you're lucky enough to score a seat at the 12-stool counter, you'll be privvy to multiple imaginative, Asian-tinged courses such as raw fluke with buttermilk, poppy

SHORTLIST

Best new
- Cabrito (p98)
- Corton (p70)
- Raines Law Room (p116)
- Scarpetta (p99)

Best revivals and revamps
- Daniel (p147)
- Minetta Tavern (p94)
- Oak Room (p132)

Best cheap eats
- Baoguette (p86)
- Ippudo NY (p87)
- Porchetta (p88)

Most hype-worthy
- Momofuku Ssäm Bar (p87)
- Pearl Oyster Bar (p99)

Best American faves
- Co. (pizza) (p105)
- Corner Bistro (burgers) (p98)
- Crif Dogs (hot dogs) (p86)

Best delis and diners
- Katz's Delicatessen (p80)
- Empire Diner (p110)
- Lexington Candy Shop (p148)

Best cocktails
- PDT (p88)
- Pegu Club (p71)
- White Star (p81)

Best dives
- Botanica (p79)
- International Bar (p87)

The classics
- Bemelmans Bar (p147)
- Grand Central Oyster Bar & Restaurant (p136)
- Russian Tea Room (p133)

Best wine bars
- Sweet & Lowdown (p80)
- Terroir (p88)

OPEN MIKE
MONDAYS
WITH HOST COLLEEN HARRIS & ACCOMPANIST MICHAEL JAMES ROY

Sing out, Louise!

EVERY MONDAY AT 9:30PM ★ No cover

RETRO JAZZ
THURSDAYS
WITH JULIAN YEO

Blending old-school soul with celebrated qualities of today

EVERY OTHER THURSDAY FROM 7 TO 9:30PM
★ No cover

KARAOKE NIGHT
WITH HOST ERIN FEHR DEPALMA

The only free karaoke left in midtown!

THURSDAYS AT 9:30PM ★ No cover

LUSH AND LIVELY
WITH DJ DAN FORTUNE

Pop hits and theater classics like you've never heard them before

LAST FRIDAY OF THE MONTH AT 9PM
★ No cover

Check newworldstages.com
for performance updates.

340 W 50TH ST
(BETWEEN EIGHTH AND NINTH AVES)

DOWNSTAIRS AT NEW WORLD STAGES

Time Out
New York
LOUNGE

Let us
entertain you.

seeds and sriracha. If not, Chang's Momofuku Ssäm Bar (p87) and Noodle Bar are both worthy alternatives.

Although New Yorkers have adventurous palates, Italian remains one of the city's most beloved cuisines. Notable newcomers include Scarpetta (p99), the 2009 *Time Out New York* Eat Out Award winner for best new Italian restaurant and the latest from chef Scott Conant. Superb dishes include foie gras stuffed ravioli (and any pasta, really). Another excellent Italian entry comes courtesy of chef Michael White. His restaurant, Convivio (p136), serves, in addition to other delicacies, some of the city's finest pastas, such as saffron gnocchetti with crabmeat and sea urchin. And Jim Lahey, the vaunted baker behind Sullivan Street Bakery, opened gourmet pizzeria Co., where unconventional pies include the Flambé, which comes topped with onions, gruyère, béchamel and lardons.

There will always be the areas that we hit for excellent Chinese (the Chinatowns in Manhattan, Flushing in Queens and Sunset Park, Brooklyn), Indian (Jackson Heights in Queens) and Japanese food (the East 40s), although other neighbourhoods attract us for more eclectic, but no less compelling, reasons. The East Village, in particular, has a knack for sprouting reasonably priced eateries that draw cult followings (see box p91).

But no discussion of New York dining is complete without mention of the second borough, increasingly becoming a first choice for foodies. If you make it to Brooklyn, consider the locally sourced comfort classics (duck meat loaf, fried chicken) at Buttermilk Channel (see box p162), the Korean-Eastern European fusion at No.7 (7 Greene Avenue, between Cumberland & Fulton Streets, Fort

Corton p70

Greene, 1-718 522 6370) and the beautifully rendered nouveau bistro staples and expert cocktails at James (605 Carlton Avenue, at St Marks Avenue, Prospect Heights, 1-718 942 4255). Reflecting its culinary status, Brooklyn now has its own Restaurant Week in spring (see www.visitbrooklyn.org for information). During the original twice-a-year Manhattan tradition (p42) you can dine at notable restaurants around town at around $25 and $35 for a three-course lunch and dinner, respectively. Also keep an eye out for recession deals and special prix fixe offers throughout the year.

Veg out

One of the city's weak spots is the relative dearth of new vegetarian dining options. Dirt Candy (430 E 9th Street, between First Avenue & Avenue A, 1-212 228 7732, closed Mon & Sun), from former Pure Food & Wine chef Amanda Cohen, serves sometimes sinful, always sophisticated meat-free eats (like a vibrant and buttery signature carrot risotto) that reminds diners that vegetarian doesn't have to mean virtuously bland. Ever-popular Chelsea mainstay Blossom (p105) has recently brought its seitan scallopine and Brazilian mock-beef stew to the Upper West Side. Raw-food specialist Pure Food & Wine (54 Irving Place, between 17th & 18th Streets, 1-212 477 1010) and Counter (105 First Avenue, between 6th & 7th Streets, 1-212 982 5870) both continue to draw devotees.

The big tipple

If you think all of the activity in the restaurant world has left the bar scene neglected, think again. Wine bars are proliferating, and becoming increasingly specialised. Terroir (p88), the latest project from the owners of neighbouring Hearth in the East Village and winner of *Time Out New York*'s 2009 Eat Out Award for best new wine bar, serves only wines that best express the land and conditions whence

Co. p105

they came. Lower East Side newcomer Sweet & Lowdown (p80) concentrates on American tipples.

But the cocktail craze continues to reign and lately it has seemed as if a nostalgic watering hole – many of them with a speakeasy theme or at least a hidden entrance – opens every week (see box p82). Two particularly noteworthy additions are cunningly concealed East Village spot PDT (p88), spotlighting the old-school stylings of mixologist Jim Meehan, and pre-Prohibition-style Raines Law Room (p82). What sets this louche Flatiron destination apart is the setup: there's no bar. Instead, the memorable libations are mixed in a cocktail kitchen of sorts, which can only be glimpsed en route to the bathroom. For excellent drinks on the other side of the river, visit cocktail doyenne Julie Reiner's Clover Club in Brooklyn (see box p162), which won our 2009 Eat Out Award for best new cocktail bar.

Where there's smoke...

A strict citywide smoking ban in 1995 changed the way smokers carouse. Now the only legal places to smoke indoors are either venues that cater largely to cigar smokers (and actually sell cigars as well as cigarettes) or spaces that have created areas specifically for smokers. Try Circa Tabac (32 Watts Street, between Sixth Avenue & Thompson Street, 1-212 941 1781) or Beekman Bar & Books (889 First Avenue, at 50th Street, 1-212 758 6600), which has a smoking room. If you like jazz with your 'baccy, check out the Carnegie Club (156 W 56th Street, between Sixth & Seventh Avenues, 1-212 957 9676). A $10 tobacco minimum buys nic fiends sofa space and live jazz. A number of bars and restaurants also have outdoor smoking gardens or terraces.

THECAST p84

Shopping

The most anticipated opening in 2009 was the arrival of British fashion behemoth Topshop (478 Broadway, at Broome Street, Soho, 1-212 966 9555, www.topshop.com), which joined Broadway's veritable United Nations of international chain stores. The four-floor emporium is a fraction of the size of the London flagship, but offers a slice of London style, including Kate Moss's line (previously only available on these shores at upmarket department store Barneys), designs by young Brit talent such as Markus Lupfer and Christopher Kane, and streetwise shoe label Office.

Although it's hard to ignore the proliferation of empty storefronts in the city – even in posh, well-trafficked areas such as Madison Avenue – we're pleased to report that most of our favourite independents are still in business and new shops continue to open. In fact, as rents in Manhattan become more affordable, young designers and boutique-owners from the outer boroughs are scoping out areas like the Lower East Side that were previously beyond their reach. Perhaps another silver-lined side effect is the rise of mixed-use businesses, such as the Smile (p90), which combines a café, fashion store, art gallery and tattoo parlour under one roof. If you don't splash out on some designer gear or a Santa Maria Novella candle,

Wanted. Jumpers, coats and people with their knickers in a twist.

From the people who feel moved to bring us their old books and CDs, to the people fed up to the back teeth with our politicians' track record on climate change, Oxfam supporters have one thing in common. They're passionate. If you've got a little fire in your belly, we'd love to hear from you. Visit us at **oxfam.org.uk**

Be Humankind **Oxfam**

Registered charity No. 202918

you may grab an open-faced fresh ricotta sandwich and an espresso.

Retail hotspots

Although many retail-rich districts are within walking distance of each other, and you can zip quickly between others on the subway, because of the dense concentration of shops in some areas (for example, the Lower East Side or Madison Avenue), you might want to limit yourself to a couple of areas in a day out. Generally speaking, you'll find the most unusual shops Downtown and in parts of Brooklyn.

Although Soho has been heavily commercialised, especially the main thoroughfares, this once edgy, arty enclave still has some idiosyncratic survivors and numerous top-notch shops. Urban fashion abounds on Lafayette Street, while Broome Street is becoming a burgeoning enclave for chic home design. To the east, Nolita has been colonised by indie designers, especially along Mott and Mulberry Streets.

Once the centre of the rag trade, the Lower East Side used to be associated with bargain outlets and bagels. Now a bar- and boutique-laden patch, it's especially good for vintage, streetwear and local designers, such as Chuck Guarino and Ryan Turner's hip menswear line THECAST (p84). Orchard, Ludlow and Rivington Streets are retail hotspots. North of here, in the East Village, you'll find a highly browsable mix of vintage clothing, streetwear and records alongside stylish home and kid's goods, but shops are more scattered than in the Lower East Side.

On the other side of the island, the one-time down-at-heel wholesale meat market, stretching south from 14th Street, has become a high-end consumer playground; the warehouses of the Meatpacking

SHORTLIST

Best new
- Bespoke Chocolates (p87)
- Samples for (eco)mpassion (p90)
- The Smile (p90)

Best vintage
- Allan & Suzi (p152)
- Edith Machinist (p81)
- Girls Love Shoes (p81)

Taste of New York
- Guss' Pickles (p83)
- H&H Bagels (p152)
- Union Square Greenmarket (p113)

Best books and music
- 192 Books (p108)
- Housing Works Bookstore Café (p72)
- Other Music (p89)

Local labels
- Alexis Bittar (p101)
- Lyell (p77)
- Nom de Guerre (p95)
- THECAST (p84)

Most unusual gifts
- Bowne & Co Stationers (p68)
- Kiosk (p72)

Best for emerging designers
- Dressing Room (p81)
- Market NYC (p78)

Best accessories
- Doyle & Doyle (jewellery) (p81)
- Fabulous Fanny's (eyewear) (p87)
- Still Life (hats) (p83)

Coolest streetwear
- Alife Rivington Club (p81)
- Reed Space (p83)

Best bargain-hunting
- Antiques Garage (p106)
- Century 21 (p68)

Get the local experience

Over 50 of the world's top destinations available.

District are now populated by a clutch of international designers, including Diane von Furstenberg, Stella McCartney and Alexander McQueen. The western strip of Bleecker Street is lined with a further cache of designer boutiques.

Most of the city's famous department stores can be found on Fifth Avenue between 42nd and 59th Streets, in the company of big-name designer flagships and chain stores. The exceptions are Bloomingdale's and Barneys, which are both on the Upper East Side. The Uptown stretch of Madison Avenue has long been synonymous with the crème de la crème of international fashion.

It's also worth venturing across the East River. Williamsburg, one subway stop from the East Village on the L train, abounds with idiosyncratic shops and one-off buys. As well as the main drag, Bedford Avenue, North 6th and Grand Streets are good hunting grounds for vintage clothes, arty housewares and record stores. There are further treasures in Cobble Hill and Boerum Hill, especially on Court and Smith Streets and Atlantic Avenue; the latter has mainly been known for antiques, but hip clothiers have started to move in.

Keep it local

As America's fashion capital, and the site of the prestigious Fashion Institute of New York and other high-profile art colleges, the city is a magnet for creative young designers from around the country. Hot local names to look out for in independent boutiques include Mociun, by Brooklyn textile designer Caitlin Mociun, who also creates her own art-influenced prints; Emma Fletcher's label Lyell (p77), whose vintage-inspired dresses and

tailoring have been picked up by the hip young Hollywood set; Built By Wendy (p72), a cool, casual line by transplanted Midwesterner Wendy Mullin; Hyden Yoo's updated menswear classics; and Nom de Guerre (p95), a historical-edged, often military-inspired upscale streetwear label designed by a New York collective.

There are also opportunities to buy goods direct from emerging designers at a couple of weekend markets: at Market NYC (p78), housed in a school gymnasium in Soho, you'll find anything from jewellery to art T-shirts, while at Brooklyn's Artists & Fleas (129 N 6th Street, between Bedford & Berry Streets, Williamsburg, 1-917 541 5760, www.artistsandfleas. com), local designers, vintage collectors and craftspeople show off a terrific range of individual and unusual clothing, homeware, accessories, jewellery and great gifts in a warehouse on Saturdays and Sundays.

Famous names

Of course, many visitors to New York will simply be looking to make the most of the incredible variety of big brands on offer in the city. For young, casual and streetwear labels, head to Broadway in Soho. Fifth Avenue heaves with a mix of designer showcases and mall-level megastores. Madison Avenue is more consistently posh, with a further parade of deluxe labels. If you prefer to do all your shopping under one roof, famous department stores Macy's (good for mid-range brands), Bloomingdale's (a mix of mid-range and designer), Barneys (cutting-edge and high-fashion) and Bergdorf Goodman (luxury goods and international designer) are all stuffed with desirable goods.

Sniffing out sales

New York is fertile bargain-hunting territory. The traditional post-season sales (which usually start just after Christmas and in early to mid June) have given way to frequent markdowns throughout the year: look for sale racks in boutiques, chain and department stores. The twice-a-year Barneys Warehouse Sale (p146) is an important fixture on the bargain hound's calendar. And of course, as New York is home to numerous designer studios and showrooms, there is a weekly spate of sample sales. The best are listed in the Seek section of *Time Out New York* magazine and updates are posted on www.timeoutnewyork.com. Top Button (www.topbutton.com) and the SSS Sample Sales hotline (1-212 947 8748, www.clothingline.com) are also useful. Chief among the permanent resources is the famous Century 21(p68) discount trove across the street from Ground Zero – it's beloved of rummagers, but detested by those with little patience for sifting through less than fabulous merchandise for the prize finds. Loehmann's (p111) and Daffy's (www.daffys.com), which has several Manhattan locations, can also come up trumps for cut-price fashion.

Have a rummage

Flea market browsing is a popular weekend pastime among New Yorkers. Chelsea's famous Annex Antiques Fair & Flea Market may be consigned to history, but the area retains the covered market Antiques Garage (p106) and some worthwhile antiques stores. Also check out the Hell's Kitchen Flea Market (p125) and, further afield, Brownstoner's Brooklyn Flea (Bishop Loughlin Memorial High School, Lafayette Avenue, between Clermont & Vanderbilt Avenues, Fort Greene, www.brownstoner.com/brooklynflea), which has more than 100 vendors selling goods in a large schoolyard across the street from a Masonic temple. The market is open on Saturdays from April to December and goods encompass everything from vintage jewellery and crafts to salvage and locally made foodstuffs. For fine antiques, with prices to match, head for Madison Avenue in the 60s and 70s.

Consumer culture

Chains like Barnes & Noble (www.barnesandnoble.com) still dominate the book scene, but several well-loved independents, such as St Mark's Bookshop (p89) and Chelsea's 192 Books (p108), are holding their own. Housing Works Bookstore Café (p72) doubles as a popular Soho hangout. For art books, as well as cool souvenirs, don't forget museum shops – the collections at the MoMA Design & Book Store (p130), the Shop at Cooper-Hewitt (p144), and the New Museum Store (p79), are all terrific.

When Other Music (p89) opened opposite gigantic Tower Records in the East Village in the mid 1990s, it boldly stood as a small pocket of resistance to corporate music. Its Goliath now shuttered, Other Music rolls on, offering a well-curated selection of indie-rock favourites, jazz, world music and experimental sounds. Old-school turntable aficionados should also check out Academy LPs (415 E 12th Street, between First Avenue & Avenue A, 1-212 780 9166, www.academy-records.com), one of the few vinyl emporiums in town that combines discerning stock with modest pricing; it's not uncommon to pick up a first-rate jazz, punk or folk title for under $5.

(Le) Poisson Rouge p96

WHAT'S BEST
Nightlife

Corner a veteran clubber – one, say, who remembers the glory days of hallowed 1970s halls Studio 54 or the Paradise Garage, '80s alt-clubbing pioneers Area or Danceteria, or even '90s hotspots Twilo and Vinyl – and ask them how they view the Gotham nightlife scene of the '00s. Actually, we'll save you the trouble – nine times out of ten, you'll get a retort that falls roughly between 'Things aren't like the good old days' and 'What nightlife scene?' And there's a bit of truth to those answers (at least, the more charitable first one); compared to previous decades, the current lay of the clubland is a bit flat.

The reasons for that are many, but a crucial one is the city's attitude towards dance clubs. The minutiae of the various laws that impact on clubs could fill this guide, but here's a telling statistic: there are currently only 173 venues in NYC with a cabaret licence, the document that allows dancing. (Yes, you need a licence to dance in New York, which says something in itself.) As recently as the 1970s, the number was in the thousands. Even the best-run clubs, like the wonderful Cielo (p102), can run foul of the administration, as happened in early 2009 when it was briefly shuttered by city decree. Then there's the rise of bottle service, a cursed scourge that led clubland down the road of selfish, 'look-at-me' banality. (With any luck, by the time you read this, the economic downturn will have led clubs that rely on reselling $25 bottles of booze for $400 to rethink their business plans.)

But comparing the scene of old with today's after-dark world is like juxtaposing Mount Everest and the Matterhorn. Sure, Everest stands twice as tall, but that Swiss peak sure does have some fancy angles.

www.treesforcities.org

Trees for Cities
Charity registration number 1032154

Travelling creates so many
lasting memories.

Make your trip mean something for
years to come - not just for you but
for the environment and for people
living in deprived urban areas.

Anyone can offset their flights,
but when you plant trees with
Trees for Cities, you'll help create
a green space for an urban
community that really needs it.

To find out more visit
www.treesforcities.org

Leave
Your
Mark

Create a green future for cities.

In New York, a lot of those angles come courtesy of forward-thinking venues that have been opened by brave optimists over the last few years. Chief among them is Studio B (259 Banker Street, between Calyer Street & Meserole Avenue, Greenpoint, 1-718 389 1880, www.clubstudiob.com). Located in a still-ungentrified corner of Brooklyn, the club scores some of the city's best bookings, attracting everyone from the electrorock superstars of Soulwax, hip-hop elder statesman Afrika Bambaataa and alt-techno doyenne Ellen Allien to its stage and DJ booth. On the island, Downtown newcomer Santos Party House (p74) splits its bills between underground house and top-flight funk nights.

The old timers have held their own as well. Sullivan Room (p96) is an unpretentious spot that regularly features some of America's best house-music talent, including the likes of Derrick Carter and Mark Farina. The aforementioned Cielo, despite its glossy vibe, gets down and dirty with weekly parties featuring dance-floor deities François K and Louie Vega. Webster Hall (p92), for years a haven for men with gold chains and women with big hair, has turned to the world's best electro and house stars to pack its massive main floor, at least on Fridays. And Love (p96)…well, it has one of the best sound systems in the world.

But it's around the edges that NYC really shines. P.S.1 Warm Up, a weekly summertime soirée held in the courtyard at P.S.1 Contemporary Art Center in Queens (p164), attracts thousands of kids who like nothing better than to boogie down to some pretty twisted DJs. The monthly Bunker bash, one of America's top techno get-togethers, takes place in Williamsburg's Public Assembly (70 N 6th Street, between Kent & Wythe Avenues, 1-718 384 4586,

S H O R T L I S T

Best new
- City Winery (p74)
- (Le) Poisson Rouge (p96)
- Santos Party House (p74)

Most storied venues
- Apollo Theater (p159)
- Lenox Lounge (p159)
- Village Vanguard (p103)

Least attitude-plagued clubs
- Love (p96)
- Studio B (left)
- Sullivan Room (p96)

Best for rising stars
- Joe's Pub (p90)
- Mercury Lounge (p84)
- Metropolitan Room (p118)
- Smalls (p103)

Best tiny rock clubs
- Cake Shop (p84)
- Union Pool (p165)

Best gay spots
- The Eagle (p111)
- Henrietta Hudson (p102)
- The Ritz (p126)
- Splash (p118)

Best for laughs
- Ars Nova (p125)
- Comix (p102)
- Upright Citizens Brigade Theatre (p112)

Best big night out
- Bowery Ballroom (p84)
- Cielo (p102)

New Yorkiest vibe
- Jazz at Lincoln Center (p155)
- Oak Room (p180)
- Radio City Music Hall (p134)

Best for partying alfresco
- P.S.1 Warm Up (p166)

DON'T MISS: 2010

www.publicassemblynyc.com), a club that consists of little more than two bare-bones concrete rooms. The wandering Giant Step (www.giant step.net) and Turntables on the Hudson (www.turntablesonthe hudson.com) parties never fail to bring the funk, wherever they are.

Live action

The world's economic meltdown has left few industries unscathed, and the music biz is certainly no exception. Yet rock clubs here are still regularly packed and big shows sell out regardless of high ticket prices. It's worth spending the dough: almost any night of the week, there's a world-class performance going down somewhere in the city.

For larger seated shows, try the posh theatres further uptown. The palatial art deco totem Radio City Music Hall (p134), Harlem's decaying benchmark the Apollo Theater (p159), and of course Carnegie Hall (plus its subterranean baby, Zankel Hall; p128) lend historic importance to even tedious performances. Jazz at Lincoln Center's Allen Room (p155), perched atop Columbus Circle in the Time Warner Center, presents shows with a glorious windowed backdrop, a million-dollar view that threatens to steal even the *good* shows.

The rock scene's heart, however, beats Downtown and across the water in Brooklyn. The clubs dotting the East Village and Lower East Side are too many to count, but include the avant-gardist fare of the Stone (p93) and the Mercury Lounge (p84), the no-nonsense spot that launched the career of the Strokes, among others. For medium-size acts, the Bowery Ballroom (p84) remains Manhattan's hub. In recent years, its owners have taken advantage of rock's resurgence by booking shows

in a smattering of larger venues. Under the Bowery Presents rubric, the company regularly books the huge Webster Hall (p92), as well as Terminal 5 (610 W 56th Street, between Eleventh & Twelfth Avenues, Hell's Kitchen, 1-212 260 4700, www.terminal5nyc.com), an even larger space on the city's western fringes. Bowery has also branched out to Brooklyn with the Music Hall of Williamsburg (see box p165). Whether the club is really challenged by Downtown fixture the Knitting Factory (p165), which is relocating to the neighbourhood, remains to be seen.

While trendspotters' attention has lately been fixed on Brooklyn, a number of promising clubs have popped up around Manhattan in recent years. In Chelsea, the slick Highline Ballroom (p112) showcases a range of acts and houses a popular weekly jam by the Roots. (Le) Poisson Rouge (p96), tucked away in a Village basement, welcomes experimental rock alongside contemporary classical music and other adventurous fare. More recently, wine bar and cabaret space City Winery (p74) has opened further downtown.

As in any town, New York's most exciting music tends to emanate from its tiniest spaces. Joe's Pub (p90), the classy cabaret room tucked inside the Public Theater, continues to present great acts of all genres. Cheaper, grubbier and louder is the Lower East Side's Cake Shop (p84), which also houses a colourful, vegan-friendly café. The sight lines are ghastly and there are certainly more comfortable places in which to hang out. But the booking is vibrant and on good nights the club has the sticky air of a high-school basement party and so is the ideal setting for a scruffy rock 'n' roll show.

Make 'em laugh, make 'em cry

The cabaret scene offers a confluence of opposites: the heights of polish and the depths of amateurism; intense honesty and airy pretense; earnestness and camp. One thing's for sure, it's a quintessentially New York experience. Classic performance rooms include Café Carlyle in the plush Upper East Side hotel (the Carlyle, 35 E 76th Street, at Madison Avenue, 1-212 744 1600, www.the carlyle.com) and the Oak Room at the Algonquin (p180), but cover is high and dinner is often compulsory. A worthy alternative is the Metropolitan Room (p118), which offers top-notch shows at reasonable prices.

If it's laughs that you're after, likewise, the city's myriad comedy clubs serve as both platforms for big names and launchpads for the stars of tomorrow and you might find some of the venues surprisingly comfortable. Unlike some dingy standup dives, the surroundings are as fresh as the talent at Ars Nova (p125) and Comix (p102), while the Upright Citizens Brigade Theatre (p112), home of the city's best improv and sketch groups, is a must for laugh addicts.

It's queer, it's here

There is a huge number of gay subcultures in New York. Promoters throw parties every night of the week for all sorts of queer scenesters, whether you're an electronica loving twink, a pumped-up circuit boy, a tattooed trannie or a glammed-out femme. Gay nightspots aren't relegated to just one neighbourhood, either; while Chelsea and the East Village have reigned for several years now, there's plenty to pull you to the West Village, Midtown and parts of Brooklyn and Queens too. Mega-clubs are practically extinct because of unfortunate city crackdowns, although a couple of the biggies – Pacha (p126) and Webster Hall (p92) – do offer frequent gay blowouts. The best, most consistent parties, though, are more intimate affairs held at spots like Splash (p118), the Ritz (p126) and the Eagle (p111), a den of sin specialising in kink. While lesbians definitely get the short end of the stick when it comes to venues – Henrietta Hudson (p102) and Cubbyhole (281 W 12th Street, at 4th Street, West Village, 1-212 243 9041, www.cubbyholebar.com) pretty much cover it in Manhattan – the girls are always welcome on the boys' turf.

Santos Party House p74

West Side Story p129

Arts & Leisure

The hoarding that has hidden much of New York's premier cultural complex, Lincoln Center, during the past few years has started to come down. Although it opened in 1962, in 2009/10 the institution celebrates the 50th year since its ground-breaking and a series of special events is planned until spring 2010. Improvements and additions to the campus – including a new visitor space (see box p127) – will continue to be unveiled throughout the next year and a half. Much excitement surrounded the spring 2009 debut of the rebuilt Alice Tully Hall (see below, Classical music & opera). Sports fans, meanwhile, said hello to not one, but two new stadiums. Beset by budget shortfalls and controversy, the Mets' and Yankee's new homes were met with general approval for increased comfort and better sight lines – yet empty seats in the Yankees' opening season bore out complaints about increased top-priced seats at the cost of affordable bleachers (see box p166). Meanwhile, the city's arts scene seems to be weathering the financial storm. Its unstoppable creative energy and boundless appetite for unusual and challenging fare supports small, adventurous spaces. While the past year has seen some casualties, there have also been welcome additions, such as multidisciplinary centre Dixon Place (p84).

Theatre

The very word 'Broadway' has long been shorthand for American stage success. For decades, however, discerning theatregoers turned their noses up at the Great White Way. Let the tourists flock to the grand jewellery-box theatres in Midtown, the argument went; insiders knew that Broadway was all flash and trash, and the real art was to be found in smaller venues beyond Times Square.

Lately, however, that story has been changing. True, Broadway is still home to long-running hit tuners, such as *Chicago*, *Jersey Boys* and *Wicked*. Musical versions of films (such as Elton John's *Billy Elliot*) and cartoons remain popular: the 2009/10 season is set to include adaptations of *Spider-Man* (directed by *The Lion King*'s Julie Taymor, with music by Bono and the Edge) and *The Addams Family*. But serious straight plays have become increasingly common on Broadway as well, often in limited runs lit by awesome star wattage; in recent years, Julia Roberts, Jane Fonda, Denzel Washington and Susan Sarandon have all appeared on the local boards. Since tickets for these shows often go fast, you may want to check websites such as www.theatermania.com and www.playbill.com for advance information. Nearly all Broadway and Off Broadway shows are served by one of the big ticketing agencies (p189), but for cheap seats, your best bet is the TKTS Discount Booth, which has just reopened after a dramatic makeover (see box p127).

As fun as big-budget productions are, sometimes you need a bit more intimacy; check out what's playing at Playwrights Horizons (416 W 42nd Street, between Ninth & Tenth Avenues, Ticket Central 1-212 279 4200) and Second Stage (307 W 43rd Street, at Eighth Avenue, 1-212 246 4422) for quality in a fairly classic mode. In the East Village, the Public Theater (p93) offers a mix of new plays and classics with excellent production

DON'T MISS: 2010

SHORTLIST

Best new or revamped
- Alice Tully Hall (p155)
- Citi Field (p166)
- Dixon Place (p84)
- Yankee Stadium (p166)

Best for cinephiles
- Anthology Film Archives (p92)
- Film Forum (p103)
- Walter Reade Theater (p156)

Most experimental
- Performance Space 122 (p92)
- Soho Rep (p75)
- The Stone (p93)

Best for unwinding
- Caudalie Vinothérapie Spa (p134)
- Chelsea Piers (p114)
- Juvenex (p121)

Best new Broadway shows
- Hair: The American Tribal Love Rock Musical (p128)
- West Side Story (p129)

Best Off Broadway
- Atlantic Theater Company (p112)
- New York Theatre Workshop (p92)
- Public Theater (p93)

Best free outdoor arts
- Bryant Park Summer Film Festival (p44)
- Lincoln Center Out of Doors Festival (p46)
- New York Philharmonic Concerts in the Parks (p45)
- Shakespeare in the Park (p44)

Essential high culture
- Carnegie Hall (p128)
- Metropolitan Opera House (p35)
- New York City Center (p129)

Best cheap tickets
- The Kitchen (p114)
- TKTS (p127)

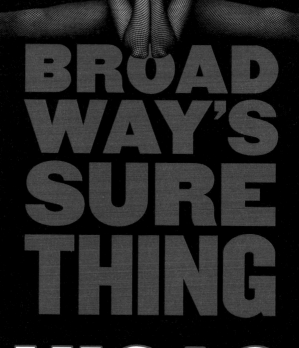

BROADWAY'S SURE THING

CHICAGO
THE MUSICAL

AMBASSADOR THEATRE · 219 WEST 49TH STREET
TELECHARGE.COM/CHICAGO 212-239-6200 · CHICAGOTHEMUSICAL.COM

values; it also puts up a pair of free Shakespeare in the Park (p44) productions every summer in Central Park.

If you need something a little more challenging and iconoclastic – and easier on the wallet – head below 14th Street or across the river to Brooklyn, where avant-garde and experimental theatre still thrive. Look for local companies such as Radiohole (www.radiohole.com), Elevator Repair Service (www.elevator.org), the Nature Theater of Oklahoma (www.oktheater.org) and the Civilians (www.thecivilians.org), which often appear at venues like Performance Space 122 (p92), Soho Rep (p75) and New York Theatre Workshop (p92).

Film

Walking around New York is like entering a film set. Every corner – even the subway – has been immortalised in celluloid, and you might even stumble upon an actual scene being shot (the Queens-based Silvercup Studios, which filmed *Gangs of New York*, *The Devil Wears Prada* and *Sex and the City*, is expanding). So it's not surprising that New York has a special relationship with the movies. The calendar is packed with festivals, including Tribeca, the New York Film Festival and several others organised by the excellent Film Society of Lincoln Center (p156). Summer brings the wonderful tradition of free outdoor screenings at Bryant Park (p44) and other park and riverside venues (check www.timeoutnewyork.com for listings). Cinephiles love Film Forum (p103) for its wide range of revivals and new indie features, while Anthology Film Archives (p92) specialises in experimental programming. The Museum of

Modern Art (p130) and Lincoln Center's Walter Reade Theater (p156) also offer well-curated series and impeccable screening conditions; the facilities at Lincoln Center will be boosted considerably in early 2011, when the Elinor Bunin-Munroe Film Center opens with two additional screens, a gallery and café.

Classical music & opera

Change is the operative word at Lincoln Center (p155). The newly renovated Alice Tully Hall has drawn near-unanimous raves for its exceptional acoustics, handsome interiors and bold, angular glass façade; if this is the direction the rest of the complex means to take during this, its 50th anniversary season, then any sense of fustiness should soon be shed, with programming likely to follow suit. Even with belts somewhat tightened, the Metropolitan Opera is forging ahead with new productions from William Kentridge (*The Nose*), Bart Sher (*Les Contes d'Hoffmann*), Richard Eyre (*Carmen*), Luc Bondy (*Tosca*) and Mary Zimmerman (*Armida*), populated with the customary constellation of star performers.

Things are less certain across the plaza at the recently refurbished and rechristened David H Koch Theater, where New York City Opera – newly led by George Steel, formerly the wunderkind behind the success of Columbia University's Miller Theatre – is expected to mount a foreshortened season while laying groundwork for the future. At the New York Philharmonic, the arrival of Alan Gilbert as music director began to provoke a buzz of anticipation before the first downbeat was given. In addition to these resident institutions, Lincoln Center also presents such series as Great Performers and American

Make the most of London life

Songbook, as well as its three staple offerings of the summer: Lincoln Center Out of Doors, the Mostly Mozart Festival and the Lincoln Center Festival.

A few blocks away, the venerable shrine to musical genius Carnegie Hall is currently under the leadership of Clive Gillinson, formerly of the London Symphony Orchestra. It continues to burst forth at its well-packed seams, spilling its festival offerings out into other venues around the city. One emphasis during the 2009/10 season is the explosive growth of Western classical music in China (p40).

Dance

Tradition and innovation live side by side in New York, where the art form has remarkable breadth. Dance, of course, is not just a pointed foot: choreographers today are intent on exploring the more complex notions of performance and the body. Performance practice is honed within laboratories like Movement Research (www.movementresearch. org), an organisation devoted to the investigation of dance and movement-based forms. In recent years, this intimate, visceral approach has manifested itself at smaller theatres and performance spaces in Brooklyn (Center for Performance Research, Greenbelt, Unit 1, 361 Manhattan Avenue, at Jackson Street, Williamsburg, 1-718 577 2700, www.cprnyc.org) and Queens (the Chocolate Factory, 5-49 49th Avenue, at Vernon Boulevard, Long Island City, 1-718 482 7069, www.chocolatefactorytheater.org). But that's not to suggest that New York is lacking in more established quarters. For ballet fans, there is no greater place to bask in the world of George Balanchine and Jerome Robbins than the New York City Ballet (at the David H Koch Theater,

Alice Tully Hall p155

p156, in the winter and spring). American Ballet Theatre – recently joined by extraordinary Russian choreographer Alexei Ratmansky – presents a mix of full-length classics with one-act ballets by Twyla Tharp and Antony Tudor (at the Metropolitan Opera House, p156, in spring and at New York City Center, p129, in the autumn). The latter is the home of British transplant Christopher Wheeldon; the one-time resident choreographer of NYCB has formed his own group, Morphoses, where he hopes to 'restore ballet as a force of innovation'.

New York is still the centre of modern and postmodern dance, where choreographers like Trisha Brown, Merce Cunningham, Mark Morris and Paul Taylor continue to push their own artistic boundaries. And individual contemporary voices like Sarah Michelson, John Jasperse and Ralph Lemon challenge the notion of what dance means today. Delightfully and defiantly, they prove that there is no right answer.

Discover the city from your back pocket

Essential for your weekend break, 25 top cities available.

Calendar

Pride March p44

Dates highlighted in **bold** are public holidays.

September 2009

Early Sept **Howl!**
East Village, p85
www.howlfestival.com
Five days of art events, films, readings and more, in the East Village.

5-7, 12, 13 **Washington Square Park Outdoor Art Exhibit**
Greenwich Village, p93
www.washingtonsquareoutdoor artexhibit.org
Artists display their wares in the streets around the park.

7 Labor Day

10-20 **Feast of San Gennaro**
Little Italy, p75
www.sangennaro.org
Eleven-day Italian-American street fair along Little Italy's main drag, with a marching band and plenty of eating.

Mid Sept **Broadway on Broadway**
Times Square, p123
www.broadwayonbroadway.com
Stars perform their Broadway hits for free in Times Square.

17 Sept **Aretha Franklin**
Radio City Music Hall, p134
www.radiocity.com

17 Sept-17 Jan **Georgia O'Keeffe: Abstraction**
Whitney Museum of American Art, p147
www.whitney.org
The first large-scale show to focus on this aspect of the artist's work.

18 Sept-10 Jan **Kandinsky**
Solomon R Guggenheim Museum, p147
www.guggenheim.org

25 Sept-11 Oct
New York Film Festival
Lincoln Center, p155
www.filmlinc.com

October 2009

Ongoing Georgia O'Keeffe:
Abstraction (see Sept);
Kandinsky (see Sept); New
York Film Festival (see Sept)

10, 11 **Open House New York**
Various locations
www.ohny.org
Architectural sites that are normally
off-limits open their doors for two days.

12 **Columbus Day**

13 October-24 Jan **American
Stories: Paintings of Everyday
Life, 1765-1915**
Metropolitan Museum of Art, p144
www.metmuseum.org
See box p145.

21 Oct-10 Nov **Ancient
Paths, Modern Voices**
Carnegie Hall, p128
www.carnegiehall.org
The esteemed hall heads up a citywide
festival of Chinese culture.

20-24 **CMJ Music Marathon
& FilmFest**
Various locations
www.cmj.com
Showcase for new musical acts, as well
as music-related films.

31 **Village Halloween Parade**
Greenwich Village, p93
www.halloween-nyc.com

November 2009

Ongoing Georgia O'Keeffe:
Abstraction (see Sept); Kandinsky
(see Sept); American Stories:
Paintings of Everyday Life, 1765-
1915 (see Oct); Ancient Paths,
Ancient Voices (see Oct)

1 **New York City Marathon**
Various locations
www.nycmarathon.org
Starting on Staten Island, the course
runs through Brooklyn, Queens and the
Bronx before finishing in Central Park.

11 **Veterans' Day**

13 Nov-30 Dec **Radio City
Christmas Spectacular**
Radio City Music Hall, p134
www.radiocity.com
The Rockettes' holiday show.

22 Nov-26 Apr **Tim Burton**
Museum of Modern Art, p130
www.moma.com
This retrospective combines a gallery
show and film series.

25, 26 **Macy's Thanksgiving
Eve Balloon Blowup &
Thanksgiving Day Parade**
Various locations
www.macys.com
The stars of this annual parade are the
gigantic, inflated balloons.

26 **Thanksgiving Day**

Late Nov-early Jan
The Nutcracker
Lincoln Center, p155
www.nycballet.com

Late Nov-late Jan **Seaport
Music Winter Festival**
South Street Seaport, p58
www.seaportmusicfestival.com
See box p44.

December 2009

Ongoing Georgia O'Keeffe:
Abstraction (see Sept); Kandinsky
(see Sept); American Stories:
Paintings of Everyday Life,
1765-1915 (see Oct); Radio
City Christmas Spectacular (see
Nov); Tim Burton (see Nov); The
Nutcracker (see Nov); Seaport
Music Winter Festival (see Nov)

2 **Christmas Tree
Lighting Ceremony**
Rockefeller Center, p131
www.rockefellercenter.com
Marvel at the giant evergreen.

22 **National Chorale
Messiah Sing-In**

Greater expectations

P.S.1 and MoMA's NYC-centric joint quinquennial.

In the last decade or so, there's been a boom in major contemporary art shows and fairs taking place every two or three years – making biennials and triennials seem like a dime a dozen. Much rarer are the surveys mounted in five-year increments, like the famous Documenta, which has been held in Kassel, Germany, since 1954.

The infrequency of such shows makes them a bigger deal, of course, since the five-year interval offers the advantages of greater historical depth. That could be why, after P.S.1 Contemporary Art Center became affiliated with the Museum of Modern Art in 2000, the two institutions decided to follow the Documenta model when they jointly instituted a regular, curated survey of contemporary artists. Called **Greater New York** (p43), the first edition launched that very same year with a roster of 140 artists, most of them

newly emerging, and all of them, as the exhibition title suggests, working in New York City and environs. The next iteration in 2005 included 162 participants. In spring 2010 the show will be mounted a third time. It's a don't-miss event – not least because if you do, you'll have to wait until 2015 for the next one.

So, what to expect? Firstly, artists who push boundaries while working in a plethora of media and styles. Some of the biggest names in art got their first exposure at 'Greater New York', including painters Julie Mehretu, Cecily Brown and Dana Schutz, and video artists Jeremy Blake and Paul Pfeiffer. Secondly, lots of art. The huge exhibition will take up P.S.1's entire space – all 145,000 square feet of it – and the pieces won't be limited to the museum's proper gallery spaces. The works often spill out into the hallways, as if to fill every nook and cranny of the building.

Mermaid Parade p44

Lincoln Center, p155
www.nationalchorale.org
Join a chorus of 3,000 for an evening performance of Handel's *Messiah*.

25 Christmas Day

31 Dec-1 May **Carmen**
Metropolitan Opera House, p156
www.metoperafamily.org
Angela Gheorghiu takes the main role.

31 New Year's Eve Ball Drop
Times Square, p123
www.timessquarenyc.org
See the giant illuminated ball descend.

31 New Year's Eve Fireworks
Central Park, p137
www.centralparknyc.org
The fireworks explode at midnight.

January 2010

Ongoing Georgia O'Keeffe: Abstraction (see Sept); Kandinsky (see Sept); American Stories: Paintings of Everyday Life, 1765-1915 (see Oct); Tim Burton (see Nov); The Nutcracker (see Nov); Carmen (see Dec); Seaport Music Winter Festival (see Nov)

1 New Year's Day

1 New Year's Day Marathon Poetry Reading
East Village, p85
www.poetryproject.com
Big-name bohos step up to the mic in this spoken-word spectacle.

18 Martin Luther King, Jr Day

22-31 **Winter Antiques Show**
Midtown East, p134
www.winterantiquesshow.com
One of the world's most prestigious antiques shows.

Late Jan-early Feb **Winter Restaurant Week**
Various locations
www.nycvisit.com
Sample gourmet food at low prices for two weeks (weekdays only; see also p44).

February 2010

Ongoing Tim Burton (see Nov); Carmen (see Dec)

Mid Feb **Chinese New Year**
Chinatown, p75
www.explorechinatown.com

Parades, performances and delicious food during the two weeks of the Lunar New Year.

16 Presidents' Day

March 2010

Ongoing Tim Burton (see Nov)

Early Mar **Whitney Biennial**
Whitney Museum of American Art, p147
www.whitney.org

4-7 **The Armory Show**
Piers 92 & 94, Midtown West, p104
www.thearmoryshow.com
A huge contemporary art mart.

17 **St Patrick's Day Parade**
Fifth Avenue, p104
www.saintpatricksdayparade.com
The traditional huge march of green-clad merrymakers.

April 2010

Ongoing Tim Burton (see Nov); Whitney Biennial (see Mar); Carmen (see Dec)

4 **Easter Parade**
Fifth Avenue, p104
Admire the myriad creative Easter bonnets on show at this one-day event.

Mid Apr **SOFA New York**
Park Avenue Armory, Upper East Side, p143
www.sofaexpo.com
Giant four-day show of Sculptural Objects and Functional Art.

Late Apr **Tribeca Film Festival**
Tribeca, p68
www.tribecafilmfestival.org
Two-week Robert De Niro-organised festival of independent films.

May 2010

Ongoing Whitney Biennial (see Mar)

Early May **Bike New York: The Great Five Boro Bike Tour**
www.bikenewyork.org
Thousands of cyclists take part in a 42-mile Tour de New York.

Early May-Sept **Greater New York**
P.S.1 Contemporary Art Center, p164
www.ps1.org
See box p41.

Late May **Lower East Side Festival of the Arts**
Lower East Side, p78
www.theaterforthenewcity.net
Theatre, poetry readings, films and family-friendly programming, over three days.

29-31, 5, 6 June **Washington Square Park Outdoor Art Exhibit**
Greenwich Village, p93
www.washingtonsquareoutdoor artexhibit.org
See Sept 2009.

31 Memorial Day

June 2010

Ongoing Whitney Biennial (see Mar); Greater New York (see May); Washington Square Park Outdoor Art Exhibit (see May)

Early June **Museum Mile Festival**
Various locations
www.museummilefestival.org
Nine major museums are free of charge to the public for one day every year.

Early June **National Puerto Rican Day Parade**
Fifth Avenue, p104
www.nationalpuertoricandayparade.org
Celebrate the city's largest Hispanic community, and its culture.

Early June-Aug **Central Park SummerStage**
Central Park, p137
www.summerstage.org
Rockers, symphonies, authors and dance companies take over the stage.

DON'T MISS: 2010

Chilling by the river

Cool winter sounds come to South Street Seaport.

Long the preserve of chain restaurants and banal retailers, the South Street Seaport has undergone an impressive image overhaul over the past few years. Come July, the vanilla tourist trap is transformed into one of the premier music venues in the city, when cutting-edge artists – from Animal Collective to Battles – take to the outdoor stage as part of the **River to River Festival** (right). The free concerts have become an essential summertime activity for New Yorkers (not to mention quite a party), right up there with picnics in Central Park or fleeing to the New Jersey shore at the weekend.

But why limit a good thing? The folks behind the summer series have now launched a separate **Seaport Music Winter Festival** (p40), running from late November to late January. It may be chillier, but the river view is still a joy, the margaritas have given way to hot chocolate and a waterside ice rink has been added into the mix. (Although admission to concerts is free, there's a $5 charge for ice-skating, plus $7 if you need to rent skates.) Most importantly, the organisers showed the same curatorial prowess in the winter season's inaugural run last year, which saw hip local acts like Neckbeard Telecaster and Heloise & the Savoir Faire rock the masses.

Early June-Aug **Shakespeare in the Park**
Delacorte Theater, Central Park, p143
www.publictheater.org
Join the queue for free alfresco theatre.

Early June-mid Sept
River to River Festival
Various locations Downtown
www.rivertorivernyc.com
More than 500 free events, from walks to concerts at waterfront venues.

Mid June-Aug **Bryant Park Summer Film Festival**
Bryant Park, Midtown
www.bryantpark.org
Free alfresco films on Monday nights.

23 June-19 Sept **Craft Revolution: The American Studio Movement, 1945-1970**
Museum of Arts & Design, p150
www.madmuseum.org

Late June **Broadway Bares**
Roseland Ballroom, Midtown
www.broadwaycares.org
This one-day charity fundraiser features Broadway's hottest bodies sans costumes.

Late June **Mermaid Parade**
Coney Island, Brooklyn
www.coneyisland.com
Decked-out, made-up mermaids and mermen share the parade route with elaborate, kitschy floats.

Late June **NYC LGBT Pride March**
Greenwich Village, p93
www.nycpride.org
Downtown is a sea of rainbow flags.

Late June/early July
Summer Restaurant Week
See Jan Winter Restaurant Week

Late June-Aug **Met in the Parks**
Central Park, p137
www.metopera.org
The Metropolitan Opera stages free performances. Grab a blanket, pack a picnic and show up early to get a good spot.

July 2010

Ongoing Greater New York
(see May); Central Park
SummerStage (see June);
Shakespeare in the Park (see
June); River to River Festival
(see June); Bryant Park Summer
Film Festival (see June); Craft
Revolution: The American
Studio Movement, 1945-1970
(see June); Met in the Parks
(see June)

4 **Independence Day**

4 **Nathan's Famous July 4
Hot Dog Eating Contest**
Coney Island, Brooklyn
www.nathansfamous.com
The granddaddy of all pig-out contests.

4 **Macy's Fireworks Display**
East River
www.macys.com
World-famous annual display.

Early July **Midsummer
Night Swing**
Lincoln Center Plaza, p155
www.lincolncenter.org
Dance under the stars to salsa, Cajun,
swing and other music most nights for
almost three weeks.

Mid July **New York Philharmonic
Concerts in the Parks**
Central Park and various locations
www.newyorkphilharmonic.org
Performances of classical music in the
city's larger parks.

Late July-late Aug
Mostly Mozart Festival
Lincoln Center, p155
www.lincolncenter.org
Four weeks of works by Mozart and
his contemporaries.

Late July-late Aug **Harlem Week**
Harlem, p157
www.harlemweek.com
'Week' is a misnomer: live music, art
and food are on tap for around a month.

August 2010

Ongoing Greater New York
(see May); Central Park
SummerStage (see June);
Shakespeare in the Park (see
June); River to River Festival
(see June); Bryant Park Summer
Film Festival (see June); Craft
Revolution: The American Studio
Movement, 1945-1970 (see
June); Mostly Mozart (see July);
Met in the Parks (see June);
Harlem Week (see July)

River to River Festival

1 Aug-1 Nov The Original Copy: Photography of Sculpture, 1839 to Today
Museum of Modern Art, p130
www.moma.org

Aug Lincoln Center Out of Doors Festival
Lincoln Center, p155
www.lincolncenter.org
Several weeks of free family-friendly classical and contemporary works.

Aug New York International Fringe Festival
Various locations
www.fringenyc.org
Wacky, weird and sometimes great. Hundreds of performances over 16 days.

September 2010

Ongoing Greater New York (see May); River to River Festival (see June); Craft Revolution: The American Studio Movement, 1945-1970 (see June); The Original Copy: Photography of Sculpture, 1839 to Today (see Aug)

6 Labor Day

Early Sept Howl!
See above Sept 2009.

4-6, 11, 12 Washington Square Park Outdoor Art Exhibit
See above Sept 2009.

Mid Sept Feast of San Gennaro
See above Sept 2009.

Mid Sept Broadway on Broadway
See above Sept 2009.

Late Sept-early Oct New York Film Festival
See above Sept 2009.

October 2010

Ongoing New York Film Festival (see Sept); The Original Copy: Photography of Sculpture, 1839 to Today (see Aug)

Early Oct Open House New York
See above Oct 2009.

11 Columbus Day

Late Oct CMJ Music Marathon & FilmFest
See above Oct 2009.

31 Oct Village Halloween Parade
See above Oct 2009.

November 2010

Early Nov New York City Marathon
See above Nov 2009.

11 Veterans' Day

Mid Nov Radio City Christmas Spectacular
See above Nov 2009.

24, 25 Macy's Thanksgiving Eve Balloon Blowup & Thanksgiving Day Parade
See above Nov 2009.

25 Thanksgiving Day

Late Nov The Nutcracker
See above Nov 2009.

December 2010

Ongoing Radio City Christmas Spectacular (see Nov); The Nutcracker (see Nov)

Early Dec Christmas Tree Lighting
See above Dec 2009.

Late Dec National Chorale Messiah Sing-in
See above Dec 2009.

25 Christmas Day

31 New Year's Eve Ball Drop
See above Dec 2009.

31 New Year's Eve Fireworks
See above Dec 2009.

Itineraries

New York Times Building p50

High Points

In *Here is New York*, EB White wrote that the city's iconic skyline 'is to the nation what the white church spire is to the village – the visible symbol of aspiration and faith, the white plume saying that the way is up.' The comment still resonates with locals and newcomers alike. From City Hall's neoclassical rotunda (1811) to the impressive International style slab of Chase Manhattan Plaza (1960) to the glass façade of Renzo Piano's New York Times Building (2007), New York's architecture still manages to awe.

Above all, this is a city of skyscrapers, so the logical starting point for a tour is the **Skyscraper Museum** in the Financial District (p66). If you want to complete your tour in one day, it's best to arrive as soon as the museum opens. Here you can see large-scale photographs of lower Manhattan's skyscrapers from 1956, 1974 and 2004, a 1931 silent film documenting the Empire State Building's construction, as well as fascinating architectural artefacts, like original models of the World Trade Center Towers and the 1,776-foot-tall Freedom Tower, currently under construction on the site.

Head out the door, make a left and follow Battery Place across West Street and along the northern edge of Battery Park. Turn left up Greenwich Street, and at Moore Street (look for the Blarney Stone pub) walk along Trinity Place to make a brief stop at **Trinity Church** (p65). In stark contrast to the skyscrapers that surround it, Trinity – the third church to stand on this spot – remains frozen in Gothic Revival style, but it was the island's tallest structure when it was completed in 1846. The churchyard, which dates back to 1697, is one of New York's oldest cemeteries. Alexander Hamilton (the nation's first secretary of the treasury – check out his mug on the $10 bill) is buried here.

Afterwards, it's time to visit one of the most powerfully moving sites in recent history: **Ground Zero** (p65), where the mighty Twin Towers once stood. From the church, continue up Trinity Place for two more blocks and cross over Liberty Street. The fenced-off building site to your left is Ground Zero. Construction of the new World Trade Center complex, including the Freedom Tower, a museum and memorial, is extremely slow-going, but work continues.

From the tragedy of Ground Zero, it's onwards and upwards to the spot where the race to the heavens began. Walk along Church Street, past Vesey Street and then left on to Barclay Street. On the corner, at 233 Broadway, is the **Woolworth Building**. Note the flamboyant Gothic terracotta cladding designed by Cass Gilbert in 1913. The 55-storey, 793-foot 'Cathedral of Commerce' was the world's tallest structure for 16 years until it was topped by the Chrysler Building.

The Woolworth Building overlooks City Hall Park, which is where you are now headed. Walk through the park and aim for the foot of the **Brooklyn Bridge** (p162). Our sojourn is about buildings, not bridges – but we wouldn't mind one bit if you made a detour here; it takes about an hour to walk out to the middle of the bridge and back, allowing plenty of time to gaze upon the East River and marvel at the web of steel cables. Back to the current plan: once you've passed through the park (bordered to the east by Park Row), look for a subway entrance to your left. Board the Uptown 4 or 5 train to Grand Central-42nd Street. On the subway, consider this: it took ten years of unflagging effort for Jacqueline Kennedy Onassis to save **Grand Central Terminal** (p135).

After the glorious (original) Pennsylvania Station was demolished in 1964, developers unveiled plans to wreck Grand Central and erect an office tower in its place. Jackie O would have none of it and rallied politicians and celebrities to her cause. In 1978 her committee won a Supreme Court decision affirming landmark status for the beloved Beaux Arts building. When you exit the subway, head upstairs and take in the thrilling main concourse. Curiously, the constellations on the ceiling are drawn in reverse, as if you were staring down from space.

By now you'll likely be famished. Head back downstairs to one of Manhattan's most famous eateries, the **Grand Central Oyster Bar & Restaurant** (Lower Concourse; p136), for a late lunch. Before heading inside, linger a moment under the low ceramic arches, dubbed the 'whispering gallery'. Instruct a friend to stand in an opposite, diagonal corner from you and whisper sweet nothings to each other – they'll sound as clear as if you were face to face.

Revitalised, you're ready for the next stop: **Columbus Circle**. Either hop back on the subway (S to Times Square, transfer to the Uptown 1 train and get off at 59th Street-Columbus Circle) or, preferably, you can hoof it there in about 40 minutes. Exit Grand Central on 42nd Street and head west. At Fifth Avenue, you'll pass by another Beaux Arts treasure from the city's grand metropolitan era, the sumptuous white-marble **New York Public Library** (p130). Built on a former Revolutionary War battleground, the library now sits on the greensward known as Bryant Park. When you get to Broadway, make a right and head north into Times Square. Imposing, sentinel-like skyscrapers mark the southern

ITINERARIES

entry to the electric carnival here; the **Condé Nast Building** (4 Times Square) and the **Reuters Building** (No.3), both by Fox & Fowle, complement Kohn Pedersen Fox's postmodern **5 Times Square** and the recent addition of David Childs's **Times Square Tower** (No.7). Take a detour if you want to see Renzo Piano's sparkling **New York Times Building** (620 Eighth Avenue, between W 40th & 41st Streets), one block west and a couple of blocks' south. The glass-walled design is a literal representation of the newspaper's desire for transparency in reporting.

Back on Broadway, walk north on the pedestrian-packed sidewalks until you spot Christopher gazing out from his perch in the centre of Columbus Circle at 59th Street. The recently renovated traffic circle,with its ring of fountains and benches, is the perfect place to contemplate another set of twin towers, the **Time Warner Center** (p152), also designed by David Childs.

Woolworth Building p49

Increasingly, skyscrapers are incorporating green design, to minimise the impact of construction on the environment. Lord Norman Foster's extraordinary 2006 **Hearst Magazine Building** (959 Eighth Avenue, at W 57th Street) is a shining example. Look south-west and you can't miss it; it's the one that resembles a giant greenhouse.

At this point you have two options. The first is to end the day | at the Time Warner Center and enjoy the staggering view from a leather chair in the **Mandarin Oriental Hotel**'s Lobby Lounge, perched 35 floors in the air. The drinks prices here are equally staggering, but the Fifth Avenue and Central Park South skylines make it worth the splurge. Alternatively, you can hail a cab and top off a day of skyscraper gazing with a panoramic view from either New York's tallest tower, the **Empire State Building** (p129), or the **Top of the Rock** observation deck at Rockefeller Center (p131). The latter has an edge as it affords a great view of the former. Also look out for William Van Alen's silver-hooded **Chrysler Building** (p134). The acme of art deco design, it was part of a madcap three-way race to become the world's tallest building just before the Depression. The competitors were the now-forgotten 40 Wall Street and the Empire State Building. Van Alen waited for 40 Wall Street to top out at 927 feet before unveiling his secret weapon – a spire assembled inside the Chrysler's dome and raised from within to bring the height to 1,046 feet. At 102 storeys and 1,250 feet, the Empire State Building surpassed it only 11 months later.

Now that you're done, one last landmark awaits: grab a cocktail in the **Rainbow Room** on the 65th floor and let your spirits soar.

Camaradas El Barrio p53

Coming to America

Between the middle of the 19th century and the 1920s, America witnessed an influx of immigrants that was as unprecedented in volume as it was ethnically diverse. More than 12 million people (of Irish, German, Italian, Jewish, Russian, Eastern European and numerous other extractions) sailed into New York Harbor, and were either absorbed by the rapidly growing city or continued on, fanning out all over the United States. Those that remained in the metropolis soon gave life to neighbourhoods that contributed to the diversity that supplies New York's lifeblood.

If coming to the New World symbolised a form of rebirth for the immigrants, Ellis Island, lying in New York Harbor, just north of the Statue of Liberty, was where their umbilical cords to the Old were cut. Over 40 per cent of America's population can trace its ancestry back to someone who passed through the former depot at Ellis Island, which served as the principal immigration centre from 1892 to 1954. Today, the **Ellis Island Immigration Museum** (p67) is an extremely poignant tribute to their diverse experiences. Among the highlights are the enormous registry room with its high-vaulted tiled ceiling (where criminals, polygamists and the politically unsavoury were held before being sent home) and the very affecting recorded memories of actual immigrants, taped in the 1980s.

Many of the newcomers found themselves living on the slums of the Lower East Side, a neighbourhood of nightmarish squalour around the turn of the 19th century. Few would have found the brick tenements with their narrow, overcrowded apartments and lack of adequate plumbing the answer to their immigrant dreams. The **Lower East Side Tenement Museum** (p78) captures their experience in a landmark 1863

building, accessible only by guided tour. The four different tours (which regularly sell out, so it's wise to book ahead) evoke the daily life of typical tenement-dwelling immigrant families in the museum's restored apartments. 'Getting By' visits the homes of an Italian and a German-Jewish clan; 'Piecing It Together' explores the apartments of two Eastern European Jewish families as well as a garment shop where many of the locals would have found employment; 'The Moore Family Tour' unfurls the life of an Irish family coping with the loss of their child; and the 'Confino Family Living History Program' takes in the homes of Sephardic Jewish occupants with the help of an interpreter in period costume. From April to December, the museum also conducts 90-minute 'Immigrant Soles' walking tours of the Lower East Side on the weekends.

While the LES has undergone an intense gentrification that would have stunned most of its earlier inhabitants, there are a few traces of the old neighbourhood they would surely recognise. Most of these vestiges come from the area's former Jewish population, such as the **Eldridge Street Synagogue** (p79), built in 1887 by Eastern European Orthodox Jews. Originally a place of worship for thousands, it fell into disuse as Jews began to leave the area, then into disrepair. The synagogue has recently been restored and you can tour the resplendent interior. An on-site museum features photographic exhibits and interactive displays on the history of Jewish immigration. Heading east down Canal Street, you'll see the façade of the **Sender Jarmulowsky Bank** (on the corner of Canal & Orchard Streets), which catered to immigrants until its collapse in 1914; note the reclining classical figures of the sculpture above the door, bookending the clock. Further down Canal, at the corner of Ludlow, is the former home of the **Kletzker Brotherly Aid Association**, a Jewish lodge for immigrants from Belarus still marked by the Star of David and the year of its opening, 1892.

If you need refreshment, skip the array of hipster cafés, trendy

ITINERARIES

bars and upscale restaurants, and make your way north to **Yonah Schimmel Knish Bakery** (137 E Houston Street, between First & Second Avenues, 1-212 477 2858). This 'knishery' has been doling out its carborific goodies since 1910. Traditional potato, kasha and spinach knishes are the most popular varieties, but sweet potato and blueberry fillings are also available. The latkes (potato pancakes) are a true city secret.

Most Chinese arrived in the city not via Ellis Island but from the West, many having worked on the country's new railroads. Despite facing racist restrictions, such as the 1882 Chinese Exclusion Act, many were able to settle in Chinatown. The **Museum of Chinese in America** (p76) recounts their history in a brand new space, designed by Vietnam Veterans Memorial architect Maya Lin and centred on a sky-lit courtyard. The permanent collection and temporary installations focus on the Chinese-American experience. Most notable of the exhibits is the Chinatown Film Project, which explores Chinatown through the cameras of ten NYC filmmakers. Best of all are the walking tours of the bustling neighbourhood ($15; $12 reductions). When you're done, stop off for lunch at **Peking Duck House** (p77). The signature dish, aromatic, crisp-skinned and succulent, is the perfect restorative before continuing on your travels.

Hailing from all over South and Central America as well as the Caribbean, New York's Hispanic community is uniquely diverse. It is also one of the largest ethnic groups (representing over a quarter of the city's population), spread out all over the five boroughs. East Harlem, aka Spanish Harlem, is better known to its primarily Puerto Rican residents as 'El Barrio'. Here, on the northern end of Museum Mile, the **Museo del Barrio** (p146) is dedicated to the work of Latino artists who reside in the US as well as Latin American masters. After big renovations, the museum re-opens in September 2009 with 'Nexus: New York 1900-1945', an exhibition devoted to Latino artists' impressions of the city.

End the day at Spanish Harlem's most vibrant nightspot, **Camaradas El Barrio** (p158). At this tapas bar, benches, exposed brick and a modest gallery create a hangout for kicking back over a pitcher of sangria. The place provides a glimpse of young Puerto Rican nightlife, which draws off the island's cultural heritage and is at the same time intrinsically part of New York. Camaradas has an irresistible menu of small plates and a throbbing music programme that takes in live Latin funk and jazz, the Afro-Rican rhythms of local band Yerba Buena and DJs spinning salsa, hip hop and 1980s hits.

Chinatown

Washington Square

Literary Greenwich Village

Although its genteel townhouses and upscale restaurants might seem at odds with its bohemian reputation, Greenwich Village was once the city's answer to Paris's Left Bank. As the rich moved uptown following World War I, free thinkers and artists – most notably writers – from all over the world began to move in, taking advantage of the cheap rents and large apartments. In the 1950s the Beat poets moved in and made the area their own. You'd need a lot more than a struggling writer's salary to inhabit its leafy streets today, but the literary landmarks remain.

We suggest taking this half-day outing in the afternoon. Start with an espresso at the oldest coffeehouse in the village, **Caffe Reggio** (119 MacDougal Street, between 3rd Street & Minetta Lane, 1-212 475 9557), open since 1927. The carved wooden chairs, marble-topped tables and relaxed vibe maintain the cosy feel that earned it cameos in *The Godfather II* and the original *Shaft*, and appealed to Jack Kerouac, native Villager Gregory Corso and other Beat poets. Sadly, this is the only true Beat hangout still operating in the locale, but you can pay tribute to their decadence by indulging in a delectable sfogliatella pastry.

Heading north, you'll pass the **Provincetown Playhouse** (133 MacDougal Street, between 3rd & 4th Streets), former home to the Provincetown Players (1916-29), a seminal group that introduced the works of its leading member, Eugene O'Neill, as well as plays by Djuna Barnes and Edna St Vincent Millay, among others. Although as a troupe the Players didn't survive the Crash of 1929, the Playhouse continued as one of America's foremost independent theatres, premiering the works of David Mamet and John Guare, as well as the first New York production of Edward Albee's *Zoo Story*, the city's quintessential drama. Today, the building is owned by New York University, which is renovating it for its law faculty; its façade will be restored to the original.

If the stately townhouses along the northern fringe of **Washington Square** still evoke Henry James's novel of that name, it's no small tribute to their preservation. In fact, 21 Washington Square North was used as Jennifer Jason Leigh's house in the 1997 film remake. Although the actual inspiration for the novel (James's grandmother's home at No.14) has not survived, the townhouses along Washington Square North provide a good indication of its august world. James himself lived at No.1, as did – at different points – Edith Wharton and the literary critic William Dean Howells. Diagonally across the square, at 38 Washington Square South, Eugene O'Neill consecrated his first New York residence by having an affair with journalist Louise Bryant, while her husband, John Reed (author of *Ten Days That Shook the World*) was in hospital.

Leave the square via Fifth Avenue and head north, turning left on Tenth Street, which brings you to Sixth Avenue and the local landmark **Jefferson Market Library**. Just behind it, off Tenth, lies Patchin Place, one of Greenwich Village's true gems and former home to some of the leading luminaries of New York's literary pantheon. This cul-de-sac lined with brick houses built during the mid-19th century is off-limits to the public, but through the gate you can make out No.1, which Reed and Bryant made their home; No.4, where the poet and foe of capitalisation e.e. cummings resided from 1923 to 1962; and No.5, where

Djuna Barnes, author of *Nightwood*, lived from 1940 to 1982. Ezra Pound, Theodore Dreiser and John Cowper Powys also lived here briefly, while numerous other literary figures passed through, but it managed to retain a quirky sense of community.

The favourite watering hole of self-destructive Welsh poet Dylan Thomas – the **White Horse Tavern** (567 Hudson Street, at 11th Street, 1-212 243 9260) – was also beloved of Kerouac, James Baldwin, Norman Mailer, Anaïs Nin and today's dire circus of frat boys. It was Thomas, however, who made the place his own, and several portraits of the poet adorn the walls – although the story of him drinking 18 straight whiskeys and expiring on the premises is a myth. Thomas (who was already taking medication for depression) gave his mistress that highly unlikely figure upon returning from the White Horse on 4 November 1953, then slept it off before heading back to the bar for two glasses of beer. Returning to the Chelsea Hotel (where he lived in his final years), he collapsed and later died at St Vincent's Hospital. Although the place serves pub grub, we recommend solemnly raising a glass before repairing to nearby **Corner Bistro** (p98) at the junction of W 4th and Jane Streets, where the burgers are consistently rated among the city's best.

If you want to end the tour in the neighbourhood, stop by the **Cherry Lane Theatre** (38 Commerce Street, at Barrow Street, 1-212 989 2020, www.cherrylanetheatre.org), the city's longest continually running Off Broadway theatre. Or catch a cab to the East Village for a slam at **Nuyorican Poets Café** (236 East 3rd Street, between Avenues B & C, 1-212 505 8183, www.nuyorican.org), where Allen Ginsberg occasionally read, and where today's lyricists square off.

New York by Area

South Street Seaport

Downtown

The southern tip of Manhattan has always been the city's financial, legal and political powerhouse. It's where New York began, and where the 19th-century influx of immigrants injected the city with new energy. Yet with much of it off the Big Apple's orderly grid, Downtown doesn't conform to the standard. The landscape shifts from block to block. In the Financial District, gleaming skyscrapers rub shoulders with 18th-century landmarks; Tribeca's haute cuisine dining spots are only a short hop from Chinatown's frenetic food markets; and around the corner from the clubs of the Meatpacking District, impeccably dressed matrons tend to the delicate gardens of their West Village brownstones.

Financial District

Since the city's earliest days as a fur-trading post, commerce has been the backbone of its prosperity. The southern point of Manhattan quickly evolved into the Financial District because, in the days before telecommunications, banks established their headquarters near the city's active port. Wall Street, which took its name from a defensive wooden wall built in 1653 to mark the northern limit of New Amsterdam, is synonymous with the world's greatest den of capitalism. On the eastern shore of lower Manhattan, old buildings in the disused South Street Seaport area were redeveloped in the mid-1980s into restaurants, bars, chain stores and a museum. Also check out the fine views of Brooklyn Bridge (p162).

Sights & museums

City Hall

City Hall Park, from Vesey to Chambers Streets, between Broadway & Park Row (1-212 639 9675/www.nyc.gov/design commission). Subway J, M, Z to Chambers Street; R, W to City Hall; 2, 3 to Park Place; 4, 5, 6 to Brooklyn Bridge-City Hall. **Open** *Tours* (individuals) noon Wed, 10am Thur; (groups) 10am Mon, Tue, Wed, Fri. **Admission** free. **Map** p60 C2 ➊

Designed by French émigré Joseph François Mangin and native New Yorker John McComb Jr, the fine, Federal-style City Hall was completed in 1812. Tours take in the rotunda, with its splendid coffered dome; the City Council Chamber; and the recently restored Governor's Room, which houses a collection of 19th-century American political portraits as well as historic furnishings (including George Washington's desk). Individuals can book the Thursday-morning tour (at least two days in advance); alternatively, sign up at the Heritage Tourism Center at the southern end of City Hall Park on the east side of Broadway, at Barclay Street, for Wednesday's first-come, first-served tour at noon. Group tours should be booked at least one week in advance.

Federal Reserve Bank

33 Liberty Street, between Nassau & William Streets (1-212 720 6130/ www.newyorkfed.org). Subway 2, 3, 4, 5 to Wall Street. **Open** *Tours* 9.30am, 10.30am, 11.30am, 1.30pm, 2.30pm, 3.30pm Mon-Fri. Tours must be booked at least 1wk in advance (phone or see website). **Admission** free. **Map** p60 C3 ➋

Descend 50ft below street level and you'll find roughly a quarter of the world's gold (more than $100 billion worth), stored in a gigantic vault that rests on the solid bedrock of Manhattan Island. Visitors on hour-long tours learn about the precious metal's history and the role of the New York Fed in its safeguarding.

Fraunces Tavern Museum

2nd & 3rd Floors, 54 Pearl Street, at Broad Street (1-212 425 1778/www. frauncestavernmuseum.org). Subway J, M, Z to Broad Street; 4, 5 to Bowling Green. **Open** noon-5pm Mon-Sat. **Admission** $10; free-$5 reductions. No credit cards. **Map** p60 C4 ➌

This 18th-century tavern was favoured by General George Washington, and was the site of his famous farewell to the troops at the Revolution's close. During the mid to late 1780s, the building housed the fledgling nation's departments of war, foreign affairs and treasury. In 1904, it became a repository for artefacts collected by the Sons of the Revolution in the State of New York. Highlights include a portrait gallery devoted to Washington, and one of the first president's false teeth. The tavern and restaurant (1-212 968 1776) serve hearty fare at lunch and dinner from Monday to Saturday.

Governors Island

1-212 440 2202/www.govisland.com. Subway R, W to Whitehall Street; 1 to South Ferry; 4, 5 to Bowling Green; then take ferry from Battery Maritime Building at Slip no.7. **Open** *Late May-mid Oct* 10am-5pm Fri; 10am-7pm Sat, Sun. **Admission** free. **Map** p60 C5 ➍

A seven-minute ride on a free ferry takes you to this seasonal island sanctuary, a scant 800 yards from lower Manhattan. Thanks to its strategic position in the middle of New York Harbor, Governors Island was a military outpost and off-limits to the public for 200 years. It finally opened to summer visitors in 2006. The verdant, 172-acre isle still retains a significant chunk of its military-era architecture, including Fort Jay, started in 1776, and Castle Williams, completed in 1812 and for years used as a prison. Today, the island is jointly run by the

A

WATTS ST
DESBROSSES ST
VESTRY ST
LAIGHT ST
HUBERT ST
BEACH ST
NORTH MOORE ST
FRANKLIN ST

HUDSON ST
COLLISTER ST
ERICKSON PL

B
VARICK ST
ST JOHN'S LN

See p62

CANAL ST

MERCER ST
HOWARD ST

C
Museum of
Chinese in
America

LISPENARD ST
WALKER ST

37

WEST SIDE HWY

26
25
HARRISON ST
STAPLE ST
JAY ST
GREENWICH ST

WEST BROADWAY

WHITE ST
FRANKLIN ST
LEONARD ST
WORTH ST
THOMAS ST
DUANE ST
READE ST

45 25
CORTLANDT ALLEY
LAFAYETTE ST
41
43
BROADWAY
CENTRE ST

CHINATOWN
Colum
Park
FOLEY
SQ
HAMILL PL
CARDINAL
BAXTER ST

TRIBECA

27 26
22
1,2,3
CHAMBERS ST
WARREN ST
PARK PL W
MURRAY ST

CHURCH ST

African
Burial Ground

J,M,Z,
4,5,6
A,C

City Hall
Park

City Hall
1

PARK ROW
FRANKFOR
SPRUCE ST

R,W

VESEY ST
PARK PL
BARCLAY ST
VESEY ST

2,3
BEEKMAN ST
ANN ST

RIVER TERR
NORTH END AVE
VESEY ST
PL

A,C,J,M,Z,
2,3,4,5
J,M,Z,
2,3,4,5
FULTON ST

GOLD ST

J,M,Z,
2;3,4,5

World Financial
Center

Ground
Zero
5

E
DEY ST
18
CORTLANDT

R,W

J,M,Z,
2,3,4,5
WILLIAM ST
PLATT ST
JOHN ST

BATTERY
PARK CITY

PUBLIC
PL
LIBERTY ST
CEDAR ST
ALBANY ST
THAMES ST

GREENWICH ST
CEDAR ST

Federal
Reserve
Bank
2
MAIDEN

Trinity
Church
8

NASSAU ST

Museum of
American Finar

RECTOR PL
S END AVE

CARLISLE ST
WASHINGTON ST
RECTOR ST

PINE ST

R,W
4,5
2,3

6
WAL
HANOVER

HANDVE
SQ

NY Stock
Exchange

EXCHANGE PL

BEAVER ST
S WILLIAM ST
PEARL ST
WATER ST

W THAMES ST

FINANCIAL DISTRICT

NEW ST
BROAD ST
MARKETFIELD

STONE ST

3
Fraunces
Tavern

THIRD PL
MORRIS ST
SECOND PL
FIRST PL

Bowling
Green
BATTERY PL

BEAVER ST
BRIDGE ST

S WILLIAM ST
COENTIES
SLIP

WHITEHALL ST

MOORE ST

Museum of
Jewish Heritage
Skyscraper
Museum

9
Museum of the
American Indian
7

4

Castle
Clinton

Battery
Park

12
1
Ferry to
Statue of
Liberty

11
Staten Is
Ferry Tern

BROOKLYN-BATTERY
TUNNEL

Hudson River

Downtown 1

THE BOWERY

D **E** EAST BROADWAY **F**

East River Park

1

See p63
Seward
Park

Eldridge St Synagogue

Confucius Plaza

First Shearith Israel Graveyard

2

MANHATTAN BRIDGE

ROOSEVELT DR

FRANKLIN

BROOKLYN BRIDGE

South Street Seaport

19
18

South St Seaport Museum
17
16
15
14

New York City Police Museum
13

11
9

BROOKLYN

3

4

0   200 m
0   200 yds
© Copyright Time Out Group 2009

5

PARK ROW

❶	Sights & museums
❷	Eating & drinking
❶	Shopping
❶	Nightlife
❶	Arts & leisure

Legend
- ❶ Sights & museums
- ❶ Eating & drinking
- ❶ Shopping
- ❶ Nightlife
- ❶ Arts & leisure

Ask New York City about New York City all night

nycgo.com

city, the state and the National Park
Service. As well as providing a peaceful setting for cycling (bring a bike on
the ferry, or rent from Bike & Roll
once there), the island hosts a programme of events, such as concert
series and art exhibitions (see website
for schedule). And where else can you
have a picnic directly across from the
Statue of Liberty?

Ground Zero

*Subway 1, 2, 3 to Chambers Street;
R, W to Cortlandt Street.* **Map**
p60 B3 ❺
The streets around Ground Zero, the
former site of the World Trade Center,
have been drawing continual crowds
since the terrorist attacks of 2001.
While people come to pay their
respects to the nearly 2,800 people
who lost their lives on 9/11, there's not
much to see. The area is surrounded
by a high fence and it's unlikely that
the new World Trade Center complex
– due to include office buildings, a
museum and memorial and the 1,776-
ft Freedom Tower – will be completed
by the 2011 target date.

Museum of American Finance

*48 Wall Street, at William Street
(1-212 908 4110/www.financial
history.org). Subway 2, 3, 4, 5 to
Wall Street; 1 to Rector Street.* **Open**
10am-4pm Tue-Sat. **Admission** $8;
free-$5 reductions. **Map** p60 C4 ❻
Situated in the old headquarters of the
Bank of New York, the Museum of
American Finance's permanent collection traces the history of Wall Street
and America's financial markets.
Displays in the august banking hall
include a bearer bond made out to
President George Washington and
ticker tape from the morning of the
stock market crash of 1929. The recent
addition of a timeline exhibit tracking
the evolution of the credit crisis from
2006 to the present helps to clarify the
current global predicament.

National Museum of the American Indian

*George Gustav Heye Center, Alexander
Hamilton Custom House, 1 Bowling
Green, between State & Whitehall
Streets (1-212 514 3700/www.nmai.
si.edu). Subway R, W to Whitehall
Street; 1 to South Ferry; 4, 5 to
Bowling Green.* **Open** 10am-5pm
Mon-Wed, Fri-Sun; 10am-8pm Thur.
Admission free. **Map** p60 C4 ❼
This branch of the Smithsonian displays its collection around the grand
rotunda of the 1907 Custom House, at
the southern tip of Broadway (which,
many moons ago, began as an Indian
trail). Although New York's first inhabitants are long gone, the life and culture
of Native Americans are presented in
rotating exhibitions, from intricately
woven fibre Pomo baskets to ceremo-
nial costumes.

St Paul's Chapel & Trinity Church

*St Paul's Chapel 209 Broadway,
between Fulton & Vesey Streets (1-212
233 4164/www.saintpaulschapel.org).
Subway A, C to Broadway-Nassau
Street; J, M, Z, 2, 3, 4, 5 to Fulton
Street. Trinity Church 89 Broadway,
at Wall Street (1-212 602 0872/
www.trinitywallstreet.org). Subway R,
W to Rector Street; 2, 3, 4, 5 to Wall
Street.* **Open** *St Paul's Chapel* 10am-
6pm Mon-Sat; 8am-4pm Sun. *Trinity
Church* 7am-6pm Mon-Fri; 8am-4pm
Sat; 7am-4pm Sun. **Admission** free.
Map p60 B3 ❽
Trinity Church was the island's tallest
structure when it was completed in
1846 (the original burned down in 1776;
a second was demolished in 1839). A
set of gates north of the church on
Broadway allows access to the adjacent cemetery, where cracked and
faded tombstones mark the final resting places of dozens of past city
dwellers, including signatories of the
Declaration of Independence and the
Constitution. The church museum displays an assortment of historic diaries,

Battery Park City

photographs, sermons and burial records. Trinity's satellite, St Paul's Chapel, is more important architecturally. The oldest building in New York still in continuous use (it dates from 1766), it is one of the nation's most valued Georgian structures. Both houses of worship host the inexpensive lunchtime Concerts at One series (see websites for details).

Skyscraper Museum

39 Battery Place, between Little West Street & 1st Place (1-212 968 1961/ www.skyscraper.org). Subway 4, 5 to Bowling Green. **Open** noon-6pm Wed-Sun. **Admission** $5; $2.50 reductions. **Map** p60 B4 ❾
The only institution of its kind in the world, this modest space explores high-rise buildings as objects of design, products of technology, real-estate investments and places of work and residence. Recent exhibits have covered architectural fantasies of the early 20th century, and charted the progress of the new World Trade Center complex.

South Street Seaport Museum

Visitors' centre, 12 Fulton Street, at South Street (1-212 748 8786/www. southstreetseaportmuseum.org). Subway A, C to Broadway-Nassau Street; J, M, Z, 2, 3, 4, 5 to Fulton Street. **Open** *Apr-Dec* 10am-6pm Tue-Sun. *Jan-Mar* 10am-5pm Mon, Fri-Sun. **Admission** $10; free-$8 reductions. **Map** p61 D3 ❿
Occupying 11 blocks along the East River, this museum is an amalgam of galleries, historic ships, 19th-century buildings and a visitors' centre. Wander around the rebuilt streets and pop in to see an exhibition on marine life and history before climbing aboard the four-masted 1911 barque *Peking* or the 1930 tug *WO Decker*.
Event highlights 'New Amsterdam, The Island at the Center of the World' (12 Sept 2009-7 Jan 2010).

Staten Island Ferry

Battery Park, South Street, at Whitehall Street (1-718 727 2508/ www.siferry.com). Subway 1 to South

Ferry; 4, 5 to Bowling Green.
Tickets free. **Map** p60 C5 ⑪
During this commuter barge's 25-minute crossing, you get superb panoramas of lower Manhattan and the Statue of Liberty. Boats leave South Ferry at Battery Park and run 24 hours a day.

Statue of Liberty & Ellis Island Immigration Museum

1-212 363 3200/www.nps.gov/stli & www.ellisisland.org. Subway R, W to Whitehall Street; 1 to South Ferry; 4, 5 to Bowling Green; then take Statue of Liberty ferry (1-877 523 9849/ www.statuecruises.com), departing roughly every 30mins from gangway 4 or 5 in southernmost Battery Park.
Open ferry runs 9.30am-3.30pm daily. Purchase tickets online, by phone or at Castle Clinton in Battery Park. **Admission** $12; free-$10 reductions. **Map** p60 B5 ⑫
The sole occupant of Liberty Island, *Liberty Enlightening the World* stands 305-ft tall from the bottom of her base to the tip of her gold-leaf torch.

Intended as a gift from France on America's 100th birthday, the statue was designed by Frédéric Auguste Bartholdi (1834-1904). Construction began in Paris in 1874, her skeletal iron framework crafted by Gustave Eiffel (the man behind the Tower), but only the arm with the torch was finished in time for the centennial. The celebrated limb was exhibited at the Centennial Exhibition in Philadelphia and then spent six years on display in Madison Square Park. In 1884, the statue was finally completed – only to be taken apart to be shipped to New York, where it was unveiled by President Grover Cleveland in 1886. It served as a lighthouse until 1902 and as a welcoming beacon for millions of immigrants. These 'tired…poor…huddled masses' were evoked in Emma Lazarus's poem *The New Colossus*, written in 1883 to raise funds for the pedestal and engraved inside the statue in 1903. With a Monument Pass, which is free but only available with ferry tickets reserved in advance, you can enter the pedestal and view the statue's interior through a glass ceiling. The crown is off limits for security reasons, but the views of New York City and the harbour from the observation deck are sensational.

A half-mile across the harbour from Liberty Island is 32-acre Ellis Island, gateway to the country for over 12 million people who arrived between 1892 and 1954. In the Immigration Museum (a former check-in depot), three floors of photos, interviews, interactive displays and exhibits pay tribute to the hopeful souls who made the voyage, and the nation they helped transform. Visitors can also search the museum's registry database and print copies of an ancestor's record.

Eating & drinking

Bin No. 220

220 Front Street, between Beekman Street & Peck Slip (1-212 374 9463/ www.binno220.com). Subway A, C to

NEW YORK BY AREA

Broadway-Nassau; J, M, Z, 2, 3, 4, 5 to Fulton Street. **Open** 4pm-midnight daily. **Wine bar**. Map p61 D3 ⑬

Located on a picturesquely historic street, this sleek wine bar offers refuge from the South Street Seaport tourist scene. Most patrons come for the selection of 60 wines (20 are available by the glass), but a well-stocked bar satisfies those who prefer the hard stuff. A selection of cured meats, cheeses and bread served with olive oils is available to soak up the booze.

Bridge Café

279 Water Street, at Dover Street (1-212 227 3344). Subway A, C to Broadway-Nassau Street; J, M, Z, 2, 3, 4, 5 to Fulton Street. **Open** 11.45am-10pm Mon, Sun; 11.45am-11pm Tue-Thur; 11.45am-midnight Fri; 5pm-midnight Sat. **$$**. **American creative**. Map p61 D3 ⑭

Standing since 1794, this wood-framed old timer (which once housed a brothel) is currently a cosy tavern slinging icy beers, stellar American wines and elevated pub grub. Former New York mayor Ed Koch was such a fan, he swung by twice a week – turning a blind eye to the beer-guzzling bookie regulars.

Financier Pâtisserie

62 Stone Street, between Hanover Square & Mill Lane (1-212 344 5600/ www.financierpastries.com). Subway 2, 3 to Wall Street. **Open** 7am-8pm Mon-Fri; 8.30am-6.30pm Sat. **$**. **Café**. Map p60 C4 ⑮

Tucked away on a cobblestoned street, this sweet gem offers tasty café fare to office workers, tourists and locals seeking a pleasant alternative to the Financial District's pubs and delis. Hot pressed sandwiches (try the croque-monsieur), salads and quiches are all delicious. But the pastries are where it excels, including miniature financiers, which are free with each coffee.

Other locations 35 Cedar Street, at William Street (1-212 952 3838); 3-4 World Financial Center (1-212 786 3220).

Jack's Stir Brew Coffee

222 Front Street, between Beekman Street & Peck Slip (1-212 227 7631/ www.jacksstirbrew.com). Subway A, C to Broadway-Nassau Street. **Open** 7am-6pm Mon-Fri; 8am-6pm Sat, Sun. **$**. No credit cards. **Café**. Map p61 D3 ⑯

Java fiends convene at this award-winning Downtown caffeine spot that offers organic, shade-grown beans and a homely vibe. Coffee is served by chatty, quick-to-grin espresso artisans with a knack for oddball concoctions, such as the super-silky Mountie latte, infused with maple syrup.

Shopping

Bowne & Co Stationers

South Street Seaport Museum, 211 Water Street, at Fulton Street (1-212 748 8651). Subway A, C, J, M, Z to Broadway-Nassau Street. **Open** 10am-5pm Tue-Sun. Map p61 D3 ⑰

South Street Seaport Museum's re-creation of an 1870s-style print shop doesn't just look the part: the 19th-century platen presses, hand-set using antique type and powered by a treadle, turn out everything from prints to calling cards using Crane & Co stationery.

Century 21

22 Cortlandt Street, between Broadway & Church Street (1-212 227 9092/ www.c21stores.com). Subway R, W to Cortlandt Street. **Open** 7.45am-9pm Mon-Wed; 7.45am-9.30pm Thur, Fri; 10am-9pm Sat; 11am-8pm Sun. Map p60 C3 ⑱

A Gucci men's suit for $300? A Marc Jacobs cashmere sweater for less than $200? No, you're not dreaming – you're shopping at Century 21. You may have to rummage to unearth a treasure, but with savings from 25% to 75% or more off regular prices, it's often worth it.

Tribeca & Soho

A former industrial wasteland, Tribeca (the Triangle Below Canal

Street) is now one of the city's most expensive areas, where upscale shops and haute eateries cater to the well-heeled locals. Likewise, Soho (the area South of Houston Street) was once a hardscrabble manufacturing zone with the derisive nickname Hell's Hundred Acres. Earmarked for destruction in the 1960s, its signature cast-iron warehouses were saved by the artists who inhabited them. Although the large chain stores and sidewalk-encroaching street vendors along Broadway create a shopping-mall-at-Christmas crush at weekends, there are some fabulous shops, galleries and eateries in the locale.

Sights & museums

Rock & Roll Hall of Fame Annex NYC

NEW *76 Mercer Street, between Broome & Spring Streets (1-646 786 6680/www.rockannex.com). Subway R, W to Prince Street.* **Open** 11am-7pm Tue-Thur, Sun; 11am-9pm Fri, Sat. **Admission** $24.50; free-$22.50 reductions. **Map** p62 C4 ⑲
See box p73.

Eating & drinking

Balthazar

80 Spring Street, between Broadway & Crosby Street (1-212 965 1414/ www.balthazarny.com). Subway N, R, W to Prince Street; 6 to Spring Street. **Open** 7.30am-4pm, 5.45pm-midnight Mon-Thur; 7.30am-4pm, 5.45pm-1am Fri; 8-10am, 5.45pm-1am Sat; 8am-10am, 5.30pm-midnight Sun. $$.
French. **Map** p62 C4 ⑳
At dinner, this iconic eaterie is perennially packed with rail-thin lookers dressed to the nines. But it's not only fashionable – the kitchen rarely makes a false step and the service is surprisingly friendly. The $110 three-tiered seafood platter casts an impressive shadow, and the roast chicken on mashed potatoes for two is *délicieux*.

Boqueria

171 Spring Street, between West Broadway & Thompson Street (1-212 343 4255/www.boquerianyc.com). Subway C, E to Spring Street. **Open** noon-midnight daily. $$. **Spanish**. **Map** p62 C4 ㉑
Given that Boqueria is named for Barcelona's centuries-old food market, you might expect the menu to lean

Soho

toward the classics. Not quite. Chef Seamus Mullen's bacalao (salt cod), a standard tapas ingredient, is served here as an airy and crisp beignet. The most successful sangria is an unorthodox beer-based version that mixes lager, pear purée, lemon juice and triple sec.

Bouley Market

120 West Broadway, at Duane Street (1-212 219 1011/www.davidbouley. com). Subway A, C, E, 1, 2, 3 to Chambers Street. **Open** 7.30am-8.30pm daily. **$-$$. American creative/café**. Map p60 B2
High-profile chef David Bouley has rejigged his collection of restaurants. Bouley Bakery & Market, now in the space once occupied by fine-dining room Bouley (which has moved to nearby Duane Street), has dropped the 'Bakery' tag in name only; it still offers heavenly loaves. There's also a fine cheese selection and great takeout and eat-in options, including soups and sandwiches. Less expensive than Bouley proper, Bouley Upstairs now occupies all of Bouley Market's old, bi-level space – got that? Essentially an expanded version of the original second-floor eatery, it offers a mostly French menu with some small Asian twists, and a sushi bar.
Other locations Bouley Upstairs, 130 West Broadway, at Duane Street (1-212 608 5829); Bouley, 163 Duane Street, at Hudson Street (1-212 964 2525).

Corton

NEW *239 West Broadway, between Walker & White Streets (1-212 219 2777/www.cortonnyc.com). Subway A, C, E to Canal Street; 1 to Franklin Street.* **Open** 5.30-10.30pm Mon-Thur; 5.30-11pm Fri, Sat. **$$$. French**. Map p60 B1
A meal at Corton, which has been given six stars – the highest rating – by *Time Out New York* magazine's critics, is an extraordinary experience. Veteran restaurateur Drew Nieporent's white-on-white sanctuary focuses all attention on chef Paul Liebrandt's finely wrought food. The presentations, in the style of the most esteemed modern kitchens of Europe, are Photoshop flawless: sweet bay scallops, for example, anchor a visual masterpiece featuring wisps of radish, marcona almonds and sea urchin.

Fanelli's Café

Fanelli's Café

*94 Prince Street, at Mercer Street
(1-212 226 9412). Subway N, R, W
to Prince Street.* **Open** 10am-1.30am
Mon-Thur, Sun; 10am-3.30am Fri, Sat.
$. **American/bar.** Map p62 C4 ㉔
On a lovely cobblestoned corner, this
1847 joint claims to be the second-old-
est continuously operating bar and
restaurant in New York, and the basic
menu includes one of the city's best
burgers. The long bar, prints of boxing
legends and check tablecloths all add
to the charm.

M1-5

*52 Walker Street, between Broadway
& Church Street (1-212 965 1701/
www.m1-5.com). Subway J, M, N, Q,
R, W, Z, 6 to Canal Street.* **Open** 4pm-
4am daily. **Bar.** Map p60 C1/p62 C5 ㉕
The name of this huge, red-walled hangout refers to Tribeca's zoning ordinance,
which permits trendy restaurants to co-
exist with warehouses. The mixed-use
concept also applies to M1-5's crowd:
suited brokers, indie musicians and
baby-faced screenwriters play pool and
order from the full, well-stocked bar specialising in stiff martinis.

Megu

*62 Thomas Street, between Church
Street & West Broadway (1-212 964
7777/www.megunyc.com). Subway A,
C, 1, 2, 3 to Chambers Street.* **Open**
5.30-10.30pm Mon-Wed, Sun; 5.30-
11.30pm Thur-Sat.* **$$$.** **Japanese.**
Map p60 B2 ㉖
Since the day this awe-inspiring temple
of Japanese cuisine opened in 2004, din-
ers have criticised its overblown prices
and unwieldy, complicated menu. But
critics often forget to mention that this
is one of the most thrilling meals you'll
find in New York. Spring for one of the
tasting menus: a parade of ingenious lit-
tle bites and surprising presentations.

Odeon

*145 West Broadway, between Duane
& Thomas Streets (1-212 233 0507/*
*www.theodeonrestaurant.com). Subway
A, C, 1, 2, 3 to Chambers Street.* **Open**
11.45am-1am Mon-Wed; 11.45am-2am
Thur, Fri; 10am-2am Sat, Sun. **$$.**
French. Map p60 B2 ㉗
The Odeon has been part of the
Downtown scene for so long that it's
hard to remember a time when Tribeca
wasn't home to the iconic bistro. It's
still a great destination for drinks, and
diners can't go wrong with the tried-
and-true standards: French onion soup
blanketed with bubbling gruyère,
crunchy fried calamari made to be
dipped in tartare and spicy chipotle
sauces, and steak au poivre with fries.

Pegu Club

*77 W Houston Street, at West
Broadway (1-212 473 7348/www.
peguclub.com). Subway B, D, F, V to
Broadway-Lafayette Street; N, R to
Prince Street.* **Open** 5pm-2am Mon-
Wed, Sun; 5pm-4am Thur-Sat. **Bar.**
Map p62 C4 ㉓
Audrey Saunders, the drinks maven
who turned Bemelmans Bar (p147) into
one of the city's most respected cocktail
lounges, is behind this sleek, second-
storey liquid destination, inspired by a
British officers' club in Burma. The bev-
erage programme features classics
culled from decades-old booze bibles,
and gin is the star ingredient – try the
eponymous signature cocktail, made
with gin, bitters and orange curaçao.

Savoy

*70 Prince Street, at Crosby Street
(1-212 219 8570/www.savoynyc.com).
Subway N, R, W to Prince Street; 6 to
Spring Street.* **Open** noon-10.30pm
Mon-Thur; noon-11pm Fri, Sat; 6-10pm
Sun. **$$$.** **American creative.**
Map p62 C4 ㉙
Chef Peter Hoffman maintains his rep-
utation as one of the godfathers of the
local foods movement at this comfort-
able Soho stalwart, outfitted with a
wood-burning fireplace (in use during
colder months) and a congenial, semi-
circular bar. Hoffman makes daily

NEW YORK BY AREA

pilgrimages to the Union Square Greenmarket to assemble Savoy's farm-forward, aggressively seasonal menus, which include the likes of flaky halibut perched over a verdant fava bean purée.

Shopping

Built by Wendy

7 Centre Market Place, at Grand Street (1-212 925 6538/www.builtbywendy. com). Subway B, D to Grand Street; J, N, Q, R, M, W, Z, 6 to Canal Street. **Open** noon-7pm Mon-Sat; noon-6pm Sun. **Map** p63 D4 ➂⓪

Chicago-bred designer Wendy Mullin started selling handmade clothes and guitar straps in record stores in 1991. Today, her youthful men's and women's garb still maintains a home-spun look and Midwestern vibe, via men's plaid flannel shirts and girlish dresses, as well as cool graphic T-shirts. Stylish rockers, take note: guitar straps are still available in colour-ful Ultrasuede.

Dean & DeLuca

560 Broadway, at Prince Street (1-212 226 6800/www.deananddeluca.com). Subway N, R, W to Prince Street. **Open** 7am-8pm Mon-Fri; 8am-8pm Sat, Sun. **Map** p62 C4 ➂①

Dean & DeLuca's flagship store provides the most sophisticated selection of speciality food items in the city, but prices are high.

Housing Works Bookstore Café

126 Crosby Street, between Houston & Prince Streets (1-212 334 3324/ www.housingworksubc.com). Subway B, D, F, V to Broadway-Lafayette Street; R, W to Prince Street; 6 to Bleecker Street. **Open** 10am-9pm Mon-Fri; noon-7pm Sat, Sun. **Map** p62 C4 ➂②

This endearing, two-level place – which stocks a range of literary fiction, non-fiction, rare books and collectibles – is a peaceful spot for browsing, attending literary events or relaxing over coffee or wine. All proceeds from the café go to providing support services for homeless people living with HIV/AIDS.

Jacques Torres Chocolate

350 Hudson Street, between Charlton & King Streets, entrance on King Street (1-212 414 2462/www.mr chocolate.com). Subway 1 to Houston Street. **Open** 9am-7pm Mon-Sat; 10am-6pm Sun. **Map** p62 B4 ➂③

Walk into Jacques Torres's glass-walled shop and café, and you'll be sur-rounded by a Willy Wonka-esque factory that turns raw cocoa beans into luscious chocolate goodies before your eyes. As well as selling the usual assort-ments, truffles and bars (plus quirkier delicacies like chocolate-covered corn-flakes), the shop serves deliciously rich hot chocolate, steamed to order.

Kiki de Montparnasse

79 Greene Street, between Broome & Spring Streets (1-212 965 8150/ www.kikidm.com). Subway R, W to Prince Street; 6 to Spring Street. **Open** noon-7pm Mon, Sun; noon-8pm Tue-Sat. **Map** p62 C4 ➂④

This erotic boutique channels the spirit of its namesake, a 1920s sexual icon and Man Ray muse, with a posh array of tastefully provocative contem-porary lingerie in satin and French lace, including such novelties as cotton tank tops with built-in garters and knickers embroidered with saucy leg-ends. Bedroom accoutrements, includ-ing molten crystal 'dilettos' and feather ticklers, give new meaning to the expression 'satisfied customer'.

Kiosk

95 Spring Street, between Broadway & Mercer Street (1-212 226 8601/ www.kioskkiosk.com). Subway 6 to Spring Street. **Open** 1-7pm Tue-Sat. **Map** p62 C4 ➂⑤

Don't be put off by the unprepossessing, graffiti-covered stairway that leads up to this gem of a shop. Alisa Grifo has collected an array of inexpensive items

Rock this town

New York City gave birth to many of popular music's most influential artists and storied venues, yet it took an out-of-towner to give the city its first repository of rock. An offshoot of the Cleveland original, the **Rock & Roll Hall of Fame Annex NYC** (p69) traces the history of the genre through artefacts, video installations and special exhibitions. 'We thought it would be a good place to do a smaller version, given New York City's central place in the history of rock 'n' roll,' says Jim Henke, vice-president of exhibitions and curatorial affairs. And it shows: one whole gallery is devoted to all things NYC; relics include the awning from defunct club CBGB and David Byrne's big suit from the film *Stop Making Sense*.

'Everyone has a different definition of rock 'n' roll,' says Henke. 'We try to define it very broadly, so there's something for everyone.' As you'd expect, the collection includes some legendary axes: a Les Paul that survived famous guitar-destroyer Pete Townshend on The Who's 1973 Quadrophenia tour, and the white Mosrite wielded by the late Johnny Ramone in The Ramones' last show. But the Annex has a varied array of holdings: one of the earliest manuscripts of 'Purple Haze', which Jimi Hendrix scrawled on notebook paper in a London nightclub dressing room, a pair of John Lennon's glasses and some of Madonna's old gear – including the iconic, pointy-cupped gold Jean-Paul Gaultier bustier that the Material Girl wore on her Blond Ambition tour. '*Rolling Stone* called it the best tour of 1990,' says Henke. 'Her use of sexuality onstage made it controversial, and Pope John Paul II even called on people to boycott concerts in Italy.' The museum also hosts a rockin' roster of temporary shows; 'John Lennon: The New York Years', created by Yoko Ono, will run through late autumn 2009. If the crowds paying their respects at Central Park's Strawberry Fields are anything to go by, it's bound to be a smash hit.

– mostly simple and functional but with a strong design aesthetic – from around the world, such as hairpins in a cool retro box from Mexico, Finnish licorice, colourful net bags from Germany and a butterfly can-opener from Japan.

Matter

405 Broome Street, between Centre & Lafayette Streets (1-212 343 2600/ www.mattermatters.com). Subway 6 to Spring Street. **Open** noon-7pm Mon-Sat; noon-6pm Sun. **Map** p63 D4 ㊱

The Soho spin-off of Brooklyn design store Matter offers an eclectic international selection of furniture, home accessories and jewellery, including Iraqi-Brit architect Zaha Hadid's interlocking Nekton stools and hot duo Fredrikson Stallard's provocative cross-shaped clothes brushes. There are some great New York-centric gifts too: look out for limited-edition metal manhole-cover coasters by Curios.

Opening Ceremony

35 Howard Street, between Broadway & Lafayette Street (1-212 219 2688/ www.openingceremony.us). Subway J, M, N, Q, R, W, Z, 6 to Canal Street. **Open** 11am-8pm Mon-Sat; noon-7pm Sun. **Map** p62 C5 ㊲

Opening Ceremony offers a stylish trip around the world in a tri-level, warehouse-size space gussied up with grape-coloured walls and crystal chandeliers. The name references the Olympic Games, and each year the store assembles hip US designers and pits them against the competition from abroad; the Japanese focus is wrapping up in autumn 2009, when the new country will be revealed. Also in autumn/winter 2009, look out for high-profile collaborations, including Chloë Sevigny's menswear line, which channels preppy style.

3.1 Phillip Lim

115 Mercer Street, between Prince & Spring Streets (1-212 334 1160/ www.31philliplim.com). Subway R, W to Prince Street; 6 to Spring

Street. **Open** 11am-7pm Mon-Sat; noon-6pm Sun. **Map** p62 C4 ㊳

Since Phillip Lim debuted his collection in 2005, he has amassed a devoted international following for his simple yet strong silhouettes and beautifully constructed tailoring-with-a-twist. His boutique gathers together his award-winning womens- and menswear and accessories under one roof.

Nightlife

City Winery

NEW *155 Varick Street, at Vandam Street (1-212 608 0555/www.city winery.com). Subway 1 to Houston Street.* **Map** p62 B4 ㊴

Grapes are crushed and aged on the premises at this high-end wine bar; fancy cheese and dinner are also available. But the intimate space doubles as a music venue. Opened by Knitting Factory founder Michael Dorf, the quintessentially New York yuppie haven has already presented an impressive array of performers, including Aimee Mann, Marianne Faithfull and Rufus Wainwright.

Jazz Gallery

290 Hudson Street, between Dominick & Spring Streets (1-212 242 1063/ www.jazzgallery.org). Subway A, C, E to Spring Street. **Map** p62 B4 ㊵

The fact that there's no bar here should be a tip-off: the Jazz Gallery is a place to witness true works of art, from the sometimes obscure but always interesting jazzers who play the club (Henry Threadgill and Steve Coleman, to name a couple) to the photos and artefacts displayed on the walls. The diminutive room's acoustics are sublime.

Santos Party House

NEW *100 Lafayette Street, at Walker Street (recorded message 1-212 714 4646/www.santospartyhouse.com; box office 1-212 584 5492). Subway J, M, N, Q, R, W, Z, 6 to Canal Street.* **Map** p60 C1 ㊶

Launched by a team that includes rocker Andrew WK, this two-floor club was three years in the making, though you'd never guess it from the generic decor. The place is committed to resuscitating Downtown's underground scene, with top spinners of off-kilter house, cosmic disco, funk and soul regularly taking to the decks, including A Tribe Called Quest's Q-Tip and Rich Medina.

SOB's

204 Varick Street, at Houston Street (1-212 243 4940/www.sobs.com). Subway 1 to Houston Street.
Map p62 B4 ㊷

The titular Sounds of Brazil (SOB, geddit?) are just some of the many global genres that keep this spot hopping. Hip hop, soul, reggae and Latin beats all figure in the mix, with Seu Jorge, Zap Mama and Wyclef Jean each appearing of late. The drinks are expensive, but the sharp-looking clientele doesn't seem to mind.

Arts & leisure

Flea Theater

41 White Street, between Broadway & Church Street (1-212 226 2407/ www.theflea.org). Subway A, C, E, J, M, N, Q, R, W, Z, 1, 6 to Canal Street.
Map p60 C1/p62 C5 ㊸

Founded in 1997, Jim Simpson's cosy, well-appointed venue has presented avant-garde experimentation (such as the work of Mac Wellman) and politically provocative satires (mostly by AR Gurney).

HERE

145 Sixth Avenue, between Broome & Spring Streets (1-212 647 0202/ Smarttix 1-212 868 4444/www.here. org). Subway C, E to Spring Street.
Map p62 C4 ㊹

This recently renovated Soho arts complex, dedicated to not-for-profit arts enterprises, has been the launch pad for such well-known shows as

Eve Ensler's *The Vagina Monologues*. More recently, it has showcased the talents of puppeteer Basil Twist, singer Joey Arias and the brilliantly imaginative playwright-performer Taylor Mac.

Soho Rep

46 Walker Street, between Broadway & Church Street (1-212 868 4444/ box office 1-212 941 8632/www.soho rep.org). Subway A, C, E, N, R, 6 to Canal Street; 1 to Franklin Street.
Map p60 C1/p62 C5 ㊺

A couple of years ago, this Off-Off mainstay moved to an Off Broadway contract, but tickets for most shows are still cheap for Off Broadway. Artistic director Sarah Benson's programming is diverse and adventurous; the 2008/9 line-up included the New York première of Sarah Kane's brutal, controversial 1995 play *Blasted*.

Chinatown, Little Italy & Nolita

Take a walk in the area south of Broome Street and west of Broadway, and you'll feel as though you've entered a different continent. New York's Chinatown is one of the largest Chinese communities outside Asia. The crowded streets are lined by fish-, fruit- and vegetable-stocked stands, and Canal Street is infamous for its (illegal) knock-off designer handbags, perfumes and other goods among the numerous cheap gift shops. But the main attraction is the food: Mott Street, between Kenmare and Worth Streets, is lined with restaurants.

Little Italy once stretched from Canal to Houston Streets, between Lafayette Street and the Bowery, but these days a strong Italian presence can only truly be observed on the blocks immediately surrounding Mulberry Street.

Ethnic pride remains, though: Italian-Americans flood in from across the city during the 11-day Feast of San Gennaro (p39). Nolita (North of Little Italy) became a magnet for pricey boutiques and trendy eateries in the 1990s. Elizabeth, Mott and Mulberry Streets, between Houston and Spring Streets, in particular, are home to hip designer shops.

Sights & museums

Museum of Chinese in America

NEW *211-215 Centre Street, between Grand & Howard Streets (1-212 619 4785/www.mocanyc.org). Subway J, M, N, Q, R, W, Z, 6 to Canal Street.* **Open** 11am-5pm Mon, Fri; 11am-9pm Thur; 10am-5pm Sat, Sun. **Admission** $7; free-$4 reductions. **Map** p61 D1/ p63 D5 ⓐ

MOCA's former space on Mulberry Street closed last year, and its new home, designed by Vietnam Veterans Memorial architect Maya Lin, was due to open as this guide went to press. The Chinese-American experience is the main focus of the permanent collection, but the additional gallery space allows for more contemporary programming, such as 'Archaeology of Change' in autumn 2009, which tracks Chinatown's gentrification by spotlighting five erstwhile landmarks (including the museum itself, the former Grand Machinery Exchange).

Eating & drinking

Café Habana

17 Prince Street, at Elizabeth Street (1-212 625 2001/www.ecoeatery.com). Subway N, R, W to Prince Street; 6 to Spring Street. **Open** 9am-midnight daily. **$**. **Cuban**. **Map** p63 D4 ⓐ

Trendy Nolita types storm this chrome corner fixture for the addictive grilled corn: golden ears doused in fresh mayo, chargrilled, and generously sprinkled with chilli powder and grated *cotija* cheese. Staples include a Cuban sandwich of roasted pork, ham, melted Swiss and sliced pickles, and crisp beer-battered catfish with spicy mayo. At the takeout annexe next door (open May-Oct), you can get that corn-on-a-stick to go.

Ed's Lobster Bar

Ed's Lobster Bar

222 Lafayette Street, between Kenmare & Spring Streets (1-212 343 3236/ www.lobsterbarnyc.com). Subway B, D, F, V to Broadway-Lafayette Street. **Open** noon-3pm, 5-11pm Tue-Thur; noon-3pm, 5pm-midnight Fri; noon-midnight Sat; noon-9pm Sun. **$$.** **Seafood**. **Map** p62 C4 ㊽

Chef Ed McFarland (of Pearl Oyster Bar; p99) takes on the shellfish shack formula at this tiny Soho spot. If you secure a place at the 30-seat marble bar or one of the few tables in the white-washed eaterie, expect superlative raw-bar eats, delicately fried clams and lobster served every which way: steamed, grilled, broiled, chilled, stuffed into a pie and, the crowd favourite, the lobster roll.

Golden Bridge Restaurant

50 Bowery, between Bayard & Canal Streets (1-212 227 8831). Subway B, D to Grand Street; J, M, N, Q, R, W, Z, 6 to Canal Street. **Open** 9am-midnight daily. **$.** **Chinese**. **Map** p61 D1/p63 D5 ㊾

In this dim sum house, carts patrol a spacious dining room that overlooks the Manhattan Bridge. Flag one of them down to procure fresh Cantonese standards such as clams in black bean sauce and pillowy pork buns, plus more unusual items, including an egg tart with a soft taro crust. Look for the elusive cart with the mysterious wooden bucket: it's filled with sweetened tofu.

Lombardi's

32 Spring Street, between Mott & Mulberry Streets (1-212 941 7994/ www.firstpizza.com). Subway 6 to Spring Street. **Open** 11.30am-11pm Mon-Thur, Sun; 11.30am-midnight Fri, Sat. **$.** No credit cards. **Pizza**. **Map** p63 D4 ㊿

New York's oldest pizzeria, Lombardi's, has been serving thin-crust pies since 1905. The setting is classic pizza-parlour style, with wooden booths and red and white checked tablecloths, and the place bakes a hot contender for the city's best pie in its coal-fired oven. The pepperoni is fantastic, as are the killer meatballs.

Peking Duck House

28 Mott Street, between Mosco & Pell Streets (1-212 227 1810/www.pekingduckhousenyc.com). Subway J, M, N, Q, R, W, Z, 6 to Canal Street. **Open** 11.30am-10.30pm Mon-Thur, Sun; 11.45am-11pm Fri, Sat. **$.** **Chinese**. **Map** p61 D1/63 D5 (51)

At this duck specialist, select the 'three-way' and your bird will yield the main course, a vegetable stir-fry with left-over bits of meat, and a cabbage soup made with the remaining bone.

Shopping

Lyell

173 Elizabeth Street, between Kenmare & Spring Streets (1-212 966 8484/ www.lyellnyc.com). Subway J, M, Z to Bowery; 6 to Spring Street. **Open** noon-7pm Mon-Sat; noon-6pm Sun. **Map** p63 D4 (52)

Lyell creator Emma Fletcher's exquisite 1930s-inspired tea dresses and

Market NYC

clean-lined silk blouses are all impeccably tailored in New York City; the line has been adopted by such stylish young stars as Zooey Deschanel and Michelle Williams.

Market NYC

268 Mulberry Street, between Houston & Prince Streets (1-212 580 8995/ www.themarketnyc.com). Subway B, D, F, V to Broadway-Lafayette Street; N, R, W to Prince Street; 6 to Bleecker Street. **Open** 11am-7pm Sat, Sun. No credit cards. **Map** p63 D4 ⑬

Every weekend, independent clothing and accessories designers set up shop in the gymnasium of a church's youth centre, giving shoppers the chance to buy a variety of unique wares direct from the makers.

Sigerson Morrison

28 Prince Street, between Elizabeth & Mott Streets (1-212 219 3893/ www.sigersonmorrison.com). **Open** 11am-7pm Mon-Sat; noon-6pm Sun. **Map** p63 D4 ⑭

The culty footwear brand recently hatched a deluxe Madison Avenue depot, but the original store displays the full range of sleek – often 1960s-inspired – boots and pixie-like flats (from around $300). The Belle line is more cheaply priced.

Other locations Belle, 242 Mott Street, between Houston & Prince Streets, Nolita (1-212 941 5404).

Lower East Side

Once better known for bagels and bargains, this old immigrant area is now brimming with vintage and indie-designer boutiques, speakeasy-style bars and, since the **New Museum of Contemporary Art** opened a $50 million building on the Bowery in late 2007, dozens of storefront galleries.

Sights & museums

Lower East Side Tenement Museum

Visitors' centre: 108 Orchard Street, at Delancey Street (1-212 982 8420/ www.tenement.org). Subway F to Delancey Street; F, J, M, Z to

Delancey-Essex Streets. **Open** *Visitors' centre & gift shop* 11am-6pm daily. *Tours* every 15mins 11.15am-5pm daily. **Admission** $17; $13 reductions. **Map** p63 E4 ⑤

This fascinating museum – actually a series of restored tenement apartments at 97 Orchard Street – is accessible only by guided tour. Tickets are purchased at the visitors' centre at 108 Orchard Street, and it's wise to book ahead. Costumed interpreters recount the daily lives of individual immigrant clans that called the building home over the decades. 'Piecing it Together' pays a call on the Russian Rogarshevsky family, mourning the loss of patriarch Abraham, a garment worker who died of tuberculosis in 1918, while a new tour, 'The Moores: An Irish Family in America', revisits a Dublin family who lived in the building in 1869. From April to December, the museum also offers weekend walking tours of the Lower East Side ($17; $13 reductions).

Museum at Eldridge Street Synagogue (Eldridge Street Synagogue)

NEW *12 Eldridge Street, between Canal & Division Streets (1-212 219 0302/ www.eldridgestreet.org). Subway F to East Broadway.* **Open** *Tours* every 30mins 10am-3pm Mon-Thur, Sun. **Admission** $10; free-$8 reductions. **Map** p61 D1/63 E5 ⑤

Established in 1887, the Eldridge Street Synagogue was among the earliest temples founded in America by the new wave of Eastern European Jews. For its first 50 years, the Moorish Revival shul had a congregation of thousands and doubled as a mutual-aid society for new arrivals. But the synagogue fell into disrepair, and by the 1950s the badly damaged main sanctuary was closed. Following a 20-year, $20 million facelift that rejuvenated its 70ft vaulted ceilings and breathtaking stained-glass rose windows, it is now open for hour-long guided tours.

New Museum of Contemporary Art

235 Bowery, at Prince Street (1-212 219 1222/www.newmuseum.org). Subway F, V to Lower East Side-Second Avenue. **Open** noon-6pm Wed, Sat, Sun; noon-9pm Thur, Fri. **Admission** $12; free-$10 reductions. **Map** p63 D4 ⑦

After 30 years of occupying various sites around town, New York City's only contemporary art museum finally got its own purpose-built space in late 2007 – the first new art museum ever constructed below 14th Street. Dedicated to emerging media and important but under-recognised artists, the seven-floor space is worth a look for the architecture alone – a striking, off-centre stack of aluminium-mesh-clad boxes designed by the cutting-edge Tokyo architectural firm Sejima + Nishizawa/SANAA. On weekends, don't miss the fabulous views from the minimalist, seventh-floor Sky Room.

Eating & drinking

Back Room

NEW *102 Norfolk Street, between Delancey & Rivington Streets (1-212 228 5098). Subway F, J, M, V, Z to Delancey-Essex Streets.* **Open** 7.30pm-4am Tue-Sat. **Bar**. **Map** p63 E4 ⑤ See box p82.

Botanica

47 E Houston Street, between Mott & Mulberry Streets (1-212 343 7251). Subway B, D, F, V to Broadway-Lafayette Street; 6 to Bleecker Street. **Open** 5pm-4am Mon-Fri; 6pm-4am Sat, Sun. **Bar**. **Map** p63 D4 ⑤

The thrift-store decor (mismatched chairs with sagging seats, statues of the Virgin Mary and a faux fireplace) makes for a charmingly shabby backdrop at this Downtown dive, a favourite among laid-back creative types and the occasional gaggle of NYU students. The libations range

NEW YORK BY AREA

from basic brews (eight on tap) to house cocktails like the Mean Bean martini, made with vodka and spicy green beans from Rick's Picks. DJs spin on most nights of the week.

Clinton Street Baking Company

4 Clinton Street, between E Houston & Stanton Streets (1-646 602 6263/ www.clintonstreetbaking.com). Subway F to Delancey Street; J, M, Z to Delancey-Essex Streets. **Open** 8am-4pm, 6-11pm Mon-Fri; 10am-4pm, 6-11pm Sat; 10am-4pm Sun. $. **Café**. Map p63 E4 ⑥⓪
The warm buttermilk biscuits and fluffy plate-size pancakes at this pioneering little eaterie give you reason enough to face the guaranteed brunchtime crowds. If you want to avoid the onslaught, however, the homely spot is just as reliable at both lunch and dinner; drop in between 6pm and 8pm for the daily $10 beer-and-burger special, consisting of 8oz of Black Angus topped with Swiss cheese and caramelised onions, served with a Brooklyn Lager.

Freemans

2 Freeman Alley, off Rivington Street, between Bowery & Chrystie Street (1-212 420 0012/www.freemans restaurant.com). Subway F, V to Lower East Side-Second Avenue; J, M, Z to Bowery. **Open** 11am-4pm, 6-11.30pm daily. $$. **American**. Map p63 D4 ⑥①
Up at the end of a graffiti-marked alley, Freemans' appealing colonial-tavern-meets-hunting-lodge style has found a welcome home with retro-loving Lower East Siders. Garage-sale oil paintings and moose antlers serve as backdrops to a curved zinc bar, while the menu recalls a simpler time – devils on horseback (prunes stuffed with stilton and wrapped in bacon); rum-soaked ribs, the meat falling off the bone with a gentle nudge of the fork; and stiff cocktails that'll get you good and sauced.

Katz's Delicatessen

205 E Houston Street, at Ludlow Street (1-212 254 2246/www.katzdeli.com). Subway F, V to Lower East Side-Second Avenue. **Open** 8am-9.45pm Mon, Tue; 8am-10.45pm Wed, Thur; 8am-2.45am Fri, Sat; 8am-10.45pm Sun. $. **American**. Map p63 E4 ⑥②
This cavernous old dining hall is a repository of living history – not because of the photos of celebrity diners that plaster the walls, but the old-school setting and Jewish-American fare. The crisp-skinned, all beef hotdogs are without peer, the pastrami is simply da best, and everything tastes better with the hoppy house lager.

Schiller's Liquor Bar

131 Rivington Street, at Norfolk Street (1-212 260 4555/www.schillersny.com). Subway F to Delancey Street; J, M, Z to Delancey-Essex Streets. **Open** 8am-2am Mon, Tue; 8am-3am Wed-Fri; 10am-3am Sat; 10am-2am Sun. $. **Eclectic**. Map p63 E4 ⑥③
The menu at Schiller's is a mix of French bistro (steak-frites), British pub (fish and chips) and good ol' American (cheeseburger), while the wine menu famously hawks a down-to-earth hierarchy: Good, Decent, Cheap. As at Keith McNally's other establishments, Balthazar (p69) and Pastis, folks pack in for the scene, triple-parking at the bar for elaborate cocktails and star sightings.

Sweet & Lowdown

NEW *123 Allen Street, between Delancey & Rivington Streets (1-212 228 7746). Subway F to Delancey Street; J, M, Z to Delancey-Essex Streets.* **Open** 6pm-2am daily.
Wine bar. Map p63 D4 ⑥④
More than just a novelty act, this Yankee-focused wine bar has one of the smartest, most thoughtful selections of American wine we've seen in town. In addition to the expected California and Finger Lakes options, the rotating list of 25 to 30 wines by the glass includes

four unusual selections from Virginia producer Kluge (try the succulent viognier, which pits pear and tropical fruits against a commanding acidity). Informed and attentive servers and fine nibbles – including a $5 pickle plate – complete the package.

White Star

NEW *21 Essex Street, between Canal & Hester Streets (1-212 995 5464). Subway F to East Broadway.* **Open** 6pm-3am daily. **Bar. Map** p63 E5 ⑥⑤

Last year, mix master Sasha Petraske (the man behind exclusive Milk & Honey, 134 Eldridge Street, between Broome & Delancey Streets, no phone, www.mlkhny.com) veered away from the cocktail trend as it was reaching fever pitch, focusing on straight spirits at this tiny bar, hung with the celestial Moroccan lamps for which it is named. The opening concept has since been abandoned, and the bar now cranks out classics such as Sazeracs. Absinthe (available in short 35ml pours) is still the centrepiece, but as the liquor's snail-pace preparation slows down service (icy water is dribbled over a slotted, sugar-topped spoon), you might want to stick with mixed drinks.

Shopping

Alife Rivington Club

158 Rivington Street, between Clinton & Suffolk Streets (1-212 375 8128/ www.rivingtonclub.com). Subway F to Delancey Street; J, M, Z to Delancey-Essex Streets. **Open** noon-7pm Mon-Sat; noon-6pm Sun. **Map** p63 E4 ⑥⑥

To become a member of this 'club', you have to find it: there's no sign outside the shop. But Alife is arguably the best spot in the city for exclusive or limited-edition kicks from Nike, Converse and Adidas. T-shirts, jackets, hoodies and hats come courtesy of the in-house brand or in collaboration with Nike and Lacoste.

BBlessing

181 Orchard Street, between Houston & Stanton Streets (1-212 378 8005/ www.bblessing.com). Subway F, V to Lower East Side-Second Avenue. **Open** 1-9pm Mon-Fri; noon-8pm Sat, Sun. **Map** p63 D4 ⑥⑦

A collaboration between design collectives Surface to Air and Breakbeat Science (the name's double B is a homage to their first joint project, BBS Tokyo), this men's outpost has an interior that's as chic as the threads within it. You'll find relaxed, high-end clothing from the likes of Rag & Bone, Raf Simons and the store's eponymous label, and a selection of music, films, decorative objects and accessories make it a great stop for gifts.

Doyle & Doyle

189 Orchard Street, between Houston & Stanton Streets (1-212 677 9991/ www.doyledoyle.com). Subway F, V to Lower East Side-Second Avenue. **Open** 1-7pm Tue, Wed, Fri; 1-8pm Thur; noon-7pm Sat, Sun. **Map** p63 D4 ⑥⑧

Whether your taste is art deco or nouveau, Victorian or Edwardian, gemologist sisters Pam and Elizabeth Doyle, who specialise in estate and antique jewellery, will have that one-of-a-kind item you're looking for, including engagement and eternity rings. The artfully displayed pieces within wall-mounted wood-frame cases are just a fraction of what they have in stock.

Dressing Room

75A Orchard Street, between Broome & Grand Streets (1-212 966 7330/ www.thedressingroomnyc.com). Subway B, D to Grand Street; F to Delancey Street. **Open** 1pm-midnight Tue, Wed, Sun; 1pm-2am Thur-Sat. **Map** p63 E4 ⑥⑨

At first glance, the Dressing Room may look like any Lower East Side lounge, thanks to a handsome wood bar, but stylist and designer Nikki Fontanella's quirky co-op-cum-watering-hole rewards

Covert cocktails

PDT

Blame it on Sasha Petraske, who stirred up the thirst for clandestine drinking establishments almost a decade ago with his members-only Milk & Honey. Recently, so many 'speakeasy'-style bars have cropped up, the genre is, ironically, nearing overexposure. Still, there is a treasure-hunt excitement in seeking out secretive dens behind hidden doors and seemingly blind alleys.

Just inside gourmet hot dog mecca Crif Dogs (p86) is an old wooden phonebooth. Slip inside, pick up the receiver and the host opens a secret panel to **PDT** ('Please Don't Tell'; p88). The dark, narrow space is decorated with a touch of self-parody (the obligatory taxidermy, but one stag sports a bowler hat). Reserve a booth, or sidle up to the bar to sample Jim Meehan's extensive cocktail menu. These are serious drinks that surpass the gimmicky entry: try the house Old-Fashioned, made with bacon-infused bourbon.

In a twist on the theme, **Raines Law Room** (p116), overseen by a Petraske alumnus, doesn't even have a bar; at this nostalgically louche lounge, the pre-Prohibition classic drinks are mixed behind the scenes (the name refers to an 1896 law designed to curb liquor consumption). More faithful to the popular image of the speakeasy, the **Back Room** (p79) is hidden in an industrial building on a desolate street. Look for the 'Lower East Side Toy Company' sign, pass through the adjoining gate, down an alleyway, up a metal staircase and open the door. Inside you'll find a huge mirrored bar where cocktails are served in teacups and bottled beer is disguised in brown paper bags. Chandeliers, velvet wallpaper and vintage music recreate an authentic vibe.

Although there's no password, gaining entry to the **Eldridge** (247 Eldridge Street, between E Houston & Stanton Streets, 1-212 505 7600) is a challenge. The plush lounge, behind a faux bookstore front, has only 13 tables. It helps to have connections (or try emailing reservations@theeldridge.com), but getting a drink should never be this difficult. Speakeasies may be in, but Prohibition's over.

the curious. The adjoining room displays designs by indie labels, which rotate every four months, while downstairs is a cache of vintage finds.

Edith Machinist

104 Rivington Street, between Essex & Ludlow Streets (1-212 979 9992). Subway F to Delancey Street; J, M, Z to Delancey-Essex Streets. **Open** 1-8pm Mon-Fri; noon-8pm Sat, Sun. **Map** p63 E4 ⓖ

This vintage trove has one of the city's best collections of (mostly) fine vintage leather bags, not to mention an army of shoes and boots – arranged by size – and a well-edited clothing selection.

Girls Love Shoes

29 Ludlow Street, between Canal & Hester Streets (1-212 966 7463/ www.glsnewyork.com). Subway F to East Broadway; F to Delancey Street; J, M, Z to Delancey-Essex Streets. **Open** noon-7pm Tue-Sun. **Map** p63 E5 ⓗ

Sisters Zia and Dana Zilprin have handpicked ladies' shoes – all aged to perfection – and arranged them by size on floor-to-ceiling racks. Vintage shoe fetishists can find styles from every era beginning with the 1930s.

Guss' Pickles

85-87 Orchard Street, between Broome & Grand Streets (1-212 334 3616). Subway F to Delancey Street; J, M, Z to Delancey-Essex Streets. **Open** 11am-6pm Mon-Thur, Sun; 11am-4pm Fri. **Map** p63 E4 ⓘ

A survivor of the Lower East Side's old pickle district, this shrine to the brine offers an array of sours and half-sours, pickled peppers, watermelon rinds and sauerkraut.

Reed Space

151 Orchard Street, between Rivington & Stanton Streets (1-212 253 0588/ www.thereedspace.com). Subway F to Delancey Street; J, M, Z to Delancey-Essex Streets. **Open** 1-7pm Mon-Fri; noon-7pm Sat, Sun. **Map** p63 D4 ⓙ

The brainchild of Staple Design, which has worked on product design and branding with the likes of Nike, Timberland and New Era, Reed Space displays a collection of local (Pegleg, 3Sixteen and Staple's own label, among others) and international streetwear brands – plus art books, culture mags, music and DVDs – in its super-cool shop.

Russ & Daughters

179 E Houston Street, between Allen & Orchard Streets (1-212 475 4880/ www.russanddaughters.com). Subway F, V to Lower East Side-Second Avenue. **Open** 9am-7pm Mon-Sat; 8am-5.30pm Sun. **Map** p63 D4 ⓚ

Russ & Daughters, which has been open since 1914, sells eight kinds of smoked salmon and many Jewish-inflected Eastern European delectables, along with dried fruits, chocolates and caviar.

Still Life

77 Orchard Street, between Broome & Grand Streets (1-212 575 9704/ www.stilllifenyc.com). Subway F to Delancey Street; J, M, Z to Delancey-Essex Streets. **Open** noon-7pm daily. **Map** p63 E4 ⓛ

See box p113.

Suite Orchard

145A Orchard Street, at Rivington Street (1-212 533 4115/www.suite orchard.com). Subway F, V to Second Avenue-Lower East Side; J, M, Z to Delancey Street. **Open** noon-7pm Tue, Wed, Fri, Sun; noon-8pm Thur, Sat. **Map** p63 D4 ⓜ

Fashion veterans and sisters Cindy and Sonia Huang worked at Diane von Furstenberg and Chloé, respectively, before joining forces to make their mark on the Lower East Side. The boudoir-inspired spot pays tribute to their well-honed aesthetic via gamine pieces from Alexander Wang, Sonia by Sonia Rykiel and the siblings' own Soni & Cindy line.

THECAST

Lower Level, 119 Ludlow Street, between Rivington & Delancey Streets (1-212 228 2020/www.thecast.com). Subway F, V to Second Avenue-Lower East Side. **Open** noon-8pm Mon-Sat; noon-7pm Sun. **Map** p63 E4 ⑦

A chalkboard set next to an open metal hatch in the sidewalk is the only marker for the subterranean outpost of this idiosyncratic menswear label. Chuck Guarino and Ryan Turner launched THECAST with a collection of artful T-shirts in 2004; these are still central to a collection that spans well-cut jeans to dapper suits. The space is an anarchic jumble of Victorian-style wallpaper and Gothic knick-knacks, including mounted game trophies and a human skull (bought on eBay).

Nightlife

Bowery Ballroom

6 Delancey Street, between Bowery & Chrystie Street (1-212 533 2111/www.boweryballroom.com). Subway B, D to Grand Street; J, M, Z to Bowery; 6 to Spring Street. **Map** p63 D4 ⑦⑧

It's probably the best venue in the city for seeing indie bands, either on the way up or holding their own. Still, the Bowery also manages to bring in a diverse range of artists from home and abroad. Expect a clear view and bright sound from any spot. The spacious downstairs lounge is a great place to relax and socialise between (or during) sets.

Cake Shop

152 Ludlow Street, between Rivington & Stanton Streets (1-212 253 0036/www.cake-shop.com). Subway F, V to Lower East Side-Second Avenue. **Open** 5pm-2am daily. **Map** p63 E4 ⑦⑨

It can be hard to see the stage in this narrow, stuffy basement, but Cake Shop gets big points for its keen indie and underground-rock bookings, among the most adventurous in town. True to its name, the venue sells vegan pastries and coffee upstairs, and record-store ephemera in the street-level back room.

Mercury Lounge

217 E Houston Street, between Essex & Ludlow Streets (1-212 260 4700/www.mercuryloungenyc.com). Subway F, V to Lower East Side-Second Avenue. **Map** p63 E4 ⑧⓪

The unassuming, boxy Mercury Lounge is both an old standby and pretty much the number-one indie rock club in town, with solid sound and sight lines (and a cramped bar in the front room). There are four-band bills most nights, though they can seem stylistically haphazard and set times are often later than advertised. It's a good idea to book bigger shows in advance.

205 Club

205 Chrystie Street, at Stanton Street (1-212 477 6688/www.myspace.com/205club). Subway F, V to Second Avenue-Lower East Side. **Open** 10.30pm-4am Wed-Sat. **Map** p63 D4 ⑧①

The decor is nothing to speak of – the street level has a definite dive-bar ambience, while the basement, despite an effort to convey a Factory-esque vibe, is still just a basement. No matter, though, because the subterranean space contains a top-tier Phazon sound system, which lures some of the city's best DJs. You'll hear a lot of electro, space-disco and other hipster-friendly sounds, but the bookers toss in plenty of curveballs, so it's best to check the MySpace page before venturing out.

Arts & leisure

Dixon Place

NEW *161 Chrystie Street, at Delancey Street (1-212 219 0736/www.dixonplace.org). Subway F, V to Lower East Side-Second Avenue; J, M, Z to Bowery-Delancey Streets.* **Map** p63 D4 ⑧②

Girls Love Shoes p83

More than 22 years after it started hosting experimental performances in a loft on the Bowery, this plucky organisation has finally opened its gorgeous new space. The multidisciplinary arts centre, which includes a lounge, mainstage theatre and studio, supports the work of emerging actors, dancers, musicians, choreographers and writers. The roster of events includes summer's annual HOT! festival of lesbian and gay arts.

East Village

The area east of Broadway between Houston and 14th Streets has a long history as a countercultural hotbed. From the 1950s to the '70s, St Marks Place (8th Street, between Lafayette Street & Avenue A) was a hangout for artists, writers, radicals and musicians, including WH Auden, Lenny Bruce and Abbie Hoffman. It's still packed until the wee hours, but these days, it's with crowds of college students and tourists browsing for bargain T-shirts, used CDs and pot paraphernalia. While legendary music venues such as CBGB are no more, a few bohemian hangouts endure, and the East Village has also evolved into a superior cheap-eats hotspot. In the neighbourhood's renovated green space, Tompkins Square Park, bongo beaters, guitarists, yuppies and the homeless all mingle.

Eating & drinking

Abraço

86 E 7th Street, between First & Second Avenues (1-212 388 9731/ www.abraconyc.com). Subway F, V to Lower East Side-Second Avenue; L to First Avenue; 6 to Astor Place. **Open** 8am-6pm Tue-Sat; 9am-6pm Sun. No credit cards. **$**. **Café**. **Map** p63 D3 ㉝
See box p91.

Back Forty

190 Avenue B, between 11th & 12th Streets (1-212 388 1990/www.back fortynyc.com). Subway L to First Avenue. **Open** 6-11pm Mon-Thur; 6pm-midnight Fri, Sat; noon-3.30pm, 6-10pm Sun. **$$**. **American**. **Map** p63 E2 ㉞

Chef-restaurateur Peter Hoffman (of Savoy fame; p71) is behind this East Village seasonal-eats tavern, where modern farmhouse chic prevails in the decor and on the menu. The offerings vary, but the veggies consistently shine: in season, baby cauliflower gratin with leeks and gruyère is explosively flavourful, and you'll rarely taste better brussels sprouts (marinated in shallot butter and dotted with dried cherries). Though some mains are middling, the creamy stout float is one of many reasons you'll be coming back.

Baoguette

NEW *37 St Marks Place, between Second & Third Avenues (1-212 380 1487/www.baoguette.com). Subway N, R, W to 8th Street-NYU; 6 to Astor Place.* **Open** 11am-midnight Mon-Wed, Sun; 11am-2am Thur-Sat. **$.**
Vietnamese. Map p63 D3 ❽
See box p91.

Bourgeois Pig

NEW *111 E 7th Street, between First Avenue & Avenue A (1-212 475 2246/www.bourgeoispigny.com). Subway F, V to Lower East Side-Second Avenue; 6 to Astor Place.* **Open** 6pm-2am Mon-Thur, Sun; 6pm-3am Fri, Sat.
Wine bar. Map p63 E3 ❽
Ornate mirrors and antique chairs give this small, red-lit wine and fondue joint a decidedly decadent feel. The wine list is well chosen, and although the hard stuff is verboten, mixed concoctions based on wine, champagne or beer – such as the thick Marin Port Flip featuring port, espresso and egg yolk – cater to cocktail aficionados.

Caracas Arepa Bar

91 E 7th Street, between First Avenue & Avenue A (1-212 228 5062/www.caracasarepabar.com). Subway F, V to Lower East Side-Second Avenue; 6 to Astor Place. **Open** 5.30-10.30pm Mon-Fri;

noon-10.30pm Sat; noon-9.30pm Sun.
$. Venezuelan. Map p63 D3 ❻
This endearing spot, with flower-patterned, vinyl-covered tables, zaps you straight to Caracas. The secret is in the arepas themselves: each cornmeal patty is made from scratch daily before it's stuffed with a choice of 18 fillings, such as chicken and avocado or mushrooms with tofu. Top off your snack with a cocada, a thick and creamy milkshake made with freshly grated coconut and cinnamon.

Crif Dogs

113 St Marks Place, between First Avenue & Avenue A (1-212 614 2728). Subway L to First Avenue; 6 to Astor Place. **Open** noon-2am Mon-Thur; noon-4am Fri, Sat; noon-1am Sun.
$. American. Map p63 D3 ❽
Crif's snappy hot dogs, which come deep-fried or grilled, have a cult following among tube-steak aficionados, who swarm the St Marks Place joint at all hours for combos such as the Spicy Redneck (bacon-wrapped and covered in chilli, coleslaw and jalapeños) and the Chihuahua (bacon-wrapped with sour cream and avocado). If you fancy a drink, sleuth out the hidden bar, PDT, in the back (see p88 and box p82).

Death & Company

433 E 6th Street, between First Avenue & Avenue A (1-212 388 0882/www.deathandcompany.com). Subway F, V to Lower East Side-Second Avenue; 6 to Astor Place. **Open** 6pm-midnight daily. **Bar**. Map p63 E3 ❾
The nattily attired mixologists are deadly serious about drinks at this pseudo speakeasy with Gothic flair (don't be intimidated by the imposing wooden door). Black walls and cushy booths combine with chandeliers to set the luxuriously sombre mood. Patrons bored by shot-and-beer bars can sample the inventive cocktails as well as top-notch grub including bacon-swaddled filet mignon bites.

Back Forty p85

Elsa

NEW *217 E 3rd Street, between Avenues B & C (1-917 882 7395). Subway F, V to Lower East Side-Second Avenue.* **Open** 7pm-2am daily. **Bar**. Map p63 E3 ⑩

At this stylish boîte, named for the iconoclastic 1930s clothing designer Elsa Schiaparelli, nods to couture include framed fashion sketches and three tap lines that flow through a vintage sewing machine. White leather banquettes are the sole perches from which to enjoy cocktails like the Elsa (applejack, sparkling wine, lemon and orange bitters), all designed by Freemans (p80) barkeep Kevin Jaszek. If you're inspired by the bespoke trappings, indulge yourself at the Hanger, the owners' adjacent custom-suit shop.

International Bar

120½ First Avenue, between St Marks Place & E 7th Street (1-212 777 1643). Subway F, V to Lower East Side-Second Avenue; L to First Avenue. **Open** noon-2.30am Mon-Wed, Sun; noon-3.30am Thur-Sat. **Bar**. Map p63 D3 ㉛

The walls have been cleared of graffiti, but the second coming of this legendary saloon stays true to its dive bar roots (the original shuttered in 2005 after more than 40 years of business). A scuffed mahogany bar and vintage film posters make up the decor, and the jukebox is still killer (Black Flag, Nina Simone). The cheap booze and grimy vibe foster the feeling that I-Bar never left.

Ippudo NY

NEW *65 Fourth Avenue, between 9th & 10th Streets (1-212 388 0088). Subway 6 to Astor Place.* **Open** 11am-4pm, 5pm-midnight Mon-Thur; 11am-4pm, 5pm-1am Fri, Sat; 11am-11pm Sun. **$**. **Japanese**. Map p63 D2 ㉜

See box p91.

Momofuku Ssäm Bar

207 Second Avenue, at 13th Street (1-212 254 3500/www.momofuku.com). Subway L to First or Third Avenues; L, N, Q, R, W, 4, 5, 6 to 14th Street-Union Square. **Open** 11.30am-midnight Mon-Thur, Sun; 11.30am-2am Fri, Sat. **$$**. **Korean**. Map p63 D2 ㉝

At chef David Chang's second restaurant, waiters hustle to noisy rock music in the 50-seat space, which feels expansive compared with its Noodle Bar predecessor's crowded counter dining. Try the wonderfully fatty pork-belly steamed bun with hoisin sauce and cucumbers or one of the ham platters, but you'll need to come with a crowd to sample the house speciality, *bo ssäm* (a slow-roasted hog butt that is consumed wrapped in lettuce leaves, with a dozen oysters and other accompaniments); it serves six to eight people and must be ordered in advance. David Chang has further expanded his E Vill empire with a sweet annexe at this location, Momofuku Bakery & Milk Bar.

NEW YORK BY AREA

Other locations Momofuku Ko, 163 First Avenue, at 10th Street, East Village (no phone); Momofuku Noodle Bar, 171 First Avenue, between 10th & 11th Streets, East Village (1-212 777 7773).

PDT

NEW *113 St Marks Place, between First Avenue & Avenue A (1-212 614 0386). Subway L to First Avenue; 6 to Astor Place.* **Open** 6pm-2am Mon-Thur, Sun; 6pm-4am Fri, Sat. **Cocktail bar**. Map p63 D3 94
See box p82.

Porchetta

NEW *110 E 7th Street, between First Avenue & Avenue A (1-212 777 2151). Subway F, V to Lower East Side-Second Avenue; L to First Avenue; 6 to Astor Place.* **Open** 11.30am-10pm Mon-Thur, Sun; 11.30am-11pm Fri, Sat. **$**.
Sandwiches. Map p63 E3 95
See box p91.

Terroir

NEW *413 E 12th Street, between First Avenue & Avenue A (no phone/ www.wineisterroir.com). Subway L to First Avenue; L, N, Q, R, W, 4, 5, 6 to 14th Street-Union Square.* **Open** 5pm-2am Mon-Sat. No credit cards. **Bar**. Map p63 D2 96
Oeno-evangelist Paul Grieco preaches the powers of terroir – grapes that express a sense of place – at this tiny, sparse wine haunt. The super-knowledgeable waiting staff aptly help patrons navigate the 36 by-the-glass options on the menu, including a robust Le Bouchet cabernet franc. Equally tempting is the line-up of wine and beer cocktails, including the frothy Abby Flip (Ommegang Abbey Ale, coriander syrup, pomegranate molasses and egg), and the restaurant-calibre small plates (such as sage-wrapped lamb sausages). So, stellar sips and a menu to match: hallelujah! See also box p91.

Bourgeois Pig p86

NEW YORK BY AREA

Shopping

Bespoke Chocolates

NEW *6 Extra Place (off E 1st Street), between Bowery & Second Avenue (1-212 260 7103/www.bespoke chocolates.com). Subway F, V to Lower East Side-Second Avenue.* **Open** 11am-7pm Tue-Fri; noon-8pm Sat, Sun. **Map** p63 D3 ③⑦
See box p100.

Bond No.9

9 Bond Street, between Broadway & Lafayette Street (1-212 228 1732/www.bondno9.com). Subway B, D, F, V to Broadway-Lafayette Street; 6 to Bleecker Street. **Open** 11am-8pm Mon-Fri; 10am-7pm Sat; noon-6pm Sun. **Map** p63 D3 ③⑧
The collection of scents here pays olfactory homage to New York City. Choose from 34 'neighbourhoods' and 'sensibilities', including Wall Street, Park Avenue, Eau de Noho, even Chinatown (but don't worry, it smells of peach blossom, gardenia and patchouli, not fish stands). The arty bottles and neat, colourful packaging are highly gift-friendly.

Bond Street Chocolate

NEW *63 E 4th Street, between Bowery & Second Avenue (1-212 677 5103/www.bondstchocolate.com). Subway 6 to Bleecker Street.* **Open** noon-8pm Tue-Sat; 1-5pm Sun. **Map** p63 D3 ③⑨
See box p100.

Dave's Quality Meat

7 E 3rd Street, between Bowery & Second Avenue (1-212 505 7551/www.davesqualitymeat.com). Subway F, V to Lower East Side-Second Avenue. **Open** 11.30am-7.30pm Mon-Sat; 11.30am-6.30pm Sun. **Map** p63 D3 ⑩⓪
Dave Ortiz – formerly of ghetto urban threads label Zoo York – and professional skateboarder Chris Keefe stock a range of top-shelf streetwear in their wittily designed shop. In addition to a line-up of the latest sneaks by

Adidas, Nike and Vans, DQM's graphic-print tees and hoodies are displayed in the deli case.

Fabulous Fanny's

335 E 9th Street, between First & Second Avenues (1-212 533 0637/www.fabulousfannys.com). Subway L to First Avenue; 6 to Astor Place. **Open** noon-8pm daily. **Map** p63 D2 ⑩①
Formerly a Chelsea flea market booth, this two-room shop is the city's best source of period glasses, stocking more than 30,000 pairs of spectacles, from Jules Verne-esque wire rims to 1970s rhinestone-encrusted Versace shades.

Kiehl's

109 Third Avenue, between 13th & 14th Streets (1-212 677 3171/www.kiehls.com). Subway L to Third Avenue; N, Q, R, W, 4, 5, 6 to 14th Street-Union Square. **Open** 10am-8pm Mon-Sat; 11am-6pm Sun. **Map** p63 D2 ⑩②
The apothecary founded on this East Village site in 1851 has morphed into a major skincare brand widely sold in upscale department stores, but the products, in their minimal-frills packaging, are still good value and produce great results. The lip balms and thick-as-custard Creme de Corps have become cult classics.

Other Music

15 E 4th Street, between Broadway & Lafayette Street (1-212 477 8150/www.othermusic.com). Subway R, W to 8th Street-NYU; 6 to Astor Place. **Open** 11am-9pm Mon-Fri; noon-8pm Sat; noon-7pm Sun. **Map** p62 C3 ⑩③
This wee audio temple is dedicated to small-label new and used CDs and LPs across numerous genres, from American roots and indie to electronica, soul and La Decadanse (lounge, Moog and slow-core soundtracks).

St Mark's Bookshop

31 Third Avenue, between 8th & 9th Streets (1-212 260 7853/www.stmarks bookshop.com). Subway R, W to 8th

Street-NYU; 6 to Astor Place. **Open**
10am-midnight Mon-Sat; 11am-
midnight Sun. **Map** p63 D3 ⓘ04
Students, academics and arty types
gravitate to this East Village bookseller,
which maintains strong inventories on
cultural theory, graphic design, poetry
and film, as well as numerous avant-
garde journals and 'zines. The fiction
section is one of the finest in the city.

Samples for (eco)mpassion

NEW *2 Great Jones Street, between
Broadway & Lafayette Street (1-212
777 0707/www.greenfinds.com).
Subway B, D, F, V to Broadway-
Lafayette Street; 6 to Bleecker
Street.* **Open** noon-7pm Thur-Sun.
Map p62 C3 ⓘ05
A marriage of founder Ike Rodriguez's
defunct Find Outlet and his earth-con-
scious e-tailer, greenfinds.com, this
charity-focused shop donates 5% of
the proceeds to a different non-profit
organisation each month. You can
expect heavy discounts on wares from
indie stars such as Lauren Moffatt and
eco-designer Linda Loudermilk.

The Smile

NEW *26 Bond Street, at Lafayette
Street (no phone/www.thesmilenyc.
com). Subway B, D, F, V at Broadway-
Lafayette Street; 6 at Bleecker Street.*
Open 8am-6pm Tue-Sun. **Map** p63
D3 ⓘ06
At this one-stop shop, you can grab a
bite to eat, sip espresso, cosy up by a
fireplace, buy a knitting kit, order a
pair of customised boots, admire works
displayed by rotating artists, and even
get a tattoo in the downstairs parlour.

Nightlife

The Cock

*29 Second Avenue, between 2nd &
3rd Streets (no phone/www.thecockbar.
com). Subway F, V to Lower East Side-
Second Avenue.* **Open** 11pm-4am daily.
No credit cards. **Map** p63 D3 ⓘ07

A wonderfully dark and sleazy fag-
rock spot, the Cock has nightly
soirées featuring cruising, cocktail
guzzling and heavy petting among
the rail-thin, messy-haired young
men who frequent it. Drag performers and holiday-pegged theme nights
often rock the house.

EastVille Comedy Club

NEW *85 E 4th Street, between Bowery
& Second Avenue (1-212 260 2445/
www.eastvillecomedy.com). Subway F,
V to Lower East Side-Second Avenue.*
Map p63 D3 ⓘ08
The East Village finally has its first
bonafide chuckle-hut-style stand-up
club. EastVille puts up much of the same
club-circuit talent that populates the
city's other rooms, plus up-and-coming
comics from the Downtown alt scene.

Joe's Pub

*Public Theater, 425 Lafayette Street,
between Astor Place & E 4th Street
(1-212 539 8770/www.joespub.com).
Subway N, R, W to 8th Street-NYU;
6 to Astor Place.* **Map** p63 D3 ⓘ09
Probably the city's premier small spot
for sit-down audiences, Joe's Pub
(named for Joseph Papp, the founder
of its parent, the Public Theater; p93)
brings in impeccable talent of all genres and origins. While some well-
established names play here (Gilberto
Gil, Ute Lemper), Joe's also lends its
stage to up-and-comers. A small but
solid menu and deep bar selections
seal the deal – just keep an eye on the
drinks prices.

Nublu

*62 Avenue C, between 4th & 5th
Streets (1-646 546 5206/www.nublu.
net). Subway F, V to Lower East Side-
Second Avenue.* **Open** 8pm-4am daily.
No credit cards. **Map** p63 E3 ⓘ10
Nublu's prominence on the local glob-
alist club scene has been inversely pro-
portional to its size. A pressure cooker
of creativity, the venue gave rise to the
Brazilian Girls – who started jamming

The (East) Village glutton

A gourmet crawl through NY's best budget foodie enclave.

Porchetta

With a melting pot of ethnic legacies including Ukrainian, Polish, Indian and Jewish cuisines, the East Village has long been one of the most interesting places to eat in Manhattan. Over the past decade, however, it has evolved into a genuine foodie destination, thanks in no small part to David Chang's expanding Momofuku empire, which has garnered rave reviews and acquired a cult following. The past year or so has seen an explosion in spots that offer serious fare at highly palatable prices. Starting with a morning cuppa, tiny, seatless Portuguese café **Abraço** (p85) has just about enough space to house its La Marzocco espresso machine. Order a pedigreed cortado – a rich, flavourful espresso topped with steamed milk – and a slice of olive oil cake.

Come lunchtime, consider a sandwich. In a city where designer pork inspires a fervent following, it takes some prime swine to stand out from the crowd. **Porchetta** (p88), chef Sarah Jenkins's tiny white-tiled shop, has delivered just such a contender with its namesake dish, a rendition of one of central Italy's most hallowed creations: a whole, deboned pig laced with fennel and spices, then slow-roasted until the skin is a crackling shell and the inner flesh basted with melted fat. Eat it in a ciabatta roll or straight up.

Another exceptional sandwich comes courtesy of **Baoguette** (p86), which peddles some of the city's finest *banh mi*. Choose the classic version: pâté, terrine and pulled pork stuffed into a crusty French loaf. Both superior sarnies are under a tenner.

Outrageously popular Japanese import **Ippudo NY** (p87) has fuelled the growing craze for ramen. Sample the Akamura Modern, a steaming bowl of *tonkotsu* broth (a creamy pork-bone brew) with pork belly, scallions and stretchy wheat noodles; a complex, filling meal for a mere $13.

Now for a drink. At Paul Grieco's bare-bones wine bar **Terroir** (p88) the carefully selected wine is the focus. Budget-conscious oenophiles can sample a number of 3oz 'tastes', some under five bucks. Still hungry? A menu of top-notch nibbles (like beet and gorgonzola risotto balls) complements the stellar sips.

NEW YORK BY AREA

at one late-night session and haven't stopped yet – as well as starting New York City's romance with the northern Brazilian style forró.

Pyramid

101 Avenue A, between 6th & 7th Streets (1-212 228 4888/www.the pyramidclub.com). Subway F, V to Lower East Side-Second Avenue; L to First Avenue; 6 to Astor Place. **Open** hrs vary Mon, Tue, Thur-Sun. No credit cards. **Map** p63 E3 ⓫

In a clubbing era that's long gone, the Pyramid was a cornerstone of forward-thinking queer club culture. In what could be considered a sign of the times, the venue's sole remaining gay soirée is Friday night's non-progressive '80s dancefest, 1984. Otherwise, the charmingly decrepit space features the long-running drum 'n' bass bash Konkrete Jungle, as well as an interesting rotating roster of goth and new-wave affairs.

Webster Hall

125 E 11th Street, between Third & Fourth Avenues (1-212 353 1600/ www.websterhall.com). Subway L to Third Avenue; N, Q, R, W, 4, 5, 6 to 14th Street-Union Square. **Map** p63 D2 ⓬

A great-sounding alternative for bands (and fans) who've had their fill of the comparably sized Irving Plaza, Webster Hall is booked by Bowery Presents, the folks who run Bowery Ballroom and Mercury Lounge. Expect to find high-calibre indie acts (Animal Collective, Battles, the Gossip), but be sure to show up early if you want a decent view.

Arts & leisure

Anthology Film Archives

32 Second Avenue, at 2nd Street (1-212 505 5181/www.anthologyfilm archives.org). Subway F, V to Lower East Side-Second Avenue; 6 to Bleecker Street. No credit cards. **Map** p63 D3 ⓭

This red-brick building feels a little like a fortress – and in a sense, it is one, protecting the legacy of NYC's fiercest experimenters. Anthology is committed to screening the world's most adventurous fare, from 16mm found-footage works to digital video dreams. Dedicated to the preservation, study and exhibition of independent and avant-garde film, it houses a gallery and film museum, in addition to its two screens.

Bowery Poetry Club

308 Bowery, between Bleecker & Houston Streets (1-212 614 0505/ www.bowerypoetry.com). Subway B, D, F, V to Broadway-Lafayette Street; 6 to Bleecker Street. No credit cards. **Map** p63 D3 ⓮

The name of this colourful joint reveals its roots, but it's also the truest current iteration of the East Village arts scene: All kinds of jazz, folk, hip hop and improv theatre acts can be found here.

New York Theatre Workshop

79 E 4th Street, between Bowery & Second Avenue (1-212 460 5475/ www.nytw.org). Subway F, V to Lower East Side-Second Avenue; 6 to Astor Place. **Map** p63 D3 ⓯

Founded in 1979, the New York Theatre Workshop works with emerging directors eagre to take on challenging pieces. Besides plays by world-class artists like Caryl Churchill (*Far Away, A Number*) and Tony Kushner (*Homebody/Kabul*), this company also premièred *Rent*, Jonathan Larson's Pulitzer Prize-winning musical.

Performance Space 122

150 First Avenue, at 9th Street (1-212 477 5288/www.ps122.org). Subway L to First Avenue; 6 to Astor Place. **Map** p63 D2 ⓰

One of New York's most interesting venues, this not-for-profit arts centre presents experimental theatre, dance, performance art, music, film and video.

Whoopi Goldberg, Eric Bogosian and John Leguizamo have all developed projects here. Australian trendsetter Vallejo Gantner serves as artistic director, and has been working to give the venue a more international scope.

Public Theater

425 Lafayette Street, between Astor Place & E 4th Street (1-212 539 8500/ Telecharge 1-212 239 6200/www. publictheater.org). Subway N, R, W to 8th Street-NYU; 6 to Astor Place. **Map** p63 D3 **417**

The civic-minded Oskar Eustis is artistic director of this institution dedicated to the work of new American playwrights but also known for its Shakespeare productions (Shakespeare in the Park; p44). The building, an Astor Place landmark, has five stages and Joe's Pub (p90). It's also home to one of the city's most dynamic troupes: LAByrinth Theater Company, co-founded by actor Philip Seymour Hoffman.

Anthology Film Archives

Stone

Avenue C, at 2nd Street (no phone/ www.thestonenyc.com). Subway F, V to Lower East Side-Second Avenue. No credit cards. **Map** p63 E3 **118**

Don't call sax star John Zorn's not-for-profit venture a 'club'. You'll find no food or drinks here, and no nonsense, either: the Stone is an art space dedicated to 'the experimental and the avant-garde'. If you're down for some rigorously adventurous sounds (Anthony Coleman, Okkyung Lee, Tony Conrad), Zorn has made it easy: no advance sales, and all ages admitted. The bookings are left to a different artist-cum-curator each month.

Greenwich Village

Stretching from Houston Street to 14th Street, between Broadway and Sixth Avenue, the Village has inspired bohemians for almost a century. Now that it's one of the most expensive neighbourhoods in the city, you need a lot more than a struggling artist's income to inhabit its leafy streets, but it's still a fine place for idle wandering, candlelit dining in out-of-the-way restaurants, and hopping between bars and cabaret venues.

Sights & museums

AIA Center for Architecture

536 La Guardia Place, between Bleecker & W 3rd Streets (1-212 683 0023/www.aiany.org). Subway A, B, C, D, E, F, V to W 4th Street. **Open** 9am-8pm Mon-Fri; 11am-5pm Sat. **Map** p62 C3 **119**

Completed in 2003, the centre's sweeping, light-filled design is a physical manifestation of AIA's goal of promoting transparency in its access and programming. Large slabs of flooring were cut away at the street and basement levels, converting underground spaces into bright, museum-quality galleries.

Washington Square Park

Subway A, B, C, D, E, F, V to W 4th Street-Washington Square. **Map** p62 C3 ⓬⓪

Great for people watching, Washington Square Park attracts a disparate cast of characters that takes in hippies, intellectuals, skateboarders and hip-hop kids. The park is currently in the midst of a controversial $16 million redesign; phase one, which involves revamping the plaza and fountain in the western section of the park, should be complete by publication of this guide. The iconic Washington Arch, a modestly sized replica of Paris's Arc de Triomphe, built in 1895 to honour George Washington, will remain unaltered.

Eating & drinking

Blue Hill

75 Washington Place, between Sixth Avenue & Washington Square West (1-212 539 1776/www.bluehillnyc.com). Subway A, B, C, D, E, F, V to W 4th Street. **Open** 5.30-11pm Mon-Sat; 5.30-10pm Sun. **$$$**. **American Map** p62 C3 ⓬①

More than a mere crusader for sustainability, Dan Barber is also one of the most talented cooks in town, building his menu around whatever's at its peak on his Westchester farm (home to a sibling restaurant). During fresh pea season, bright green infuses every inch of the menu, from a velvety spring pea soup to sous-vide duck breast as soft as sushi fanned over a bed of slivered sugar snap peas. Once among the most sedate restaurants in the Village, this subterranean jewel has become one of the most raucous.

La Lanterna di Vittorio

129 MacDougal Street, between 3rd & 4th Streets (1-212 529 5945/www.lalanternacaffe.com). Subway A, B, C, D, E, F, V to W 4th Street-Washington Square. **Open** 10am-3am Mon-Thur, Sun; 10am-4am Fri, Sat. **$**. **Café/ Italian**. **Map** p62 C3 ⓬②

At the most romantic café in the Village, you can sup on pizzas, salads and other light Italian fare in a 200-year-old fruit-tree-shaded garden (or by fireside in winter). None of the dishes is over $14 and there's an extensive, and reasonably priced, wine list.

Lupa

170 Thompson Street, between Bleecker & Houston Streets (1-212 982 5089/www.luparestaurant.com). Subway A, B, C, D, E, F, V to W 4th Street. **Open** noon-3pm, 5-11.30pm Mon-Fri; 11.30am-2.30pm, 5-11.30pm Sat, Sun. **$$**. **Italian**. **Map** p62 C3 ⓬③

No mere 'poor man's Babbo' (celeb-chef Mario Batali's pricier and, in our opinion, overhyped, restaurant around the corner), this convivial trattoria offers communal dining, reasonably priced wines, and hit-the-spot comfort foods. Come for classic Roman fare including punchy orecchiette with greens and sausage, and gumdrop-shaped ricotta gnocchi.

Minetta Tavern

NEW *113 MacDougal Street, between Bleecker & W 3rd Streets (1-212 475 3850/www.minettatavernny.com). Subway A, B, C, D, E, F to W 4th Street.* **Open** 5.30pm-1am daily. **$$**. **Eclectic**. **Map** p62 C3 ⓬④

Restaurateur Keith McNally (Balthazar, Pastis), along with chefs and co-owners Lee Hanson and Riad Nasr, unveils the latest, historic addition to his New York portfolio. Eight months after its shuttering, the former Hemingway haunt has new blood, including an updated kitchen, but its most beloved elements – the bar, murals and tin ceiling – remain. Expect old-world comfort foods (roasted marrow bones, crispy pigs' trotters), as well as the celebrated Black Label burger from Pat LaFrieda.

124 Rabbit Club

124 MacDougal Street, between Bleecker & W 3rd Streets (1-212 254 0575). Subway A, B, C, D, E, F, V to

W 4th Street. **Open** 6pm-2am Mon-
Thur, Sun; 6pm-4am Fri, Sat. No
credit cards. **Bar**. Map p62 C3 🔢
European suds get the speakeasy
treatment at this murky, unmarked
cellar that could double as an S&M
dungeon. Coarse brick walls and
votives sheathed in broken bottles
welcome serious beer geeks whom
you'll elbow aside for a seat at the
brass bar. Once there, you can sample
70-odd imported quaffs, such as the
tart Belgian ale Rodenbach. Be sure to
visit the loo: appropriately, it features
a re-creation of Brussels' legendary
peeing-boy statue.

Peanut Butter & Co

*240 Sullivan Street, between Bleecker
& W 3rd Streets (1-212 677 3995/
www.ilovepeanutbutter.com). Subway
A, B, C, D, E, F, V to W 4th Street.*
Open 11am-9pm Mon-Thur, Sun;
11am-10pm Fri, Sat. **$**. **Café**.
Map p62 C3 🔢
The staff at PB & Co grind peanuts
daily to create childhood throwbacks
such as the popular Elvis – the King's
infamous favourite of peanut butter,
bacon, banana and honey, grilled.
For sugar addicts, Death by Peanut
Butter is a landslide of ice-cream,
Peanut Butter Cap'n Crunch and
peanut butter chips.

Vol de Nuit Bar (aka Belgian Beer Lounge)

*148 W 4th Street, between Sixth
Avenue & MacDougal Street (1-212
982 3388/www.voldenuitbar.com).
Subway A, B, C, D, E, F, V to W 4th
Street.* **Open** 4pm-midnight Mon-Thur,
Sun; 4pm-2.30am Fri, Sat. **Bar**. Map
p62 C3 🔢
Duck through an unmarked doorway
on a busy stretch of West 4th Street
and find yourself in a red-walled
Belgian bar that serves brews exclusively from the motherland. Clusters
of European grad students knock
back glasses of De Konick and La
Chouffe – just two of 19 beers on tap

and 26 by the bottle. Moules and frites,
fittingly, are the only eats available.

Shopping

Fat Beats

*2nd Floor, 406 Sixth Avenue, between
8th & 9th Streets (1-212 673 3883/
www.fatbeats.com). Subway A, B, C,
D, E, F, V to W 4th Street.* **Open**
noon-9pm Mon-Sat; noon-6pm Sun.
Map p62 C3 🔢
Ground zero for headz seeking the latest or the most obscure in hip hop.
Everyone – Beck, DJ Evil Dee, DJ
Premier, Q-Tip – shops at this tiny
Greenwich Village shrine to vinyl for
treasured hip hop, jazz, funk and reggae releases, underground magazines
(like *Wax Poetics*) and cult flicks (such
as *Wild Style*).

Nom de Guerre

*640 Broadway, at Bleecker Street
(1-212 253 2891/www.nomdeguerre.net).
Subway 6 to Bleecker Street.* **Open**
noon-8pm Mon-Sat; noon-7pm Sun.
Map p62 C3 🔢
Fitting in nicely with its revolutionary
name, this upscale streetwear label's
Noho flagship is designed to resemble
a bunker; a forbidding caged metal
staircase leads down to the store. A
design collective founded by four New
Yorkers, the understated line has a
rugged, utilitarian look, encompassing
upscale denim, military-inspired jackets, and classic shirts and knitwear.

Strand Book Store

*828 Broadway, at 12th Street (1-212
473 1452/www.strandbooks.com).
Subway L, N, Q, R, W, 4, 5, 6 to 14th
Street-Union Square.* **Open** 9.30am-
10.30pm Mon-Sat; 11am-10.30pm Sun.
Map p63 C2 🔢
Boasting 18 miles of books, the
Strand has a mammoth collection of
over two million discount volumes,
and the store is made all the more
daunting by its chaotic, towering
shelves and surly staff. If you spend

NEW YORK BY AREA

enough time here you can find just about anything, from that out-of-print Victorian book of manners to the kitschiest of sci-fi pulp.

Nightlife

Blue Note

131 W 3rd Street, between MacDougal Street & Sixth Avenue (1-212 475 8592/www.bluenote.net). Subway A, B, C, D, E, F, V to W 4th Street. **Map** p62 C3 **131**

The Blue Note prides itself on being 'the jazz capital of the world'. Bona fide musical titans (Cecil Taylor, Charlie Haden) rub against hot young talents (the Bad Plus), while the close-set tables in the club get patrons rubbing up against each other. The Late Night Groove series and the Sunday brunches are the best bargain bets.

Comedy Cellar

117 MacDougal Street, between Bleecker & W 3rd Streets (1-212 254 3480/www.comedycellar.com). Subway A, B, C, D, E, F, V to W 4th Street. **Map** p62 C3 **132**

Despite being named one of NYC's best stand-up clubs year after year, the Cellar maintains a hip, underground feel. It gets packed, but no-nonsense comics such as Colin Quinn, Jim Norton and Marina Franklin will distract you from your bachelorette-party neighbours.

Love

179 MacDougal Street, at 8th Street (1-212 477 5683/www.musicislove.net). Subway A, B, C, D, E, F, V to W 4th Street; R, W to 8th Street-NYU. **Open** 10pm-4am Thur-Sat; hrs vary Wed, Sun. **Map** p62 C3 **133**

The focus here is squarely on the music (ranging from techno and electro to deep house and hip hop). Although the main room is a sparsely furnished box, the DJ line-up is pretty impressive – the likes of the seminal Chicago house DJ Derrick

Carter and Body & Soul's Joe Claussell have graced the decks – and the sound system is stunning.

(Le) Poisson Rouge

NEW *158 Bleecker Street, at Thompson Street (1-212 505 3474/www.lepoissonrouge.com). Subway A, B, C, D, E, F, V to W 4th Street.* **Map** p62 C3 **134**

Located beneath the site of legendary stage the Village Gate, (Le) Poisson Rouge is reviving the corner's reputation as a musical intersection. The sleek new venue, replete with table service and a dinner menu, is a far cry from the basement where Bob Dylan wrote 'A Hard Rain's A-Gonna Fall', but what really sets it apart is the adventurous booking policy of its young founders. David Handler and Justin Kantor have paired young classical artists such as pianist Simone Dinnerstein with compatible indie musicians such as singer-songwriter Essie Jain, while jazz, experimental, hip hop, kids' events, comedy and even film screenings mingle on the schedule.

Sullivan Room

218 Sullivan Street, between Bleecker & W 3rd Streets (1-212 252 2151/www.sullivanroom.com). Subway A, B, C, D, E, F, V to W 4th Street. **Open** 10pm-5am Wed-Sun. **Map** p62 C3 **135**

Where's the party? It's right here in this unmarked subterranean space, which hosts some of the best deep-house, tech-house and breaks bashes the city has to offer. It's an utterly unpretentious place, but hell, all you really need are some thumpin' beats and a place to move your feet, right? Keep a special lookout for the nights hosted by local stalwarts Sleepy and Boo.

Arts & leisure

IFC Center

323 Sixth Avenue, at 3rd Street (1-212 924 7771/www.ifccenter.com).

Sullivan Room

Subway A, B, C, D, E, F, V to W 4th Street. **Map** p62 B3 **136**

The long-darkened 1930s Waverly cinema was reborn in 2005 as the modern three-screen art house IFC Center, showing the latest indie hits, choice midnight cult items and occasional foreign classics. You may rub elbows with the actors on the screen, as many introduce their work on opening night. A high-toned café provides sweets, lattes and substantials.

West Village & Meatpacking District

The area west of Sixth Avenue to the Hudson River, from 14th Street to Houston Street, has held on to much of its picturesque charm. Bistros abound along Seventh Avenue and Hudson Street and high-rent shops, including three Marc Jacobs boutiques, proliferate on this stretch of Bleecker Street. The West Village is also a long-standing gay mecca, although the young gay scene has mostly moved north. The north-west corner of the West Village is known as the Meatpacking District, dating to its origins as a wholesale meat market in the 1930s. Until the 1990s, it was also a haunt for transexual prostitutes, but in recent years designer flagships, self-consciously hip eateries and nightclubs have moved in.

Eating & drinking

Cabrito

NEW *150 Carmine Street, between Bedford & Bleecker Streets (1-212 929 5050/www.cabritonyc.com). Subway A, B, C, D, E, F, V to W 4th Street; 1 to Christopher Street-Sheridan Square.* **Open** 5pm-midnight daily. **$$.**
Mexican. **Map** p62 B3 **137**

This artfully scuffed roadhouse, done up with Mexican wall tiles and bare filament bulbs, traffics in big, offbeat flavours. Chef David Schuttenberg favours authenticity over crowd-pleasing Tex-Mex: *jalapeños rellenos* stuffed with shredded snapper, raisins, capers and pumpkin seeds are a fiery starter, and the namesake *cabrito*, served on a banana leaf with a side of flour tortillas, offers the slow-cooked richness of a pit-roasted goat. You may find South of the Border fare this good on an outer-borough street corner, but Cabrito is a far more comfortable place to enjoy it.

Casa

72 Bedford Street, at Commerce Street (1-212 366 9410/www.casarestaurant. com). Subway 1 to Christopher Street-Sheridan Square. **Open** 6-11pm Mon-Thur; 6pm-midnight Fri; 10am-3pm, 6pm-midnight Sat; 10am-3pm, 6-11pm Sun. **$$. Brazilian. Map** p62 B3 **138**

Sure, you'll find *feijoada* and several trusty steak platters, but Casa is one of the few Brazilian restaurants in Manhattan to venture successfully into the regional cuisines of Bahia and Minas Gerais. A youthful crowd of Villagers dotted with expats fills the narrow, white-walled single room to sample the cheese bread and appetisers such as the lime-infused *lula frita* (calamari) and main dishes such as the Bahian stews cooked in palm oil.

Corner Bistro

331 W 4th Street, at Jane Street (1-212 242 9502). Subway A, C, E to 14th Street; L to Eighth Avenue. **Open** 11.30am-3.30am Mon-Sat; noon-3.30pm Sun. No credit cards. **Bar. Map** p62 B3 **139**

There's only one reason to come to this legendary pub: it serves up the city's best burgers – and beer is just $2.50 a mug (well, that makes two reasons). The patties here are cheap, delish and no-frills, served on a flimsy paper plate. To get one, you may have to wait for a good hour, especially on weekend nights. Fortunately, the game is on the tube, and a jukebox covers everything from Calexico to Coltrane.

Moustache

90 Bedford Street, between Barrow & Grove Streets (1-212 229 2220/ www.moustachepizza.com). Subway 1 to Christopher Street-Sheridan Square. **Open** noon-midnight daily. **$.** No credit cards. **Middle Eastern.** **Map** p62 B3 ❶❹⓿

Located on a leafy, brownstone-lined West Village street, this beloved cheap-eats haven serves some of the city's best Middle Eastern food. The small, exposed-brick dining room packs in a neighbourhood crowd nightly – it's not unusual to see a line outside this no-reservations spot. The freshly baked pittas are perfect for scooping up the smoky baba ghanoush.

Pearl Oyster Bar

18 Cornelia Street, between Bleecker & W 4th Streets (1-212 691 8211/ www.pearloysterbar.com). Subway A, B, C, D, E, F, V to W 4th Street. **Open** noon-2.30pm, 6-11pm Mon-Fri; 6-11pm Sat. **$$.** **Seafood.** **Map** p62 B3 ❶❹❶

There's a good reason this convivial, no-reservations, New England-style fish joint always has a line – the food is outstanding. The lemon-scented lobster roll, sweet meat laced with mayonnaise on a butter-enriched bun, is better than you could have imagined. More sophisticated dishes, such as a shellfish-packed bouillabaisse, fare equally well.

Scarpetta

NEW *355 W 14th Street, at Ninth Avenue (1-212 691 0555/www. scarpettanyc.com). Subway A, C, E to 14th Street; L to Eighth Avenue.* **Open** 5.30-11pm Mon-Thur; 5.30pm-midnight Fri, Sat; 5.30-10.30pm Sun. **$$$.** **Italian.** **Map** p62 A2 ❶❹❷

Touted as the next Mario Batali, chef Scott Conant vanished last year while his reputation and restaurants,

L'Impero and Alto, were still riding high. Now he's returned from his sabbatical with this cavernous middle-brow trattoria. His pastas, like plump duck-and-foie-gras ravioli slicked with a rich marsala-duck jus, are as ethereal as ever, but Conant's tendency towards upscale creations shows when he attempts rustic dishes – a shredded goat dish, for example – with inconsistent results.

'sNice

45 Eighth Avenue, at W 4th Street (1-212 645 0310). Subway A, C, E to 14th Street; L to Eighth Avenue. **Open** 7.30am-10pm Mon-Fri; 8am-10pm Sat, Sun. **$.** No credit cards. **Vegetarian café.** **Map** p62 B2 ❶❹❸

'Snice is nice – if what you're looking for is a cosy joint where you can read a paper, do a little laptopping, and enjoy cheap, simple and satisfying veggie fare. Far roomier than it appears from its corner windows, the exposed-brick café has what may well be the largest menu in the city scrawled on the wall, giving carefully wrought descriptions of each burrito, sandwich and salad. Standouts include the quinoa salad with mixed greens and avocado dressing, and the brie, pear and rocket baguette dressed with raspberry mustard.

Spotted Pig

314 W 11th Street, at Greenwich Street (1-212 620 0393/www.thespottedpig. com). Subway A, C, E to 14th Street; L to Eighth Avenue. **Open** noon-2am Mon-Fri; 11am-2am Sat, Sun. **$$.** **Eclectic.** **Map** p62 B3 ❶❹❹

This spot is still hopping – and even after opening more seating upstairs, a wait is always expected. Some might credit the big names involved (Mario Batali consults and April Bloomfield, of London's River Café, is in the kitchen). The burger is a must-order: a top-secret blend of ground beef grilled rare (unless otherwise specified) and covered with gobs of

Bitter sweets

Confectionery gets tough.

Bond Street Chocolates

In 1996, an indie West Village bakery kickstarted the trend for nostalgic, pastel-frosted cupcakes. After featuring on *Sex and the City*, **Magnolia Bakery**'s (p101) success was sealed. More than ten years on, lines still snake out on to Bleecker Street and, not only has it spawned a slew of cupcake copycats, in the past year it has opened branches on the Upper West Side and in the Rockefeller Center. Time for a backlash against cutesy confectionery: now a handful of bakeries and chocolate shops are giving the sweet stuff a harder edge – with delicious results. A hot contender for the anti-Magnolia, nearby bakery-cum-bar **Sweet Revenge** (p101) tops its cupcakes with spiky peaks of frosting in grown-up flavours, such as peanut butter with a ganache centre, and each one comes with a recommended beer or wine pairing. Over in the East Village, pastry chef Christina Tosi has been making waves at iconoclastic new **Momofuku**

Bakery & Milk Bar (p87). 'Compost cookies', 'crack pie' (filled with a highly addictive butter, heavy cream and sugar concoction)… this is not your grandma's bake shop. Soft-serve ice-cream comes in unusual flavours such as salted pistachio and jelly doughnut. If you're more of a chocolate junkie, look no further than the clashing flavours at **Bespoke Chocolates** (p89). Rising star Rachel Zoe Insler creates some of the best bonbons this side of the Bowery: sea-salted caramel coated in dark chocolate and crushed pretzels; a strawberry balsamic number with that telltale tang of vinegar; a Turkish coffee and cardamom truffle – all cater to sophisticated palates. Even more subversive, **Bond Street Chocolates** (p89) turns out moulded dark chocolate skulls, various gods (Jesus, Buddha) and unorthodox combinations, like corn nuts coated in milk chocolate and cocoa. Being bad has never tasted so good.

pungent roquefort. It arrives plated with a tower of crispy shoestring fries tossed with rosemary. But the kitchen saves the best treat for dessert: a delectable slice of moist orange-and-bourbon chocolate cake.

Sweet Revenge

NEW *62 Carmine Street, between Bedford Street & Seventh Avenue (1-212 242 2240/www.sweetrevenge nyc.com). Subway A, B, C, D, E, F, V to W 4th Street; 1 to Christopher Street-Sheridan Square.* **Open** 8am-11pm Mon-Thur; 8am-1am Fri; 11am-1am Sat; 11am-9pm Sun. **$. Café/ bar**. **Map** p62 B3 **145**
See box p100.

Shopping

Alexis Bittar

NEW *353D Bleecker Street, between Charles & W 10th Streets (1-212 727 1093/www.alexisbittar.com). Subway 1 to Christopher Street-Sheridan Square.* **Open** 11am-7pm Mon-Fri; noon-8pm Sat; noon-7pm Sun. **Map** p62 B3 **146**
The jewellery designer who started out selling his designs from a humble Soho street stall recently opened his second shop on upscale Bleecker Street to show off his art-object designs in his trademark Lucite, 18k vermeil and semiprecious stones; all are hand-crafted in his Brooklyn atelier.

Earnest Sewn

821 Washington Street, between Gansevoort & Little W 12th Streets (1-212 242 3414/www.earnestsewn. com). Subway A, C, E to 14th Street; L to Eighth Avenue. **Open** 11am-7pm Mon-Fri, Sun; 11am-8pm Sat. **Map** p62 A2 **147**
Established by former Paper Denim & Cloth designer Scott Morrison, this culty jeans label marries vintage American style with old-school workmanship. Each pair ($180 and up) can take up to 18 hours to make, and boasts butt-boosting pockets and flattering seams.

Flight 001

96 Greenwich Avenue, between Jane & W 12th Streets (1-212 989 0001/ www.flight001.com). Subway A, C, E to 14th Street; L to Eighth Avenue. **Open** 11am-8pm Mon-Sat; noon-6pm Sun. **Map** p62 B2 **148**
As well as a tasteful selection of luggage by the likes of Mandarina Duck, Orla Kiely and Samsonite, this one-stop shop carries everything for the chic jet-setter, including fun travel products such as Redeye Pak in-flight survival kits, eye masks, emergency totes that squash down to tennis ball size and 'essentials' such as expanding toilet-tissue tablets and single-use packets of Woolite.

Jeffrey New York

449 W 14th Street, between Ninth & Tenth Avenues (1-212 206 1272/ www.jeffreynewyork.com). Subway A, C, E to 14th Street; L to Eighth Avenue. **Open** 10am-8pm Mon-Wed, Fri; 10am-9pm Thur; 10am-7pm Sat; 12.30-6pm Sun. **Map** p62 A2 **149**
Jeffrey Kalinsky, a former Barneys shoe buyer, was a Meatpacking District pioneer when he opened his namesake store in 1999. Designer clothing abounds here – by Yves Saint Laurent, Halston, L'Wren Scott and young British star Christopher Kane, among others. But the centrepiece is without a doubt the shoe salon, which features the work of Manolo Blahnik, Prada and Christian Louboutin, as well as newer names to watch.

Magnolia Bakery

401 Bleecker Street, at 11th Street (1-212 462 2572). Subway 1 to Christopher Street. **Open** 9am-11.30pm Mon-Thur, Sun; 9am-12.30am Fri, Sat. **Map** p62 B3 **150**
Magnolia skyrocketed to fame after featuring on *Sex and the City*, and it's still oven-hot, recently spawning two branches uptown. The pastel-iced cupcakes are much vaunted, but you can also pick up other treats, including the

custardy, Southern-style banana pudding (Brits: think trifle). Comfort food doesn't get much more classy. See also box p100.

Rag & Bone

NEW *104 Christopher Street, between Bedford & Bleecker Streets (1-212 727 2990/www.rag-bone.com). Subway 1 to Christopher Street-Sheridan Square.* **Open** noon-7pm daily. **Map** p62 B3 ⑮

Born out of its founders' frustrations with mass-produced jeans, what began as a denim line in 2002 has expanded to cover clothing for both men and women, all with an emphasis on craftsmanship. The designs, in substantial, luxurious fabrics such as cashmere and tweed, nod towards tradition (riding jackets, greatcoats) while exuding an utterly contemporary vibe. This aesthetic is reflected in the brand's new flagship store – an industrial-edged brick-walled space with an elaborate tin ceiling.

Nightlife

APT

419 W 13th Street, between Ninth Avenue & Washington Street (1-212 414 4245/www.aptnyc.com). Subway A, C, E to 14th Street; L to Eighth Avenue. **Open** 7pm-4am daily. **Map** p62 A2 ⑫

Kicking back in APT's formerly exclusive street-level space (the neat design is by India Mahdavi) is like being at an impromptu party in some trust-fund babe's townhouse. Below, people looking for the perfect beat gather in a minimalist, faux-wood-panelled rectangular room. The place features an amazing array of DJs; top local spinners such as DJ Spun and the Negroclash crew and superstars like cosmic-disco dons the Idjut Boys and house-music hero Tony Humphries regularly regale the tipplers with a wide range of underground sounds.

Cielo

18 Little W 12th Street, between Ninth Avenue & Washington Street (1-212 645 5700/www.cieloclub.com). Subway A, C, E to 14th Street; L to Eighth Avenue. **Open** 10pm-4am Mon; 11pm-4am Wed; 10pm-4am Thur, Fri, Sat; hrs vary Tue, Sun. **Map** p62 A2 ⑬

You'd never guess from the Paris Hilton wannabes hanging out in the neighbourhood that the attitude inside this exclusive club is close to zero. On the sunken dancefloor, hip-to-hip crowds gyrate to deep beats from top DJs, including NYC old-schoolers François K, Tedd Patterson and Louie Vega, as well as international spinners ranging from Berlin's Ellen Allien to Dimitri from Paris. Cielo, which features a crystal-clear sound system, has won a bevy of 'best club' awards – and it deserves them all.

Comix

353 W 14th Street, between Eighth & Ninth Avenues (1-212 524 2500/www.comixny.com). Subway A, C, E to 14th Street. **Map** p62 A2 ⑭

Big names such as Richard Lewis have graced the stage in this large, sleek club, as have lesser-known but equally talented local and alt stand-ups. Downstairs, the cover-free Ochi's Lounge (one-drink minimum) provides a platform for emerging acts and experimental shows.

Henrietta Hudson

438 Hudson Street, at Morton Street (1-212 924 3347/www.henrietta hudson.com). Subway 1 to Christopher Street-Sheridan Square. **Open** 5pm-2am Mon, Tue; 4pm-4am Wed-Fri; 1pm-4am Sat, Sun. **Map** p62 B3 ⑮

A much-loved lesbian night-spot, this glam lounge attracts young hottie girls from all over the New York area. Every night's a different party, with hip hop, pop and rock music and live shows among the musical pulls. Super-cool New Yorker Lisa Cannistraci is in charge.

Henrietta Hudson

Smalls

183 W 10th Street, between Seventh Avenue South & W 4th Street (1-212 252 5091/www.smallsjazzclub.com). Subway 1 to Christopher Street-Sheridan Square. **Open** 7.30pm-4am daily. No credit cards. **Map** p62 B3 🕦
The resurrected version of this storied, youth-friendly jazz spot offers a big concession for the grown-ups: a liquor licence and a fully stocked bar. One thing hasn't changed, though: the subterranean spot is still a place to catch the best and brightest up-and-comers, as well as moonlighting stars such as the Bad Plus's Ethan Iverson and veteran baritone saxist Charles Davis.

Village Vanguard

178 Seventh Avenue South, at Perry Street, West Village (1-212 255 4037/www.villagevanguard.com). Subway A, C, E, 1, 2, 3 to 14th Street; L to Eighth Avenue. **Map** p62 B2 🕦
More than 75 years old but still going strong, the Village Vanguard is one of New York's authentic jazz meccas. History surrounds you: John Coltrane, Miles Davis and Bill Evans have all grooved in this hallowed hall. Big names both old and new continue to fill the schedule, and the 2009 Grammy Award-winning 16-piece Vanguard Jazz Orchestra has been the Monday-night regular for more than 40 years.

Arts & leisure

Film Forum

209 W Houston Street, between Sixth Avenue & Varick Street, West Village (1-212 727 8110/www.filmforum.com). Subway 1 to Houston Street. **Map** p62 B4 🕦
The city's leading tastemaking venue, Film Forum is programmed by a fest-scouring staff that takes its duties as seriously as a Kurosawa samurai. A recent renovation included new seats, all the better to take in the hottest films from Cannes, Venice and beyond.

Radio City Music Hall p134

Midtown

The area roughly between 14th Street and 59th Street, from river to river, is iconic New York: jutting skyscrapers, crowded pavements and a yellow river of cabs streaming down the congested avenues. That some of the city's most recognisable landmarks are located here, from the Empire State Building to Rockefeller Center, is of course part of the draw. But there's a lot more to Midtown than glistening towers and high-octane commerce. It contains the city's most concentrated contemporary gallery district (Chelsea), its hottest gay enclaves (Chelsea and Hell's Kitchen), some of its swankiest shops (Fifth Avenue) and the majority of its big theatres on Broadway.

Chelsea

The corridor between 14th and 29th Streets west of Sixth Avenue

emerged as the nexus of New York's queer life in the 1990s. While it's slowly being eclipsed by Hell's Kitchen to the north as a gay hotspot, and has residents of all types, it's still home to numerous bars, restaurants and shops catering to 'Chelsea boys'. The western edge of the neighbourhood is the city's major art gallery zone.

Sights & museums

Museum at FIT

Building E, Seventh Avenue, at 27th Street (1-212 217 4558/www.fitnyc.edu/museum). Subway 1 to 28th Street. **Open** noon-8pm Tue-Fri; 10am-5pm Sat. **Admission** free. **Map** p106 C3 ①
The Fashion Institute of Technology owns one of the largest and most impressive collections of clothing, textiles and accessories in the world, including some 50,000 costumes and fabrics dating from the fifth century to the present. Overseen by fashion historian Valerie Steele, the

museum showcases a selection from the permanent collection, as well as temporary exhibitions focusing on individual designers or the role fashion plays in society.

Rubin Museum of Art

150 W 17th Street, at Seventh Avenue (1-212 620 5000/www.rmanyc.org). Subway A, C, E to 14th Street; L to Eighth Avenue; 1 to 18th Street. **Open** 11am-5pm Mon, Thur; 11am-7pm Wed; 11am-10pm Fri; 11am-6pm Sat, Sun. **Admission** $10; free-$7 reductions. **Map** p106 C4 ❷
Opened in 2004, this six-storey museum (once home to Barneys New York) houses Donald and Shelley Rubin's impressive collection of Himalayan art and artefacts, as well as large-scale temporary exhibitions.

Eating & drinking

Blossom

187 Ninth Avenue, between 21st & 22nd Streets (1-212 627 1144/ www.blossomnyc.com). Subway C, E to 23rd Street. **Open** 5-10pm Mon-Thur; 12.45-2.30pm, 5-10pm Fri, Sat; 5-9pm Sun.* **$$. Vegetarian/Vegan.** **Map** p106 B4 ❸
For cautious carnivores, Blossom offers one big surprise: all the eggless pastas and mock meats actually taste pretty good. For vegans, it's a candlelit godsend. Guiltily dreaming of veal scaloppine? Try the pan-seared seitan cutlets – tender wheat gluten served with basil mash, swiss chard, a white-wine caper sauce and artichokes.

Buddakan

75 Ninth Avenue, between 15th & 16th Streets (1-212 989 6699/www. buddakannyc.com). Subway A, C, E to 14th Street; L to Eighth Avenue. **Open** 5.30-10.45pm Mon, Sun; 5.30-11.45pm Tue, Wed; 5.30pm-12.45am Thur-Sat. **$$. Chinese. Map** p106 B5 ❹
When Stephen Starr first opened this stately pleasure dome in 2006, New Yorkers flocked to gawk at the fake tapestries and Buddha statues, as well as the grand staircase leading down to the enormous golden-hued dining hall with gigantic chandeliers suspended from its 35ft ceiling. While the hordes still come, many have discovered that the real value of Buddakan lies in its gastronomy – and reasonable prices.

Co.

NEW *230 Ninth Avenue, at 24th Street (1-212 243 1105/www.co-pane.com). Subway C, E to 23rd Street.* **Open** noon-3pm, 5-11pm Tue-Sat; 11am-10pm Sun. **$. Pizza. Map** p106 B4 ❺
This unassuming pizzeria is the restaurant debut of Jim Lahey, whose Sullivan Street Bakery supplies many of the city's top restaurants. Lahey's crust is so good, in fact, it doesn't need any toppings (try the pizza bianca, dusted with sea salt and rosemary). The most compelling individual-sized pies come from non-traditional sources, such as the ham and cheese, essentially a croque-monsieur in pizza form.

Cookshop

156 Tenth Avenue, at 20th Street (1-212 924 4440/www.cookshopny.com). Subway C, E to 23rd Street. **Open** 8-11am, 11.30am-3pm, 5.30-11.30pm Mon-Fri; 11am-3pm, 5.30-11.30pm Sat; 11am-3pm, 5.30-9pm Sun. **$$. American. Map** p106 B4 ❻
Vicki Freeman and chef-husband-co-owner Marc Meyer want Cookshop to be a platform for sustainable ingredients from independent farmers. True to the restaurant's mission, the ingredients are consistently top-notch and the menu changes daily. While organic ingredients alone don't guarantee a great meal, Meyer knows how to let the natural flavours speak for themselves.

Craftsteak

85 Tenth Avenue, between 15th & 16th Streets (1-212 400 6699/www.craft restaurant.com). Subway A, C, E to 14th Street; L to Eighth Avenue.

Midtown 1

Midtown 2

A **B** **C** Strawberry Fields

1,2,3 Ⓜ W 72ND ST Ⓜ B,C

HENRY HUDSON PKWY

W 70TH ST

WEST END AVE AMSTERDAM AVE COLUMBUS AVE CENTRAL PARK WEST WEST DRIVE

W 68TH ST

1

Sheep Meadow

W 66TH ST Ⓜ

Tavern on the Green

65TH ST TRANS

RIVERSIDE BLVD

W 64TH ST

Heckscher Playground

Lincoln Center W 62ND ST

2

W 60TH ST

A,B,C,D Ⓜ

Columbus Circle

Time Warner Center

Museum of Arts & Design

99
98

W 58TH ST

Hearst Tower

97

W 57TH ST

Carnegie Hall Ⓜ N,Q,R 76

96

W 56TH ST

95

W 54TH ST

94

De Witt Clinton Park

67

HELL'S KITCHEN

92 AVE

3

NYC

92

W 52ND ST

B,D,E Ⓜ i Informa Cent

63

79

W 50TH ST

74

64

TWELFTH AVE ELEVENTH AVE TENTH AVE NINTH AVE

90

C,E Ⓜ

B

88

W 48TH ST

70 SEVENTH AVE

Intrepid Sea-Air-Space Museum

THEATER DISTRICT

1 Ⓜ N,R,

86 56

W 46TH ST

Times Squa Information C

4

65 73 71

81

84

72 51

60

75 78

TKTS

EIGHTH AVE

83 55

W 44TH ST

62

69

77

Times Square

58

W 42ND ST

Port Authority Bus Terminal

A,C,E Ⓜ

68

81

57

N,Q,R, 1,2,3

LINCOLN TUNNEL

W 40TH ST

Madame Tussaud's New York

78

66

GARMENT DISTRICT

W 38TH ST

5

SEVENTH AVE

76

Javits Center

W 36TH ST

Macy's

See p106 ▼

A,C,E Ⓜ W 34TH ST 1,2,3 Ⓜ 52

E 72ND ST

D **E** **F**

hesda Terrace

Naumburg
Bandshell

Asia Society
and Museum

The Frick
Collection

E 70TH ST

1 Sights & museums
1 Eating & drinking
1 Shopping
1 Nightlife
1 Arts & leisure

1

E 68TH ST

China
Institute

E 66TH ST

FIFTH AVE

PARK AVE

LEXINGTON AVE

THIRD AVE

SECOND AVE

FIRST AVE

FRANKLIN D ROOSEVELT DR

E 64TH ST

The
airy

Zoo

MADISON AVE

Rockefeller
University

YORK AVE

2

Wollman
Memorial
Rink

UPTOWN
(pp137-159)

E 62ND ST

E 60TH ST

TRAMWAY

N,R,W

N,R,W

QUEENSBORO
(59TH ST)BRIDGE

Grand Army
Plaza **93 102**

4,5,6

E 58TH ST

SUTTON PL

96 **97**

E 57TH ST

98

Trump Tower

E 56TH ST

SUTTON PL SOUTH

Museum of
Modern Art

90

E 54TH ST

erican
k Art
seum

82 85 91

E,V

95 87

E,V

Paley Center
for Media

E 52ND ST

MIDTOWN

BEEKMAN PL

3

Radio City
Music Hall

St Patrick's Cathedral

E 50TH ST

101

6

88

NBC

99

MITCHELL PL

kefeller
enter

Christie's

E 48TH ST

100

Japan Society

E 46TH ST

109

4

Grand Central
Terminal

Chrysler
Building

104
108

E 44TH ST

SECOND AVE

105

United Nations
Headquarters

103

B,D,F,V

7

S,4,5,6,7

E 42ND ST

FIRST AVE

107

TUDOR CITY PL

QUEENS-MIDTOWN
TUNNEL

Bryant
Park

86

106

NY Public
Library

E 40TH ST

PARK AVE SOUTH

LEXINGTON AVE

THIRD AVE

E 38TH ST

Scandinavia House:
The Nordic Center
in America

0

300 m

0

300 yds

© Copyright Time Out Group 2009

5

43

Morgan
Library

E 36TH ST

UD
RE

F,V,N,Q,R,W

Empire State
Building

6

See
p107
▼

Time Out Shortlist | New York 2010 **109**

E 34TH ST

Flatiron Building p115

Open 5.30-10pm Mon-Thur, Sun; 5.30-11pm Fri, Sat. **$$$-$$$$**. **Steakhouse**. **Map** p106 B5 ⑦
Prices here run steep even by steakhouse standards, but Tom Colicchio has methodically honed the grand, modern Craftsteak into one of the better steakhouses in New York. His pro-choice formula from the original Craft takes a beefy turn when it comes to preparation style (corn versus grass-fed, Wagyu versus 42-day ageing) and sides (30 options).

Empire Diner

210 Tenth Avenue, at 22nd Street (1-212 243 2736/www.empire-diner.com). Subway C, E to 23rd Street. **Open** 24hrs daily. **$$**. **American**. **Map** p106 B4 ⑧
This 1946 Fodero diner may look like a movie-set classic – with gleaming stainless steel walls and rotating stools – but few other hash houses have candlelight, sidewalk café tables and a pianist playing dinner music. Fewer still attempt dishes such as sesame noodles with chicken, or linguine with smoked salmon, watercress and garlic. We prefer the more standard – a juicy blue-cheese steak burger, for instance – and nostalgic desserts.

Half King

505 W 23rd Street, between Tenth & Eleventh Avenues (1-212 462 4300/ www.thehalfking.com). Subway C, E to 23rd Street. **Open** 11am-4am Mon-Fri; 9am-4am Sat, Sun. **Bar**. **Map** p106 B4 ⑨
Don't let the blasé appearance fool you – the creative types gathered at the Half King's yellow pine bar are probably as excited as you are to catch a glimpse of the part-owner, author Sebastian Junger. While you're waiting, order a draft like Widmer, a cloudy Hefeweizen or a cocktail (we like the Parisian, with Hendrick's Gin, sauvignon blanc and elderflower liquor). A reading series is held on Mondays.

Tillman's

165 W 26th Street, between Sixth & Seventh Avenues (1-212 627 8320/ www.tillmansnyc.com). Subway F, V, 1 to 23rd Street. **Open** 5pm-2am Mon, Tue; 5pm-4am Wed-Sat. **Bar**. **Map** p106 C3 ⑩
Sepia images of jazz, funk and soul legends line the walls at this warm, earth-toned cocktail emporium. Waitresses glide amid crescent-shaped leather booths, and you'll likely hear Coltrane oozing from the speakers. Given the old-fashioned aesthetic, a classic cocktail is the way to go: try a well-crafted Negroni or a bracing Dark & Stormy (dark rum, ginger beer and lime juice).

Shopping

Antiques Garage

112 W 25th Street, between Sixth & Seventh Avenues (1-212 243 5343/ www.annexmarkets.com). Subway F, V to 23rd Street. **Open** 9am-5pm Sat, Sun. No credit cards. **Map** p106 C3 ⑪

Designers (and the occasional dolled-down celebrity) hunt regularly at this flea market in a vacant parking garage. Specialities include old prints, vintage clothing and household paraphernalia. A $1 shuttle bus runs between the Garage and sister site Hell's Kitchen Flea Market (p125).

Billy's Bakery
184 Ninth Avenue, between 21st & 22nd Streets (1-212 647 9956/ www.billysbakerynyc.com). Subway C, E to 23rd Street. **Open** 8.30am-11pm Mon-Thur; 8.30am-midnight Fri, Sat; 9am-10pm Sun. **Map** p106 B4 ⑫
Amid super-sweet retro delights such as coconut cream pie, cupcakes and Famous Chocolate Icebox Cake, you'll find friendly service in a setting that will remind you of grandma's kitchen – or at least, it will if your grandmother was Betty Crocker.

Jazz Record Center
Room 804, 236 W 26th Street, between Seventh & Eighth Avenues (1-212 675 4480/www.jazzrecordcenter.com). Subway C, E to 23rd Street; 1 to 28th Street. **Open** 10am-6pm Mon-Sat. **Map** p106 C3 ⑬
The city's best jazz store stocks records (some of them rare), books, videos and other related merchandise.

Loehmann's
101 Seventh Avenue, at 16th Street (1-212 352 0856/www.loehmanns.com). Subway A, C, E to 14th Street; L to Eighth Avenue. **Open** 9am-9pm Mon-Sat; 11am-7pm Sun. **Map** p106 C5 ⑭
Although this venerable discount emporium is often crowded, its five floors offer major markdowns on current and off-season clothes (make a beeline for the back room for big names such as Prada and Armani) and accessories, as well as fragrances and housewares.

192 Books
192 Tenth Avenue, between 21st & 22nd Streets (1-212 255 4022/ www.192books.com). Subway C, E to 23rd Street. **Open** noon-6pm Mon, Sun; noon-7pm Tue-Fri; 11am-7pm Sat. **Map** p106 B4 ⑮
Owned and 'curated' by art dealer Paula Cooper and her husband, editor Jack Macrae, 192 offers a strong selection of art books and literature, as well as memoirs and books on gardening, history, politics, design and music. Regular readings, signings and discussions, some featuring well-known writers, are further good reasons to drop by.

Printed Matter
195 Tenth Avenue, between 21st & 22nd Streets (1-212 925 0325/www. printedmatter.org). Subway C, E to 23rd Street. **Open** 11am-6pm Tue, Wed; 11am-7pm Thur-Sat. **Map** p106 B4 ⑯
This non-profit organisation, which operates a public reading room as well as a shop, is exclusively devoted to artists' books, from David Shrigley's deceptively naive illustrations to provocative photographic self-portraits by Matthias Herrmann. Works by unknown and emerging artists share shelf space with those of veterans such as Edward Ruscha.

Nightlife

The Eagle
554 W 28th Street, between Tenth & Eleventh Avenues (1-646 473 1866/ www.eaglenyc.com). Subway C, E to 23rd Street. **Open** 10pm-4am Tue-Sat; 5pm-4am Sun. No credit cards. **Bar**. **Map** p106 A3 ⑰
Whatever your kink, this gay fetish bar will satisfy with its leather soirées and foot-worship fêtes, plus simple pool-playing and cruising nights. In summer, it hosts rooftop barbecues.

G Lounge
225 W 19th Street, between Seventh & Eighth Avenues (1-212 929 1085/ www.glounge.com). Subway 1 to 18th Street. **Open** 4pm-4am daily. No credit cards. **Map** p106 C4 ⑱

The neighbourhood's original slick boy nightspot – a moodily lit cave with a cool brick-and-glass arched entrance – is a favourite after-work destination for cocktails, and where an excellent roster of DJs stays on top of the mood.

Highline Ballroom

431 W 16th Street, between Ninth & Tenth Avenues (1-212 414 5994/ www.highlineballroom.com). Subway A, C, E to 14th Street; L to Eighth Avenue. **Map** p106 B5 ⑲
This club is perfect on paper: the sound is top-of-the-heap and sight lines are pretty good. The bookings are also impressive, ranging from world music (Tinariwen) to hip hop (Dizzee Rascal) via old-guard stars (Lou Reed) and indie faves (Art Brut). The overall vibe, however, can feel more LA than New York – as such, the club works best with cool R&B (Raphael Saadiq, say).

Upright Citizens Brigade Theatre

307 W 26th Street, between Eighth & Ninth Avenues (1-212 366 9176/ www.ucbtheatre.com). Subway C, E to 23rd Street; 1 to 28th Street. No credit cards. **Map** p106 B3 ⑳
The improv troupes and sketch groups anchored at UCBT are the best in the city. Stars of *Saturday Night Live*, VH1 and writers for late-night talk shows gather on Sunday nights to wow crowds in the long-running ASSSS-CAT 3000. Other teams include Reuben Williams (Saturdays) and the Stepfathers (Fridays).

Arts & leisure

Atlantic Theater Company

336 W 20th Street, between Eighth & Ninth Avenues (1-212 691 5919/ www.atlantictheater.org). Subway C, E to 23rd Street. **Map** p107 B4 ㉑
Created in 1985 as an offshoot of acting workshops taught by playwright David Mamet and film star William H Macy, the dynamic Atlantic Theater Company has presented nearly 100 plays, including Duncan Sheik and Steven Sater's *Spring Awakening*, a Tony-award-winning rock musical (based on an 1891 German play) that became a ground-breaking Broadway hit.

Flatiron Lounge p116

Old hat gets hip

JJ Hat Center

JJ Hat Center (p117) has been fitting the lids of NYC's dandies since 1911. In the panelled, chandelier-lit store, staff sporting the wares help customers choose from more than 10,000 hats (from $50 to $300). 'You're never again going to see a full Yankee Stadium where every man is wearing a fedora,' says manager Marc Williamson. But, he tells us, the age of the hat is not dying out. In fact, it's enjoying a renaissance. Walk down Bedford Avenue in Williamsburg, Brooklyn – Hipsterville's Main Street – and you'll see young blades sporting classic headwear with their skinny jeans and tees.

Former magazine designer Frenel Morris, 32, who crafts his **Still Life** (p83) line using heirloom equipment, says the trend has taken off in the past couple of years. 'When I first started making hats I'd be the only one wearing one, but within a year or two I'd go out and there would be five or six people at the bar wearing a hat.' Modified porkpies and fedoras

with reduced brims and vintage trims are displayed in his LES shop. Prices start at around $100 for a cap, $275 for felt styles.

Orchard Street is evolving into a hat enclave: **Victor Osborne** has just moved his shop-atelier from Williamsburg to No.160 (between Rivington & Stanton Streets, 1-212 677 6254, www.victorosborne. com). The 26-year-old FIT graduate says most of his customers are between 20 and 35. Designs encompass funky patterned caps (from $120), vintage-inspired cloches and fedoras ($200-$250).

Mentored by the late Isabella Blow, 29-year-old **Ryan Wilde** – hat designer for Patricia Field – has just opened her own shop in Williamsburg (109 Broadway, between Bedford Avenue & Berry Street, 1-315 430 8395, www. ryanwilde.com). The space is lined with her Gothic-tinged creations: miniature ladies' toppers and 1940s-vibe cadets are trimmed with anything from dwarf alligator claws to mink bones. Hats start at $110, but most cost $200-$250.

Chelsea Piers

Piers 59-62, W 17th to 23rd Streets, at Eleventh Avenue (1-212 336 6666/ www.chelseapiers.com). Subway C, E to 23rd Street. **Open** times vary; phone or check website for details. **Map** p106 A4 ㉒

This six-block stretch of riverfront real estate provides an Olympics-level variety of physical diversions in a bright, clean and well-maintained facility. Swingers can practise at the Golf Club (Pier 59, 1-212 336 6400); bowlers can show the locals how to roll at 300 New York's 40 lanes (between Piers 59 and 60, 1-212 835 2695); and ice skaters can enjoy carving up the indoor Sky Rink (Pier 61, 1-212 336 6100). The Field House (Pier 62, 1-212 336 6500) has a rock-climbing wall, a gymnastics training centre, batting cages, basketball courts, indoor playing fields, a toddler adventure centre and more. At the Sports Center Health Club (Pier 60, 1-212 336 6000), open to non-members, you'll find an expansive gym complete with comprehensive weight deck and 100 cardiovascular machines, plus classes in everything from triathlon training in the 25-yard pool, to boxing.

Joyce Theater

175 Eighth Avenue, at 19th Street (1-212 242 0800/www.joyce.org). Subway A, C, E to 14th Street; 1 to 18th Street; L to Eighth Avenue. **Map** p106 B4 ㉓

This intimate space is one of the finest dance stages in town. Companies and choreographers that present work here, among them Ballet Hispanico and Pilobolus Dance Theater, tend to be more traditional than experimental.

The Kitchen

512 W 19th Street, between Tenth & Eleventh Avenues (1-212 255 5793/ www.thekitchen.org). Subway A, C, E to 14th Street; L to Eighth Avenue. **Map** p106 B4 ㉔

A meeting place for the avant-garde in music, dance and theatre for more than 30 years, the Kitchen features inventive, often provocative artists. Cutting-edge choreographers such as Dean Moss have presented work here; now they mentor younger upstarts.

Flatiron District & Union Square

Taking its name from the distinctive wedge-shaped

Madison Square Park

Flatiron Building, this district extends from 14th to 29th Streets, between Sixth and Lexington Avenues. The former commercial district became more residential in the 1980s as buyers were drawn to its early 20th-century industrial architecture and 19th-century brownstones; clusters of restaurants and shops (many with an interior focus) followed. The Flatiron District has two major public spaces: **Union Square**, known for its farmers' market (p118), and the smaller, lovelier **Madison Square Park** (below).

Sights & museums

Flatiron Building

175 Fifth Avenue, between 22nd & 23rd Streets. Subway N, R, W, 6 to 23rd Street. **Map** p107 D4 ㉕
The world's first steel-frame sky-scraper, the 22-storey Beaux Arts edifice, is clad conspicuously in white limestone and terracotta, but it's the unique triangular shape that has drawn sightseers since it opened in 1902.

Madison Square Park

23rd to 26th Streets, between Fifth & Madison Avenues (www.madison squarepark.org). Subway N, R, W, 6 to 23rd Street. **Map** p107 D3/D4 ㉖
A highly desirable address when it opened in 1847, Madison Square Park became the site of several unfortunate and unsavoury events – including the murder of architect Stanford White atop one of his creations, the second Madison Square Garden, in 1901. By the 1990s, the park had become a decaying no-go zone given over to drug dealers and the homeless, but got a much-needed makeover in 2001. Now a verdant oasis, it hosts a series of summer concerts, literary readings and kids' events, organised by the Madison Square Park Conservancy. The undoubted star of the initiative is Mad Sq Art, a year-round 'gallery without walls', featuring installations from big-name artists such as Sol LeWitt and William Wegman.

Museum of Sex

233 Fifth Avenue, at 27th Street (1-212 689 6337/www.mosex.org). Subway N, R, W, 6 to 28th Street. **Open** 11am-6.30pm Mon-Fri, Sun; 11am-8pm Sat. **Admission** $14.50; $13.50 reductions. **Map** p107 D3 ㉗
Located in the former Tenderloin district, which was chockablock with dance halls and brothels in the 1800s, MoSex offers a tastefully presented collection of vintage girlie magazines, Victorian-era vibrators, blue movies and Real Dolls, plus rotating exhibits on prostitution, fetishism, homosexuality, masturbation and other semi-taboo topics. The permanent collection has recently been spiced up with several new acquisitions, including a steel-framed suspension cage used by local dominatrix Domina M. Under-18s must be accompanied by an adult.

Eating & drinking

Casa Mono/Bar Jamón

Casa Mono: *52 Irving Place, at E 17th Street.* Bar Jamón: *125 E 17th Street, at Irving Place (1-212 253 2773/ www.casamononyc.com). Subway L to Third Avenue; N, Q, R, W, 4, 5, 6 to 14th Street-Union Square.* **Open** *Casa Mono* noon-midnight daily. *Bar Jamón* 5pm-2am Mon-Fri; noon-2am Sat, Sun. $-$$. **Spanish**. **Map** p107 E4 ㉘
Offal-loving consulting chef Mario Batali and protégé Andy Nusser go where many standard Manhattan tapas restaurants fear to tread: cock's combs with cèpes, pig's feet with caper aïoli and sweetbreads dusted with almond flour and fried. Non-organ eaters should try the juicy skirt steak atop onion marmalade or soft crab with black truffle aïoli. The attached Bar Jamón serves a more casual (and cheaper) menu of treasured Ibérico hams, bocaditos and Spanish cheeses.

City Bakery

3 W 18th Street, between Fifth & Sixth Avenues (1-212 366 1414/www.the citybakery.com). Subway L, N, Q, R, W, 4, 5, 6 to 14th Street-Union Square. **Open** 7.30am 7pm Mon-Fri; 7.30am-6pm Sat; 9am-5.30pm Sun. **$**. **Café**. **Map** p107 D4 ㉙

Pastry genius Maury Rubin's loft-size City Bakery is jammed with shoppers loading up on unusual salad bar choices (grilled pineapple with ancho chilli or beansprouts with smoked tofu). There's also a small selection of soups, pizzas and hot dishes. But never mind all that: the moist 'melted' chocolate-chip cookies are divinely decadent.

Flatiron Lounge

37 W 19th Street, between Fifth & Sixth Avenues (1-212 727 7741/ www.flatironlounge.com). Subway F, N, R, V, W to 23rd Street. **Open** 5pm-2am Mon-Wed, Sun; 5pm-4am Thur-Sat. **Bar**. **Map** p107 D4 ㉚

Red leather booths, mahogany tables and globe-shaped lamps amp up the vintage vibe at this art deco space. Co-owner Julie Reiner's notable mixology skills have made the bar a destination, and her Beijing Punch (jasmine-infused vodka and white peach purée) is not to be missed. The 30ft bar, built in 1927, stays packed well into the wee hours.

Hill Country

30 W 26th Street, between Broadway & Sixth Avenue (1-212 255 4544/www. hillcountryny.com). Subway N, R, W to 28th Street. **Open** noon-10pm Mon-Wed; noon-11pm Thur-Sat; noon-10pm Sun. **$$**. **Barbecue**. **Map** p106 C3 ㉛

The guys behind Hill Country are about as Texan as Mayor Bloomberg in a Stetson, but the cooking is an authentic, world-class take on the restaurant's namesake region, and includes sausage imported from Lockhart, Texas. Beef shoulder emerges from the smoker in 20-lb slabs, and show-stealing tips-on pork ribs are hefty, with just enough fat to imbue proper flavour. Desserts,

such as jelly-filled cupcakes with peanut butter frosting, live out some kind of 1950s middle America fantasy; the two-dozen tequilas and bourbons help to address the balance.

Raines Law Room

NEW *48 W 17th Street, between Fifth & Sixth Avenues (no phone). Subway F, V to 14th Street; L to Sixth Avenue.* **Open** 5pm-2am Mon-Thur; 5pm-3am Fri, Sat; 7pm-1am Sun. **Cocktail bar**. **Map** p107 D4 ㉜

See box p82.

Shake Shack

Madison Square Park, 23rd Street, at Madison Avenue (1-212 889 6600/ www.shakeshacknyc.com). Subway N, R, W, 6 to 23rd Street. **Open** 11am-11pm daily. **$**. **Café**. **Map** p107 D4 ㉝

Restaurateur Danny Meyer takes American fast food to new heights at Shake Shack. The zinc-clad, modernist concession stand dispenses superb burgers, hot dogs and rich, creamy shakes to Madison Square Park visitors, and there's beer and wine to boot. Expect long lines.

230 Fifth

230 Fifth Avenue, between 26th & 27th Streets (1-212 725 4300/www. 230-fifth.com). Subway N, R, W to 28th Street. **Open** 4pm-4am daily. **Cocktail bar**. **Map** p107 D3 ㉞

The 14,000-sq-ft roof garden dazzles with truly spectacular views, including a close-up of the Empire State Building, but the glitzy indoor lounge – with its ceiling-height windows, wraparound sofas and bold lighting – shouldn't be overlooked. While the sprawling outdoor space gets mobbed on sultry nights, it's less crowded in the cooler months when heaters, fleece robes and hot ciders make it a winter hotspot.

Union Square Café

21 E 16th Street, between Fifth Avenue & Union Square West (1-212 243 4020/ www.unionsquarecafe.com). Subway

L, N, Q, R, W, 4, 5, 6 to 14th Street-Union Square. **Open** noon-10pm Mon-Thur, Sun; noon-11pm Fri, Sat. **$$$**.
American. Map p107 D5 ㉟

The Union Square Café's art collection and floor-to-ceiling murals have been here as long as the tuna filet mignon has been on the menu. That 1980s throwback, served with a heap of wasabi mash, remains hugely popular despite being relegated to a weekly special along with the other signature standbys. Novelty is not what keeps this New York classic packed. Danny Meyer's first New York restaurant – a pioneer in Greenmarket cooking – remains one of the city's most relaxed fine dining establishments. New chef Carmen Quagliata has wisely kept the USC standards on the menu while making his mark with lusty Italian additions, such as house-made pastas.

Shopping

ABC Carpet & Home
888 Broadway, at 19th Street (1-212 473 3000/www.abchome.com). Subway L, N, Q, R, W, 4, 5, 6 to 14th Street-Union Square. **Open** 10am-7pm Mon-Sat; 11am-6.30pm Sun.
Map p107 D4 ㊱

Most of ABC's 35,000-strong carpet range is housed in the store across the street at No.881 – except the rarest rugs, which reside on the sixth floor of the main store. Browse everything from organic soap to hand-beaded lampshades on the bazaar-style ground floor. On the upper floors, furniture spans every style, from slick European minimalism to antique oriental and mid-century modern. The huge Bronx warehouse outlet offers discounted furnishings, but don't expect incredible bargains as prices are still steep.

JJ Hat Center
310 Fifth Avenue, between 31st & 32nd Streets (1-212 239 4368/ www.jjhatcenter.com). Subway B, D, F, N, Q, R, V, W to 34th Street.

Open 9am-6pm Mon-Fri; 9.30am-5.30pm Sat. **Map** p106 C3 ㊲
See box p113.

Pippin
112 W 17th Street, between Sixth & Seventh Avenues (1-212 505 5159). Subway F, V, 1, 2, 3 to 14th Street; L to Sixth Avenue. **Open** 11am-7pm Mon-Sat; noon-6pm Sun. **Map** p106 C4 ㊳

Stephen and Rachel Cooper's brace of vintage shops, which take their name from their Cavalier King Charles spaniel, reflect their individual interests: Stephen, a trained gemologist, is behind the vintage jewellery, while his wife looks after the furniture and home goods. The former – everything from antique eternity rings to 1940s costume pieces designed by Coco Chanel herself – is displayed in a devoted shop, along with some choice vintage handbags. The latter is in a quaint 19th-century blacksmith's cottage secreted down an alleyway alongside the store. You can pick up baubles for as little as $5.

Showplace Antique Center
40 West 25th Street, between Fifth & Sixth Avenues (1-212 633 6063/ www.nyshowplace.com). Subway F, V to 23rd Street. **Open** 10am-6pm Mon-Sat; 8.30am-5.30pm Sun. **Map** p106 C3 ㊴

Set over four expansive floors, this indoor market houses more than 200 high-quality dealers selling everything from vintage designerwear to Greek and Roman antiquities. Among the highlights are Joe Sundlie Vintedge's colourful, spot-on-trend vintage pieces from the likes of Lanvin and Alaïa on the ground floor, and, upstairs, Mood Indigo – arguably the best source in the city for collectable bar accessories and dinnerware. The array of Bakelite jewellery and table accessories, Fiestaware, and novelty cocktail glasses and shakers is dazzling, and it's also a wonderful repository of vintage New York memorabilia, including souvenirs from the 1939 World's Fair.

NEW YORK BY AREA

Union Square Greenmarket

From 16th to 17th Streets, between Union Square East & Union Square West (1-212 788 7476/www.cenyc. org/greenmarket). Subway L, N, Q, R, W, 4, 5, 6 to 14th Street-Union Square. **Open** 8am-6pm Mon, Wed, Fri, Sat. **Map** p107 D4 **40**

There are more than 40 open-air Greenmarkets sponsored by the city authorities. At this, the largest and best known, small producers of cheese, herbs, fruits and vegetables hawk their goods directly to the public.

Nightlife

Metropolitan Room

34 W 22nd Street, between Fifth & Sixth Avenues (1-212 206 0440/ www.metropolitanroom.com). Subway F, R, V, W to 23rd Street. **Map** p107 D4 **41**

The Met Room has established itself as the pre-eminent venue for high-level nightclub singing that won't bust your wallet. Performers range from rising musical-theatre stars to established cabaret acts – including Baby Jane Dexter – plus legends such as Tammy Grimes, Julie Wilson and Annie Ross.

Splash

50 W 17th Street, between Fifth & Sixth Avenues (1-212 691 0073/ www.splashbar.com). Subway F, V to 14th Street; L to Sixth Avenue. **Open** 4pm-4am daily. No credit cards. **Map** p106 C4 **42**

This NYC queer institution offers 10,000sq ft of dance and lounge space, plus the famous onstage showers, where hunky go-go boys get wet and wild. The super-muscular bartenders here seem bigger than ever, and nationally known DJs still rock the house, local drag celebs give good face, and in-house VJs flash hypnotic snippets of classic musicals spliced with video visuals.

Gramercy Park & Murray Hill

A key to Gramercy Park, the tranquil, gated square at the southern end of Lexington Avenue (between 20th & 21st Streets), is the preserve of residents of the surrounding homes (and members of a couple of venerable private clubs). Murray Hill spans 30th to 40th Streets, between Third and Fifth Avenues. Townhouses of the rich and powerful were once clustered around Madison and Park Avenues, but these days, only a few streets retain their former elegance and the area is mainly populated by upwardly mobiles fresh out of university.

Sights & museums

Morgan Library & Museum

225 Madison Avenue, at 36th Street (1-212 685 0008/www.themorgan.org). Subway 6 to 33rd Street. **Open** 10.30am-5pm Tue-Thur; 10.30am-9pm Fri; 10am-6pm Sat; 11am-6pm Sun. **Admission** $12; free-$8 reductions. **Map** p107 D2/p109 D5 **43**

This Madison Avenue institution began as the private library of financier J Pierpont Morgan, and is his artistic gift to the city. Building on the collection Morgan amassed in his lifetime, the museum houses first-rate works on paper, including drawings by Michelangelo, Rembrandt and Picasso; three Gutenberg Bibles; a copy of *Frankenstein* annotated by Mary Shelley; manuscripts by Dickens, Poe, Twain, Steinbeck and Wilde; and sheet music handwritten by Beethoven and Mozart. In 2006 a massive renovation and expansion orchestrated by Renzo Piano brought more natural light into the building and doubled the available exhibition space, which hosts a varied roster of temporary shows.

Union Square Greenmarket

Eating & drinking

Artisanal

*2 Park Avenue, at 32nd Street (1-212
725 8585/www.artisanalbistro.com).
Subway 6 to 33rd Street.* **Open**
11.45pm-midnight Mon-Fri (last
seating 11pm); 10.30am-midnight
Sat (last seating 11pm); 10.30am-11pm
Sun (last seating 10pm). **$$. French.**
Map p107 D3 ❸
Terrance Brennan's high-ceilinged
deco gem makes its mark with an all-
out homage to fromage. Start with
fondue, which comes in three varie-
ties. Familiar bistro fare awaits with
such dishes as steak frites and a delec-
table glazed Scottish salmon, but the
curd gets the last word with the
cheese and wine pairings. These
flights of three cheeses, chosen by
region, style or theme (for example,
each one produced in a monastery),
are matched with three wines (or beers
or even sakés) for a sumptuous and
intriguing finale.

Les Halles

*411 Park Avenue South, between
28th & 29th Streets (1-212 679 4111/
www.leshalles.net). Subway 6 to 28th
Street.* **Open** 7.30am-midnight daily.
$$. French. Map p107 D3 ❹
Though Anthony Bourdain is just the
'chef-at-large' at Les Halles these days,
his meat-oriented philosophy still per-
meates the place, from the butcher
shop inside the restaurant to the steak
knives that appear at every place setting. With classic French fare including steak tartare and crêpes suzette
prepared tableside for a largely out-of-
towner crowd, this is almost a theme-
park restaurant. Steaks, sausages and
chops done in over a dozen different
ways are solid, but the kitchen's efforts
lack a certain joie de vivre.

Nightlife

Fillmore New York at Irving Plaza

*17 Irving Place, at 15th Street (1-212
777 6800/www.irvingplaza.com).
Subway L, N, Q, R, W, 4, 5, 6 to 14th
Street-Union Square.* **Map** p107 D5 ❹
With the rise of clubs such as Webster
Hall, the pleasantly worn Irving Plaza
lost its monopoly on concerts by mid-
size touring bands. What to do?

Rebrand! The renovations that came with the name were largely cosmetic, and nobody actually calls the club 'Fillmore New York'. Still, it's a great place to see big stars keeping a low profile (Gnarls Barkley, Wu-Tang Clan) and medium heavies on their way up.

Gramercy Theatre

127 E 23rd Street, between Park & Lexington Avenues (1-212 777 6800). Subway R, W, 6 to 23rd Street. **Map** p107 D4 **47**

The Gramercy looks exactly like what it is, a run-down former movie theatre, yet it has a decent sound system and good sight lines. Concertgoers can lounge in raised seats on the top level or get closer to the stage. Bookings have included indie stalwarts (the mighty Mekons, Múm), established stars (Dr John) and the occasional hip-hop show (Fabolous, Q-Tip).

Rodeo Bar & Grill

375 Third Avenue, at 27th Street (1-212 683 6500/www.rodeobar.com). Subway 6 to 28th Street. **Map** p107 E3 **48**

The unpretentious crowd, roadhouse vibe and absence of a cover charge help make the Rodeo Bar & Grill the city's best roots club, with a steady stream of rockabilly, country and related sounds.

Herald Square & Garment District

Seventh Avenue, aka Fashion Avenue, is the main drag of the Garment District (roughly from 34th to 40th Streets, between Broadway & Eighth Avenue), where designers – along with their seamstresses, fitters and assistants – feed America's multibillion-dollar clothing industry. The world's largest store, Macy's, looms over Herald Square (at the junction of Broadway and Sixth Avenue), named after what is now a long-gone

newspaper. To the east, the restaurants, spas and karaoke bars of Koreatown line 32nd Street, between Fifth and Sixth Avenues.

Eating & drinking

Mandoo Bar

2 W 32nd Street, between Fifth Avenue & Broadway (1-212 279 3075). Subway B, D, F, V, N, Q, R, W to 34th Street-Herald Square. **Open** 11.30am-10.30pm daily. **$. Korean**. **Map** p107 D3 **49**

If the two women painstakingly filling and crimping dough squares in the front window don't give it away, we will. This wood-wrapped industrial-style spot elevates *mandoo*, Korean dumplings, above mere appetiser status. Six varieties of the tasty morsels are offered here, filled with such delights as subtly piquant kimchi, juicy pork, succulent shrimp and vegetables. Try them miniaturised as in 'baby mandoo', swimming in a soothing beef broth or sitting atop springy, soupy ramen noodles.

New York Kom Tang Kalbi House

32 W 32nd Street, between Fifth Avenue & Broadway (1-212 947 8482). Subway B, D, F, N, Q, R, V, W to 34th Street-Herald Square. **Open** 24hrs Mon-Sat. **$$. Korean**. **Map** p107 D3 **50**

Tender *kalbi* (barbecued short ribs) are indeed the stars here; their signature smoky flavour comes from being cooked over *soot bul* (wood chips). The city's oldest Korean restaurant also makes crisp, seafood-laden *haemool pajun* (pancakes); sweet, juicy *yuk hwe* (raw beef salad); and garlicky *bulgogi*. *Kom tang*, or 'bear soup', is a milky beef broth that's deep and soothing.

Shopping

B&H

420 Ninth Avenue, at 34th Street (1-212 444 6615/www.bhphotovideo.com). Subway A, C, E to 34th Street-Penn

Station. **Open** 9am-7pm Mon-Thur; 9am-1pm Fri; 10am-6pm Sun. **Map** p106 B2 ❺❶

In this huge, busy store, goods are transported from the stock room via an overhead conveyor belt. Whether you're a professional or a keen amateur, B&H is the ultimate one-stop shop for all your photographic, video and audio needs. Note that due to the largely orthodox Jewish staff, it's closed on Saturdays.

Macy's

151 W 34th Street, between Broadway & Seventh Avenue (1-212 695 4400/ www.macys.com). Subway B, D, F, N, Q, R, V, W to 34th Street-Herald Square; 1, 2, 3 to 34th Street-Penn Station. **Open** 10am-9.30pm Mon-Sat; 11am-8.30pm Sun. **Map** p106 C2/p108 C5 ❺❷

It may not be as glamorous as New York's other famous retailers, but for sheer breadth of stock, the 34th Street behemoth is hard to beat. You won't find exalted labels here, though; mid-priced fashion and designers' diffusion lines for all ages are its bread and butter, along with all the big beauty names. Among the largely mainstream refreshment options is a Ben & Jerry's outpost. There's also a branch of the Metropolitan Museum of Art gift store.

Arts & leisure

Juvenex

5th Floor, 25 W 32nd Street, between Fifth Avenue & Broadway, Garment District (1-646 733 1330/www.juvenex spa.com). Subway B, D, F, N, Q, R, V, W to 34th Street. **Open** 24hrs daily. **Map** p107 D3 ❺❸

This bustling K-town relaxation hub may be slightly rough around the edges (frayed towels, dingy sandals), but we embrace it for its bathhouse-meets-Epcot feel (igloo saunas, tiled 'soaking ponds' and a slatted bridge), and 24hr availability (women only before 5pm). A basic Purification Program – including soak and sauna, face, body and hair cleansing and a salt scrub – is great value at $115.

5 High Line highlights

The transformation of a disused elevated freight-train track on Manhattan's far west side into a park took longer than expected, but as we went to press the first section of the High Line (www. thehighline.org) – from the Meatpacking District to 20th Street – was opening. (The second section, stretching to 30th Street, opens in 2010.)

1 The Gansevoort Woodland Trees have been planted near the Gansevoort Street access point, inspired by wild growth before development. The new outpost of the Whitney (p147) will be built below this section.

2 The Standard Straddling the promenade at 13th Street, this hip hotel (p175) boasts a restaurant and beer garden.

3 The Sundeck With an lovely river view, this area between 14th and 15th Streets features wooden deck chairs that can be rolled along the original tracks, a water feature, and benches.

4 Public art The old Nabisco factory that houses Chelsea Market received deliveries via the line; now this section is devoted to long-term site-specific art, with the first installation by Spencer Finch.

5 Tenth Avenue Square At 17th Street, steps descend into a sunken amphitheatre with a glass 'window' in the structure overlooking the avenue.

NEW YORK BY AREA

Madison Square Garden

Seventh Avenue, between 31st & 33rd Streets, Garment District (1-212 465 6741/www.thegarden.com). Subway A, C, E, 1, 2, 3 to 34th Street-Penn Station. **Map** p106 C3 ⑤④

Some of music's biggest acts – the White Stripes, Justin Timberlake, Madonna, for instance – come out to play at the world's most famous basketball arena (home of the New York Knicks and the ladies of the New York Liberty). Whether you'll actually be able to get a look at them depends on your seat number or the quality of your binoculars. There's also a smaller theatre within the complex.

The Theater District & Hell's Kitchen

Times Square is the gateway to the Theater District, the zone roughly between 41st Street and 53rd Street, from Sixth Avenue to Ninth Avenue. Thirty-eight of the opulent show houses here – those with more than 500 seats – are designated as being part of Broadway (plus the Vivian Beaumont Theater, uptown at Lincoln Center; p155). Just west of Times Square is Hell's Kitchen, which maintained a tough crime-ridden veneer well into the 1970s, when, in an effort to invite gentrification, local activists renamed it Clinton after one-time mayor DeWitt Clinton (the new name never really took). Today, it's emerging as the city's new queer mecca. Restaurant Row (46th Street, between Eighth & Ninth Avenues) caters to theatregoers, but Ninth Avenue itself, with its cornucopia of ethnic eateries, is a better bet.

Sights & museums

Circle Line Cruises

Pier 83, Twelfth Avenue, at 42nd Street (1-212 563 3200/www.circleline.com). Subway A, C, E

Koreatown p120

to 42nd Street-Port Authority.
Tickets $29.50; $17-$25 reductions.
Map p106 A1/p108 A4 ⑤
Circle Line's famed three-hour guided circumnavigation of Manhattan Island ($31) is a fantastic way to get your bearings and see many of the city's sights as you pass under its iconic bridges. Board at Pier 83 on the Hudson River. If you don't have time for the full round-trip, opt for a two-hour Semi-Circle tour ($27) that takes you around Downtown to the Brooklyn Bridge and back.

Intrepid Sea-Air-Space Museum

USS Intrepid, Pier 86, Twelfth Avenue & 46th Street (1-877 957 7447/ www.intrepidmuseum.org). Subway A, C, E to 42nd Street-Port Authority, then M42 bus to Twelfth Avenue or 15min walk. **Open** *Apr-Sept* 10am-5pm Mon-Fri; 10am-6pm Sat, Sun. *Oct-Mar* 10am-5pm Tue-Sun. **Admission** $19.50; free-$15.50 reductions.
Map p106 A1/p108 A4 ⑤
Commissioned in 1943, this 27,000-ton, 898ft aircraft carrier survived torpedoes and kamikaze attacks during World War II, served during Vietnam and the Cuban Missile Crisis, and recovered two space capsules for NASA. The 'Fighting I' was finally decommissioned in 1974, but real-estate mogul Zachary Fisher saved it from the scrapyard by resurrecting it as an educational institution. On its flight deck and portside aircraft elevator are stationed top-notch examples of American military might, including a Navy F-14 Tomcat, an A-12 Blackbird spy plane and a fully restored Army AH-1G Cobra gunship helicopter. (Foreign powers are represented by a British F-1 Scimitar, a French Entendard IV-M and a Polish MiG-21.) It recently returned to its Pier 86 home after a two-year, $8 million renovation that allowed the anchor chain room, general berthing quarters and machine shop to be opened to the public.

Ripley's Believe It or Not! Odditorium

234 W 42nd Street, between Seventh & Eighth Avenues (1-212 398 3133/ www.ripleysnewyork.com). Subway A, C, E to 42nd Street-Port Authority; N, Q, R, S, W, 1, 2, 3, 7 to 42nd Street-Times Square. **Open** 9am-1am daily (last entry midnight; call for reduced winter hours). **Admission** $26.95; free-$21.95 reductions. **Map** p106 C1/p108 C2 ⑤⑦
Times Square might be a little white-washed these days, but you can get a feel for the old freak show at this repository of the eerie and uncanny. Items on display include a two-headed goat, a 3,000lb meteorite, medieval torture devices and the largest collection of shrunken heads in the developed world.

Times Square

From 42nd to 47th Streets, between Broadway & Seventh Avenue. Subway N, Q, R, S, W, 1, 2, 3, 7 to 42nd Street-Times Square. **Map** p106 C1/p108 C4 ⑤⑧
Originally called Longacre Square, Times Square was renamed after the *New York Times* moved here in the early 1900s. The first electrified billboard graced the district in 1904, on the side of a bank at 46th and Broadway. The same year, the inaugural New Year's Eve party in Times Square doubled as the *Times'* housewarming party in its new HQ. More than 300,000 still gather here to watch a glittery mirrorball descend every 31 December. The paper left the building only a decade after it arrived (it now occupies a new $84 million tower on Eighth Avenue, between 40th and 41st Streets). However, it retained ownership of its old headquarters until the 1960s, and erected the world's first scrolling electric news 'zipper' in 1928. The readout, now sponsored by Dow Jones, has trumpeted breaking stories from the stock-market crash of 1929 to the 2001 World Trade Center attacks. Once the cradle of New York's sex industry, today's sanitised Times Square has a brashly commercial air, but it's impossible not to be dazzled by the spectacle.

NEW YORK BY AREA

TKTS

*Father Duffy Square, Broadway & 47th
Street (www.tdf.org). Subway N, Q, R,
S, W, 1, 2, 3, 7 to 42nd Street-Times
Square.* **Open** *Evening tickets* 3-8pm
Mon, Wed-Sat; 2 8pm Tue; 3-7pm Sun.
Same-day matinee tickets 10am-2pm
Wed, Sat; 11am-3pm Sun. **Map** p106
C1/p108 C4 ⑤

The Theatre Development Fund's discount-ticket arm recently returned to its
home in Father Duffy Square with
an architecturally striking new base.
Although there is often a line when the
booth opens for business, this has usually dispersed one to two hours later, so
it's worth trying your luck an hour or
two before the show. TKTS has two
other branches, in South Street Seaport
and Downtown Brooklyn, which are
much less busy and open earlier, so you
can secure your tickets in the morning
(the branches also sell matinee tickets the
day before a show). See also box p127.

Eating & drinking

Breeze

*661 Ninth Avenue, between 45th
& 46th Streets (1-212 262 7777/
www.breezenyc.com). Subway A, C,
E to 42nd Street-Port Authority.*
Open 11.30am-11.30pm Mon-Thur,
Sun; noon-midnight Fri, Sat. **$.**
Thai. **Map** p106 B1/p108 B4 ⑥

With a progressive look – tangerine
walls, triangular mirrors, menus printed
on DVDs – and a refined menu, Breeze
sails past many other Hell's Kitchen con-
tenders, combining French techniques
and Thai cuisine to spellbinding effect.
Addictive fried dumplings filled with
wild mushrooms and caramelised
onions are topped with a delectable soy-
black truffle foam. Nearly as tasty is the
smoky grilled salmon, which comes
glazed in a zesty fire-roasted chilli-
orange sauce.

Daisy May's BBQ USA

*623 Eleventh Avenue, at 46th Street
(1-212 977 1500/www.daisymaysbbq.*

*com). Subway A, C, E to 42nd Street-
Port Authority.* **Open** 11am-9pm Mon;
11am-10pm Tue-Fri; noon-10pm Sat;
noon-9pm Sun. **$. Barbecue**. **Map**
p106 A1/p108 A4 ⑥

Southerners know that the best barbecue comes from run-down shacks in the
worst parts of town – so don't let the
location of Daisy May's BBQ USA, on
a desolate stretch of Eleventh Avenue,
deter you: despite a few missteps (the
pulled pork we sampled was over-
stewed), this is the real down-home
deal, a masterful barbecue survey. The
Kansas City sweet and sticky pork ribs
are meaty and just tender enough,
while the creamed corn tastes like ball-
park nachos – and that's a good thing.

5 Napkin Burger

NEW *630 Ninth Avenue, at 45th Street
(1-212 757 2277/www.5napkinburger.
com). Subway A, C, E to 42nd Street-Port
Authority.* **Open** noon-midnight daily. **$.**
American. **Map** p106 B1/p108 B4 ㉜

The best reason to visit this upscale
diner is spelled out right there on the
awning. The namesake burger, a delicious Franco-American handful, features sweet caramelised onions, comté
cheese and herb-infused aïoli. Served
with golden fries, it anchors the
sprawling menu – an odd, rarely successful mash-up of big salads, over-
stuffed sushi rolls, pasta and
barbecued ribs. Stick to the burger and
all-American desserts like the rich
caramel-brownie sundae.

Omido

NEW *1695 Broadway, between 53rd
& 54th Streets (1-212 247 8110/
www.hungryperson-sysco.com/omido).
Subway B, D, E to Seventh Avenue.*
Open 11.30am-11.45pm Mon-Fri; 5-
11.45pm Sat, Sun. **$$. Japanese**. **Map** p108 C3 ㉝

As the Theater District isn't generally
known for top-notch dining, you may be
surprised to find one of the best sushi
dens in the city here. The centrepiece
of the dark-wood-appointed, AvroKO-

designed space is the glistening case of jewel-like dishes. Foie gras atop a salmon, tuna and yellowtail roll elevates the already rich fish to buttery supremacy, and a sashimi platter groans with an alluring landscape of seafood. Don't leave without sampling the Hoji blancmange – a roasted green tea custard.

Russian Samovar

256 W 52nd Street, between Broadway & Eighth Avenue (1-212 757 0168/ www.russiansamovar.com). Subway C, E, 1 to 50th Street. **Open** 5pm-4am daily. **$$**. **Russian**. Map p108 C3 ➍
At this Ruski haven, house-infused vodkas are the poison of choice. Impress friends by sampling the eye-opening pepper, or choose three of more than 20 seasonal varieties, which can include raspberry, apple-cinnamon, ginger or tarragon. If you don't want to drink on an empty stomach, try a satisfying bowl of borscht or the toothsome beef Stroganoff.

Shopping

Amy's Bread

672 Ninth Avenue, between 46th & 47th Streets (1-212 977 2670/ www.amysbread.com). Subway C, E to 50th Street; N, R, W to 49th Street. **Open** 7.30am-11pm Mon-Fri; 8am-11pm Sat; 9am-6pm Sun. Map p106 B1/p108 B4 ➎
Whether you want sweet (chocolate-chubbie cookies) or savoury (hefty French sourdough boules), Amy's never disappoints. Coffee and sandwiches are served on the premises (the grilled cheese sandwich, made with chipotle peppers, is one of the best in the city).

Hell's Kitchen Flea Market

39th Street, between Ninth & Tenth Avenues (1-212 243 5343/www. annexmarkets.com). Subway A, C, E to 34th Street-Penn Station. **Open** 9am-6pm Sat, Sun. No credit cards. Map p106 B2/p108 B5 ➏

Many of the vendors from the defunct Annex site in Chelsea packed up and moved to this stretch of road in Hell's Kitchen, where you'll find a mix of vintage clothing and textiles, furniture and other bric-a-brac miscellany.

Nightlife

Ars Nova

511 W 54th Street, between Tenth & Eleventh Avenues (1-212 489 9800/ tickets 1-212 352 3101/www.arsnova nyc.com). Subway C, E to 50th Street. Map p108 B3 ➐
Thoughtful, professional comedy productions are nurtured in the impeccably curated programme at Ars Nova. The space isn't bad, either: rather than dusty bar glasses and dripping basement fixtures, crowds are treated to comfortable cabaret seating. The midweek Tragedy Tomorrow series is a good bet.

BB King Blues Club & Grill

237 W 42nd Street, between Seventh & Eighth Avenues (1-212 997 4144/ www.bbkingblues.com). Subway A, C, E to 42nd Street-Port Authority; N, Q, R, S, W, 1, 2, 3, 7 to 42nd Street-Times Square. Map p106 C1/p108 C4 ➑
BB's Times Square joint stages one of the most varied music schedules in town. Cover bands and tributes fill the gaps between big-name bookings such as Ralph Stanley and Little Richard, but the venue has also hosted extreme metal (Napalm Death, Obituary) and neo-soul (Angie Stone). For many shows, the best seats are at the dinner tables at the front, but the menu prices are steep. On Sunday, the Harlem Gospel Choir's buffet brunch raises the roof.

Birdland

315 W 44th Street, between Eighth & Ninth Avenues (1-212 581 3080/ www.birdlandjazz.com). Subway A, C, E to 42nd Street-Port Authority. **Open** 5pm-1am daily. Map p106 B1/p108 C4 ➒

Its name is synonymous with jazz (Kurt Elling, Jim Hall), but Birdland is also a prime cabaret destination (Christine Andreas, Christine Ebersole), and the bookings in both fields are excellent. The Chico O'Farrill Afro-Cuban Jazz Orchestra owns Sundays, and David Ostwald's Louis Armstrong Centennial Band hits on Wednesdays; Mondays see cabaret's waggish Jim Caruso's Cast Party.

Carolines on Broadway

1626 Broadway, between 49th & 50th Streets (1-212 757 4100/ www.carolines.com). Subway N, R to 49th Street; 1 to 50th Street. **Map** p108 C3 ⑩
This comedy institution's long-term relationships with national headliners, sitcom stars and cable-special pros ensure that its stage always features marquee names. You'll never see anything less than professional.

Don't Tell Mama

343 W 46th Street, between Eighth & Ninth Avenues (1-212 757 0788/ www.donttellmamanyc.com). Subway A, C, E to 42nd Street-Port Authority. **Open** 4pm-4am daily. **Map** p106 B1/p108 C4 ⑪
Showbiz pros and piano bar buffs adore this dank but homely Theater District stalwart, where acts range from the strictly amateur to potential stars of tomorrow. The nightly line-up may include pop, jazz and musical theater singers, as well as female impersonators, comedians and musical revues.

Pacha

618 W 46th Street, between Eleventh & Twelfth Avenues (1-212 209 7500/ www.pachanyc.com). Subway C, E to 50th Street. **Open** 10pm-4am Fri, Sat. **Map** p106 A1/p108 A4 ⑫
The worldwide glam-club chain Pacha, with outposts in nightlife capitals such as Ibiza, London and Buenos Aires, hit the US market in 2005 with this

swanky joint helmed by superstar spinner Erick Morillo. The spot attracts heavyweights ranging from local hero Danny Tenaglia to big-time visiting jocks such as Jeff Mills and Josh Wink, but like most big clubs, it pays to check the line-up in advance if you're into underground beats.

Ritz

369 W 46th Street, between Eighth & Ninth Avenues (1-212 333 4177). Subway A, C, E to 42nd Street-Port Authority. **Open** 5pm-4am daily. **Map** p106 B1/p108 B4 ⑬
Although it's in the heart of the Theater District, this small, homey gay bar has a neighbourhood vibe. It's perfect for a pre- or post-Broadway cocktail, and late nights bring special performances and theme parties.

Therapy

348 W 52nd Street, between Eighth & Ninth Avenues (1-212 397 1700/ www.therapy-nyc.com). Subway C, E to 50th Street. **Open** 5pm-2am Mon-Thur, Sun; 5pm-4am Fri, Sat. **Map** p108 C3 ⑭
Therapy is just what the analyst ordered. The minimalist, dramatic two-level gay hotspot offers up comedy and musical performances, some clever cocktails (including the Freudian Sip) and a crowd of gorgeous guys. You'll find good food and a cosy fireplace to boot.

Arts & leisure

Billy Elliot

Imperial Theatre, 249 W 45th Street, between Broadway & Eighth Avenue (Telecharge 1-212 239 6200/ www.telecharge.com). **Map** p108 C4 ⑮
A London import, based on the beloved 2000 movie about an English mining-town boy who dreams of being a ballet dancer. With heart, grit and spectacular dancing, *Billy Elliot* is one of the most passionate and exhilarating shows to land on Broadway in years.

Not just the ticket

TKTS

People usually come to the Theater District to see two things: a Broadway show and the dazzling electronic spectacle of Times Square. The new **TKTS discount-ticket booth** (p124), which has returned to Father Duffy Square after two and a half years at a temporary spot outside a nearby hotel, facilitates both. The word 'booth' doesn't do the structure justice: its 12 ticket windows are encased in a dramatic glass structure that was almost a decade in the making. The brainchild of Australians John Choi and Tai Ropiha, who won the globe-spanning competition for a new design in 1999, it was finally unveiled in October 2008.

An expansive red staircase, illuminated from below with LED technology to create a glowing effect, rises to the roof. Not only is the 'stairway to nowhere', as wags in the press have dubbed it, a fittingly razzle-dazzle feature, it helps to solve the practical problem of slow-moving gawkers clogging up the streets. Part of a $19 million project in partnership with the Times Square Alliance to rebuild the square (doubling its size), the stairs are classified as city parkland and offer a place to relax and nosh on your own snacks; there are tables and chairs at street level as well as the 27 handy stoops. The 16-foot summit commands an uninterrupted view of the illuminated Great White Way.

Uptown, **Lincoln Center** (p155) is acquiring a striking visitor space-cum-cut-price-ticket-facility of its own. Designed by Tod Williams Billie Tsien Architects, the former Harmony Atrium (between W 62nd & W 63rd Streets, Broadway and Columbus Avenue) re-opens in November 2009 as an interior garden with lush, planted walls and a fountain, where visitors can relax and enjoy free concerts. As well as complimentary internet access and a café, it features a centralised box office where, for the first time, audiences can purchase same-day tickets to Lincoln Center performances, discounted by up to 50 per cent.

Ars Nova p125

Stephen Daldry's superb direction pulls together dance, working-class drama and domestic tear-jerking into an electrifying, transporting whole.

Carnegie Hall

154 W 57th Street, at Seventh Avenue (1-212 247 7800/www.carnegiehall.org). Subway N, Q, R, W to 57th Street. **Map** p108 C3 **76**

Artistic director Clive Gillinson continues to put his stamp on Carnegie Hall. The stars, both soloists and orchestras, still shine most brightly in the Isaac Stern Auditorium – but it's the spunky upstart Zankel Hall that has generated the most buzz, offering an eclectic mix of classical, contemporary, jazz, pop and world music. Next door, the Weill Recital Hall hosts intimate concerts and chamber music.

Hair: The American Tribal Love-Rock Musical

NEW *Al Hirschfeld Theatre, 302 W 45th Street, between Eighth & Ninth Avenues (Telecharge 1-212 239 6200/www.tele charge.com).* **Map** p106 C1/p108 C4 **77**

The hippies have taken over the Hirschfeld; you can be sure they'll be squatting on West 45th for some time. Director Diane Paulus has taken the successful summer 2008 Central Park revival indoors. If anything, this amps up the energy, and attendance at this 1968 rock-driven show – still timely, fun and bursting with peace, love and great music – will surely lead to a contact high.

In the Heights

Richard Rodgers Theatre, 226 W 46th Street, between Broadway & Eighth Avenue (Ticketmaster 1-212 307 4100/www.ticketmaster.com). **Map** p106 C1/p108 C4 **78**

This bouncy musical has plenty of good old-fashioned Broadway heart, and that heart has a thrilling new beat: the invigorating pulse of modern Latin rhythms mixed with the percussive dynamism of hip hop. Lin-Manuel Miranda's joyous score gives classic musical theatre themes (love, self-definition, overcoming adversity) a contemporary urban twist.

Jersey Boys

August Wilson Theatre, 245 W 52nd Street, between Broadway & Eighth

*Avenue (Telecharge 1-212 239 6200/
www.telecharge.com).* **Map** p108 C3 ⓲
The Broadway musical has finally
done right by the jukebox with this
nostalgic behind-the-music tale, presenting the Four Seasons' infectiously
energetic 1960s tunes, including classics 'Walk Like a Man' and 'Big Girls
Don't Cry,' as they were meant to be
performed. A dynamic cast under the
sleek direction of Des McAnuff ensures
that Marshall Brickman and Rick
Elice's script comes across as canny
instead of canned.

New York City Center

*131 W 55th Street, between Sixth &
Seventh Avenues (1-212 581 7907/
www.nycitycenter.org). Subway B, D,
E to Seventh Avenue; F, N, Q, R, W
to 57th Street.* **Map** p108 C3 ⓴
Before Lincoln Center changed New
York's cultural geography, this was the
home of the American Ballet Theatre,
the Joffrey Ballet and the New York
City Ballet. City Center's lavish decor
is golden – as are the companies that
pass through here. The ABT graces the
stage every autumn, while the Alvin
Ailey American Dance Theater, the
Paul Taylor Dance Company and
Morphoses/The Wheeldon Company,
as well as the Fall for Dance Festival
and visitors from abroad, offer superb
performances throughout the year.

West Side Story

NEW *Palace Theatre, 1564 Broadway,
at 47th Street (Ticketmaster 1-212
307 4100/www.ticketmaster.com).*
Map p106 C1/p108 C4 ㉛
Book writer and now director Arthur
Laurents has piloted his infamous
gang members, the Jets, out of lovable-
ruffian territory and into a darker
zone, where they often exude a sense
of reckless menace. Of course, the chief
glory of this classic is the Leonard
Bernstein score, terrific sounding with
a full orchestra; overall, this subtly
recalibrated revival is Broadway in
very fine form.

Fifth Avenue & around

The stretch of Fifth Avenue
between Rockefeller Center and
Central Park South showcases
retail palaces bearing names
that were famous long before
the concept of branding was
developed. Bracketed by Saks
Fifth Avenue (49th to 50th Streets)
and Bergdorf Goodman, tenants
include Chanel, Gucci, Prada
and Tiffany & Co, plus the usual
global mall suspects. A number
of landmarks and first-rate
museums are on, or in the
vicinity of, the strip.

Sights & museums

American Folk Art Museum

*45 W 53rd Street, between Fifth &
Sixth Avenues (1-212 265 1040/
www.folkartmuseum.org). Subway E,
V to Fifth Avenue-53rd Street.* **Open**
10.30am-5.30pm Tue-Thur, Sat, Sun;
10.30am-7.30pm Fri. **Admission** $9;
free-$7 reductions. **Map** p109 D3 ㉜
MoMA's next-door neighbour celebrates outsider art and traditional
crafts such as pottery, quilting,
woodwork and jewellery design. The
museum holds the world's largest
assemblage of works and ephemera
collected by the posthumously famous
self-taught artist and author Henry
Darger. The much smaller, original
Lincoln Center location is now a satellite gallery and gift shop.

Empire State Building

*350 Fifth Avenue, between 33rd
& 34th Streets (1-212 736 3100/
www.esbnyc.com). Subway B, D, F,
N, Q, R, V, W to 34th Street-Herald
Square.* **Open** 8am-2am daily (last
elevator at 1.15am). **Admission** *86th
floor* $20; free-$18 reductions. *102nd
floor* add $15. **Map** p107 D2 ㉝
Financed by General Motors executive John J Raskob at the height of

New York's skyscraper race, the Empire State sprang up in a mere 14 months, weeks ahead of schedule and $5 million under budget. Since its opening in 1931, it's been immortalised in countless photos and films, from the original *King Kong* to *Sleepless in Seattle*. Following the destruction of the World Trade Center in 2001, the 1,250ft tower resumed its title as New York's tallest building; the nocturnal colour scheme of the tower lights often honours holidays, charities or special events. The enclosed observatory on the 102nd floor is the city's highest lookout point, but the panoramic deck on the 86th floor, 1,050-ft above the street, is roomier. From here, in clear weather, you can enjoy views of all five boroughs and five neighbouring states. The line to get in can take up to two hours on busy days; we recommend buying tickets online to save time, and visiting late at night. Alternatively, springing for an express pass ($45) allows you to cut to the front.

International Center of Photography

1133 Sixth Avenue, at 43rd Street (1-212 857 9700/www.icp.org). Subway B, D, F, V to 42nd Street-Bryant Park; N, Q, R, S, W, 1, 2, 3, 7 to 42nd Street-Times Square. **Open** 10am-6pm Tue-Thur, Sat, Sun; 10am-8pm Fri. **Admission** $12; free-$8 reductions. **Map** p109 D4 ⨾

Since 1974 the ICP has served as a preeminent library, school and museum devoted to the photographic image. Photojournalism remains a vital facet of the centre's programme, which also includes fine art photography and video. Recent shows in the two-floor gallery have focused on the work of Edward Steichen, W Eugene Smith and Susan Meiselas.
Event highlights Third ICP Triennial of Photography and Video (18 Sept 2009-27 Jan 2010).

Museum of Modern Art (MoMA)

11 W 53rd Street, between Fifth & Sixth Avenues (1-212 708 9400/ www.moma.org). Subway E, V to Fifth Avenue-53rd Street. **Open** 10.30am-5.30pm Mon, Wed, Thur, Sat, Sun; 10.30am-8pm Fri. **Admission** (incl admission to film programmes & P.S.1) $20; free-$16 reductions; free 4-8pm Fri. **Map** p109 D3 ⨾

After a two-year redesign by Japanese architect Yoshio Taniguchi, MoMA reopened in 2004 with almost double the space to display some of the most impressive artworks from the 19th, 20th and 21st centuries. The museum's permanent collection now encompasses seven curatorial departments: Architecture & Design, Drawings, Film, Media, Painting & Sculpture, Photography, and Prints & Illustrated Books. Highlights include Picasso's *Les Demoiselles d'Avignon* and Dalí's *The Persistence of Memory*, as well as masterpieces by Giacometti, Hopper, Matisse, Monet, O'Keeffe, Pollock, Warhol and many others. Outside, the Philip Johnson-designed Abby Aldrich Rockefeller Sculpture Garden, which houses works by Calder, Rodin and Moore, overlooks the Modern, a sleek high-end restaurant and bar run by superstar restaurateur Danny Meyer.
Event highlights 'In & Out of Amsterdam: Travels in Conceptual Art, 1960-1976' (until 5 Oct 2009); 'Bauhaus 1919-1933: Workshops for Modernity' (8 Nov 2009-25 Jan 2010); Tim Burton (22 Nov 2009-26 Apr 2010); Gabriel Orozco (13 Dec 2009-1 Mar 2010).

New York Public Library

455 Fifth Avenue, at 42nd Street (1-212 930 0830/www.nypl.org). Subway B, D, F, V to 42nd Street-Bryant Park; 7 to Fifth Avenue. **Open** 11am-6pm Mon, Thur-Sat; 11am-7.30pm Tue, Wed; 1-5pm Sun. **Admission** free. **Map** p107 D1/p109 D5 ⨾

While the New York Public Library consists of 89 individual branches, it's this austere Beaux Arts building in Bryant Park – home to 75 miles of shelves housing a massive humanities and social sciences archive – that most readily comes to mind. The library's free tours (11am, 2pm Mon-Sat; 2pm Sun) stop at the beautifully renovated Rose Main Reading Room and the Bill Blass Public Catalog Room. The programme of special exhibitions rivals those of the city's finest museums.

Paley Center for Media

25 W 52nd Street, between Fifth & Sixth Avenues (1-212 621 6600/ www.paleycenter.org). Subway B, D, F, V to 47th-50th Streets-Rockefeller Center; E, V to Fifth Avenue-53rd Street. **Open** noon-6pm Wed, Fri-Sun; noon-8pm Thur. **Admission** $10; $5-$8 reductions. No credit cards. **Map** p109 D3 ⑰
A nirvana for TV addicts and pop-culture junkies, the Paley Center (formerly the Museum of Television & Radio) houses an immense archive of more than 100,000 radio and TV shows. Head to the fourth-floor library to search the system for your favourite episode of *Star Trek* or *Seinfeld*, then walk down one flight to your assigned console. (The radio listening room operates in the same fashion.) The theatre on the concourse level hosts screenings and high-profile panel discussions.

Rockefeller Center

From 48th to 51st Streets, between Fifth & Sixth Avenues (tours 1-212 664 3700/7174/Top of the Rock 1-877 692 7625/www.rockefellercenter.com). Subway B, D, F, V to 47th-50th Streets-Rockefeller Center. **Open** 7am-11pm daily. *Tours* hourly 11am-5pm Mon-Sat; 11am-4pm Sun. *Observation deck* 8am-midnight daily (last entry 11pm). **Admission** *Rockefeller Center tours* $12.75; $10.75 reductions (under-6s not admitted). *NBC Studio tours* $19.25; $16.25 reductions (under-6s not admitted). *Observation deck* $20; free-$18 reductions. **Map** p109 D3/D4 ⑱

Constructed under the aegis of industrialist John D Rockefeller in the 1930s, this art deco city-within-a-city is inhabited by NBC, Simon & Schuster, McGraw-Hill and other media giants, as well as Radio City Music Hall, Christie's auction house and an underground shopping arcade. Guided tours of the entire complex are available daily, and there's a separate NBC Studio tour (call the number above or see website for details).

Public art installations are often on display outside 30 Rockefeller Plaza (past works have featured large-scale pieces by Jeff Koons and Anish Kapoor), but the most breathtaking sights are those seen from the 70th-floor Top of the Rock observation deck (combined tour/observation deck tickets are available). In the cold-weather months, the Plaza's sunken courtyard – eternally guarded by a bronze statue of Prometheus – transforms into a picturesque ice-skating rink.

St Patrick's Cathedral

Fifth Avenue, between 50th & 51st Streets (1-212 753 2261/www. saintpatrickscathedral.org). Subway B, D, F to 47th-50th Streets-Rockefeller Center; E, V to Fifth Avenue-53rd Street. **Open** 7am-8.30pm daily. **Admission** free. **Map** p109 D3 ⑲
The largest Catholic church in America, St Patrick's, built 1858-79, counts presidents, business leaders and movie stars among its past and present parishioners. The Gothic-style façade features intricate white-marble spires, but as impressive is the interior, including the Louis Tiffany-designed altar, solid bronze baldachin, and the rose window by stained-glass master Charles Connick.

Eating & drinking

Adour Alain Ducasse

St Regis New York, 2 E 55th Street, at Fifth Avenue (1-212 710 2277/ www.adour-stregis.com). Subway E, V to Fifth Avenue-53rd Street; F to 57th

St Patrick's Cathedral p131

Street. **Open** 5.30-10.30pm Mon-Thur, Sun; 5.30-11pm Fri, Sat.

$$$$. **French**. Map p109 D3 ⑩

Legendary chef-restaurateur Alain Ducasse teamed with the final toque at his defunct Essex House restaurant to open this temple of fine dining (and drinking). Here, wine is the muse (the list includes 70 under-$50 selections among its 1,800-strong list), and chef Tony Esnault's menu is equally decadent. Entrées, such as a sumptuous tenderloin and short ribs anointed with foie gras-truffle jus, are rich without being heavy. Ditto the desserts.

Bar Room at the Modern

9 W 53rd Street, between Fifth & Sixth Avenues (1-212 333 1220/www.the modernnyc.com). Subway E, V to Fifth Avenue-53rd Street. **Open** 11.30am-10.30pm Mon, Wed, Thur; 11.30am-2.15pm, 5-10.30pm Tue; 11.30am-11pm Fri, Sat. **$$**. **American creative**. Map p109 D3 ㉛

Those who can't afford to drop a paycheck at chef Gabriel Kreuther's formal MoMA dining room, the Modern, should drop into the equally stunning and less pricey Bar Room (which shares the same kitchen) at the front. From the 30 savoury dishes on the menu (which features several small and medium-size plates), standouts include Arctic char tartare. Desserts come courtesy of pastry chef Marc Aumont, and the wine list is extensive.

Carnegie Deli

854 Seventh Avenue, at 55th Street (1-212 757 2245/www.carnegiedeli.com). Subway B, D, E to Seventh Avenue; N, Q, R, W to 57th Street. **Open** 6.30am-4am daily. **$**. No credit cards.

American. Map p108 C3 ㉜

If the Carnegie Deli didn't invent schmaltz, it certainly perfected it. The sexagenarian legend is a time capsule of the bygone Borscht Belt era, when shtick could make up for cramped quarters, surly waiters and shabby tables – and tourists still eat it up. But when you're craving a deli classic, you can't do much better than the Carnegie's obscenely stuffed pastrami and corned beef sandwiches on rye.

Oak Room

The Plaza, 10 Central Park South, at Fifth Avenue (1-212 758 7777/

www.oakroomny.com). Subway N, R, W to Fifth Avenue-59th Street. **Open** noon-11pm daily. **$$$$**. **American**. **Map** p109 D2 ③④

This landmark restaurant has shaken off its tourist trap manacles with new talent in the kitchen: Eric Hara. Waiters in pin-striped vests deliver updated classics, like duck à l'orange with candied kumquats and cheesy polenta on the side. Close the meal with a delicate chocolate cigar, which recalls the Oak Room's beginnings as a smoky men's club. If the prices are too steep, soak up the atmosphere with a drink in the equally iconic Oak Bar.

Russian Tea Room

150 W 57th Street, between Sixth & Seventh Avenues (1-212 581 7100/ www.russiantearoomnyc.com). Subway F, N, Q, R, W to 57th Street. **Open** 11.30am-3pm, 4.45-11pm Mon-Fri; 11am-11pm Sat, Sun. **$$$**. **Russian**. **Map** p108 D2 ③④

The reborn socialite centre has never looked – or tasted – better. Nostalgia buffs will be happy to hear that nothing's happened to the gilded-bird friezes or the famously tacky crystal-bear aquarium but the food, thankfully, has not been frozen in time. Chef Mark Taxiera has at once modernised the menu – adding signature novelties like sliders – and brought back waylaid classics such as beef Stroganoff.

'21' Club

21 W 52nd Street, between Fifth & Sixth Avenues (1-212 582 7200/ www.21club.com). Subway B, D, F to 47th-50th Streets-Rockefeller Center; E, V to Fifth Avenue-53rd Street. **Open** noon-10pm Mon-Thur; noon-11pm Fri; 5.30-11pm Sat. **$$$$**. **American**. **Map** p109 D3 ③⑤

After more than 75 years, this clubby sanctum for the powerful remains true to its past while thriving in the present. Chef Erik Blauberg creates contemporary seasonal fare, but for '21 Classics', he ransacked the

archives: steak Diane, flambéed table-side, was on the restaurant's first menu.

Shopping

Bergdorf Goodman

754 Fifth Avenue, at 57th Street (1-212 753 7300/www.bergdorfgoodman.com). Subway E, V to Fifth Avenue-53rd Street; N, R, W to Fifth Avenue-59th Street. **Open** 10am-8pm Mon-Fri; 10am-7pm Sat; noon-6pm Sun. **Map** p109 D3 ⑨⑥

Known for its designer clothes (the fifth floor is dedicated to younger, trend-driven labels), luxury accessories and wide-ranging beauty department, this elegant store also stocks select home goods and stationery. The men's store is across the street at 745 Fifth Avenue.

FAO Schwarz

767 Fifth Avenue, at 58th Street (1-212 644 9400/www.fao.com). Subway N, R, W to Fifth Avenue-59th Street; 4, 5, 6 to 59th Street. **Open** 10am-6pm Mon-Wed; 10am-7pm Thur-Sat; 11am-5pm Sun. **Map** p109 D2 ⑨⑦

Giant stuffed animals, life-size Lego people, a full-service ice-cream parlour, a motion-simulator ride, plus a Madame Alexander Doll Factory, a Styled by Me Barbie area and a Hot Wheels Factory where kids can build their own toys – it all beckons at this three-storey toy box.

Henri Bendel

712 Fifth Avenue, at 56th Street (1-212 247 1100/www.henribendel.com). Subway E, V to Fifth Avenue-53rd Street; N, R, W to Fifth Avenue-59th Street. **Open** 10am-8pm Mon-Sat; noon-7pm Sun. **Map** p109 D3 ⑨⑧

While the merchandise (a mix of high-end and diffusion designer clothes, accessories and big-brand cosmetics) and prices are comparable to those of other upscale stores, the goods at Bendel's somehow seem more desirable in this opulent atmosphere – and those darling brown-striped shopping bags don't hurt, either. Bendel's is now the home of celebrity hairdresser Frédéric Fekkai's flagship salon.

Saks Fifth Avenue

611 Fifth Avenue, at 50th Street (1-212 753 4000/www.saksfifthavenue. com). Subway E, V to Fifth Avenue-53rd Street. **Open** 10am-8pm Mon-Sat; noon-7pm Sun. **Map** p109 D3 ❾❾

Although Saks maintains a presence in 25 states, the Fifth Avenue location is the original, established in 1924. The store features all the big names in women's fashion, from Armani to YSL (and an expansive designer shoe department), plus an excellent menswear department and a children's section. There are also fine household linens and an opulent beauty hall – although some might find the aggressive tactics of the sales staff a bit off-putting.

Nightlife

Oak Room

The Algonquin, 59 W 44th Street, between Fifth & Sixth Avenues (1-212 840 6800/reservations 1-212 419 9331/www.algonquinhotel.com). Subway B, D, F, V to 42nd Street-Bryant Park; 7 to Fifth Avenue. **Map** p109 D4 ⓵⓿⓿

This banquette-lined room is the perfect place in which to enjoy cabaret eminences such as Karen Akers, KT Sullivan and Andrea Marcovicci, plus rising stars such as the luminous Maude Maggart and the formidable jazz singer Paula West.

Radio City Music Hall

1260 Sixth Avenue, at 50th Street (1-212 247 4777/www.radiocity.com). Subway B, D, F, V to 47th-50th Streets-Rockefeller Center. **Map** p109 D3 ⓵⓿⓵

Few rooms scream 'New York City!' more than this gilded hall, which has recently drawn Goldfrapp, Mary J Blige and Alanis Morissette as headliners. The greatest challenge for any performer is not to be upstaged by the

awe-inspiring art deco surroundings. On the other hand, those same surroundings lend a sense of historic heft to even the flimsiest of shows. Backstage tours of the former cinema (the world's largest when it was built in 1932) are available.

Arts & leisure

Caudalie Vinothérapie Spa

NEW *4th Floor, 1 West 58th Street, at Fifth Avenue (1-212 265 3182/www. caudalie.com).* **Open** 10am-8pm Mon-Wed; 10am-9pm Thur, Fri; 9am-7pm Sat; 10am-6pm Sun. **Map** p109 D2 ⓵⓿❷

The first Vinothérapie outpost in the US – and the first not attached to a European vineyard – this original spa harnesses the antioxidant power of grapes and vine leaves. The 8,000sq-ft facility in the Plaza (p181) offers such treatments as a Red Vine bath ($75) – in one of its cherrywood 'barrel' tubs. In the wine lounge, artisanal tipples from the French, Spanish and Italian vineyards that host the other Caudalie spas are served, along with small plates from these regions.

Shopping, dining and entertainment options wane east of Fifth Avenue in the 40s and 50s. However, this area is home to a number of iconic landmarks. What the area lacks in street-level attractions it makes up for with a dizzying array of world-class architecture.

Sights & museums

Chrysler Building

405 Lexington Avenue, between 42nd & 43rd Streets. Subway S, 4, 5, 6, 7 to 42nd Street-Grand Central. **Map** p107 E1/p109 E4 ⓵⓿❸

Completed in 1930 by architect William Van Alen, the gleaming Chrysler Building is a pinnacle of art deco architecture, paying homage to the

Russian Tea Room p133

automobile with vast radiator-cap eagles in lieu of traditional gargoyles and a brickwork relief sculpture of racing cars complete with chrome hubcaps. During the famed three-way race for New York's tallest building, a needle-sharp stainless-steel spire was added to the blueprint to make it taller than 40 Wall Street, under construction at the same time – but the Chrysler Building was outdone by the Empire State Building.

Grand Central Terminal

From 42nd to 44th Streets, between Lexington & Vanderbilt Avenues (tours 1-212 340 2345/www.grand centralterminal.com). Subway S, 4, 5, 6, 7 to 42nd Street-Grand Central. **Map** p107 D1/p109 D4 **104**

Each day, the world's most famous terminal sees more than 400,000 visitors shuffle through its Beaux Arts threshold; only 125,000 of them are commuters. After its 1998 renovation, it metamorphosed from a mere transport hub into a destination in itself, with decent shopping and first-rate drinking and dining options such as the Campbell Apartment lounge (off the West Balcony) and the Grand Central

Oyster Bar & Restaurant (p136). In the 80,000-sq-ft main concourse, French painter Paul Helleu's astronomical ceiling mural depicts the Mediterranean sky, complete with 2,500 stars (some of which are illuminated). Various tour options are available (call or see website for details).

United Nations Headquarters

UN Plaza, First Avenue, between 42nd & 48th Streets (tours 1-212 963 8687/ www.un.org/tours). Subway S, 4, 5, 6, 7 to 42nd Street-Grand Central. **Tours** 9.45am-4.45pm Mon-Fri. **Admission** $13.50; $7.50-$9 reductions (under-5s not admitted). **Map** p107 F1/p109 **105**

Step inside this 18-acre complex and you'll no longer be in New York City – the UN is technically international territory under the jurisdiction of member countries. The Secretariat building, designed by Le Courbusier, is off-limits, but 45-minute public tours pay a visit to the Security Council Chamber and General Assembly Hall, and highlight stunning artwork donated by member nations – a Venetian mosaic of

Norman Rockwell's *The Golden Rule*, Yevgeny Vuchetich's *Let Us Beat Swords into Plowshares* (donated by the Soviet Union in 1957), a stained-glass window by Marc Chagall memorialising Secretary General Dag Hammarskjöld, and the Japanese Peace Bell, rung on the first day of spring and at the start of each session of the General Assembly. Visitors can sup from the vast international buffet in the Delegates Dining Room (fourth floor, 1-212 963 7626), which is open to the public 11.30am-2.30pm during the week (advance reservations and business attire are required).

Eating & drinking

Bookmarks Rooftop Lounge & Terrace

Library Hotel, 299 Madison Avenue, at 41st Street (1-212 204 5498/www.hospitalityholdings.com). Subway S, 4, 5, 6, 7 to 42nd Street-Grand Central; 7 to Fifth Avenue. **Open** 4pm-12.30am Mon-Fri; 5pm-1am Sat. **Bar**. **Map** p107 D1/p109 D5 106
The fireplace, sofas and club chairs at this rooftop bar suggest a decadent penthouse apartment. The enclosed greenhouse and outdoor terrace are both ideal perches for sipping posh cocktails – such as the Hemingway, made with rum, mint and champagne – and enjoying the multimillion-dollar view of Midtown's skyscrapers.

Convivio

NEW *45 Tudor City Place, at 43rd Street (1-212 599 5045/www.convivionyc.com). Subway S, 4, 5, 6, 7 to 42nd St-Grand Central.* **Open** noon-2.30pm, 5.30-10.30pm Mon-Thur; noon-2.30pm, 5-11.30pm Fri; 5-11.30pm Sat; 5-9.30pm Sun. **$$**. **Italian**. **Map** p107 E1/p109 F4 107
Chef Michael White's revision of Scott Conant's L'Impero has brought the Tudor City spot to new heights. The emphasis is squarely on Southern Italy, with antipasti such as country bread slathered with chicken liver mousse and hauntingly good pastas – saffron gnocchetti arrive with crabmeat, sea urchin, chilli flakes, scallion and garlic. Pastry chef Heather Bertinetti maintains the quality right through to the desserts.

Grand Central Oyster Bar & Restaurant

Grand Central Terminal, Lower Concourse, 42nd Street, at Park Avenue (1-212 490 6650/www.oysterbarny.com). Subway S, 4, 5, 6, 7 to 42nd Street-Grand Central. **Open** 11.30am-9.30pm Mon-Fri; noon-9.30pm Sat. **$$**. **Seafood**. **Map** p107 D1/p109 D4 108
At the legendary nonagenarian Grand Central Oyster Bar, located in the epic and gorgeous hub that shares its name, the surly countermen at the mile-long bar (the best seats in the house) are part of the charm. Avoid the more complicated fish concoctions and play it safe with a reliably awe-inspiring platter of iced, just-shucked oysters – there can be a whopping three-dozen varieties to choose from at any given time, from Baja to Plymouth Rock.

Sparks Steak House

210 E 46th Street, between Second & Third Avenues (1-212 687 4855/www.sparkssteakhouse.com). Subway S, 4, 5, 6, 7 to 42nd Street-Grand Central. **Open** noon-11pm Mon-Thur; noon-11.30pm Fri; 5-11.30pm Sat. **$$$$**. **Steakhouse**. **Map** p107 E1/p109 E4 109
Sparks used to be a mob hangout. Now the delightfully old-school, panelled dining room is just mobbed. Even with a reservation, you may wait for an hour at the cramped bar. It's worth it, however – especially when a starter of plump broiled shrimp with garlicky lemon butter reaches your table. The signature sirloin is a lean 16-oz hunk of prime with heft, chew and a salty, lightly charred exterior. You'll feel sorry for Gambino crime boss Paul Castellano, who was famously whacked as he approached the entrance one night in 1985: he died before enjoying his meal.

Central Park

Uptown

In the 19th century, the area above 57th Street was a bucolic getaway for locals living at the southern tip of the island. Today, much of this locale maintains an air of serenity, thanks largely to Central Park and the presence of a number of New York's premier cultural institutions.

Central Park

In 1857 the newly formed Central Park Commission chose landscape designer Frederick Law Olmsted and architect Calvert Vaux to turn a vast tract of rocky swampland into a rambling oasis of lush greenery. When it finally opened in the mid-1870s, it became the first man-made public park in the US. Although it suffered from neglect at various points in the 20th century (most recently in the 1970s, when it gained a reputation as a

dangerous spot after-dark), the park has been returned to its green glory thanks to the Central Park Conservancy. This not-for-profit civic group was formed in 1980, and ever since has been instrumental in the park's restoration and maintenance.

As well as a variety of landscapes, from open meadows to woodland, the park offers numerous child-friendly attractions and activities, from the famous Central Park Zoo (830 Fifth Avenue, between 63rd & 66th Streets, 1-212 439 6500, www.wcs.org) to marionette shows in the quaint Swedish Cottage (west side, at 79th Street). Stop by the Dairy visitor centre (midpark at 65th Street, 1-212 794 6564, www.centralparknyc.org) for information on activities and events. In winter, ice-skaters lace up at the picturesque Trump

Uptown 1

A   **B**   **C**

See p140

The Pool

W 102ND ST

COLUMBUS AVE

B,C

W 100TH ST

W 98TH ST

85TH ST TRANSVERSE

1,2,3   W 96TH ST   B,C

Central Pa

Symphony Space 35

W 94TH ST

WEST END AVE

BROADWAY

AMSTERDAM AVE

W 92ND ST

WEST DRIVE

HENRY J BROWNE BLVD

W 90TH ST

Soldiers' & Sailors' Monument

The Reservo

UPPER WEST SIDE

W 88TH ST

1   W 86TH ST   B,C

86TH ST TRANSVERSE

W 84TH ST   27

Great Lawn

W 82ND ST

B,C

Delacorte Theater

31

29   W 80TH ST   28

Luce Nature Observatory

Belvede Castle

W 79TH ST   1

American Museum of Natural History

RIVERSIDE DR

W 78TH ST

18

79TH ST TRANSVERSE

26   W 76TH ST

21

New-York Historical Society

The Ramble

Loe Boath

32

The Lake

W 74TH ST

VERDI SQUARE

22

The Dakota

Bow Bridge

1,2,3   W 72ND ST   B,C

Strawberry Fields

Betheso Terrace

W 70TH ST

25

HENRY HUDSON PKWY

WEST END AVE

AMSTERDAM AVE

BROADWAY

COLUMBUS AVE

CENTRAL PARK WEST

W 68TH ST

Sheep Meadow

FREEDOM PL

W 66TH ST   1

W 66TH ST

Tavern on the Green

85TH ST TRANSVERSE RD

34

W 64TH ST

Heckscher Playground

The Dairy

RIVERSIDE BLVD

Lincoln Center   W 62ND ST

Wollman Memorial Rink

A,B,C,D

W 60TH ST

99

33

Columbus Circle

98

W 58TH ST

Time Warner Center

30

23

20

Museum of Arts & Design

N,Q,R,W

W 57TH ST

Carnegie

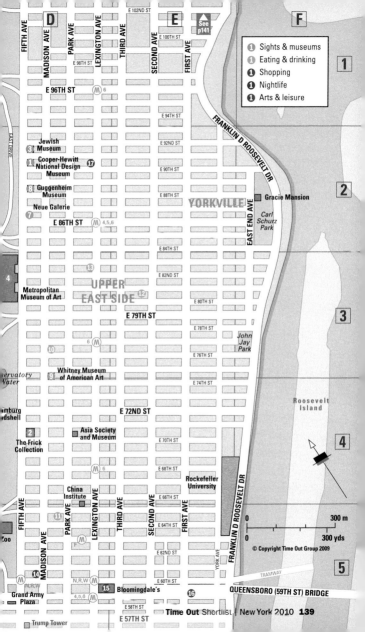

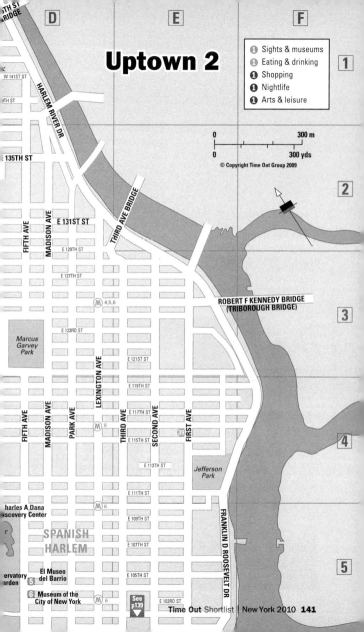

Uptown 2

D **E** **F**

1

- ① Sights & museums
- ① Eating & drinking
- ① Shopping
- ① Nightlife
- ① Arts & leisure

0   300 m
0   300 yds

© Copyright Time Out Group 2009

2

HARLEM RIVER DR

TH ST
BRIDGE

W 141ST ST

TH ST

135TH ST

THIRD AVE BRIDGE

E 131ST ST

FIFTH AVE

MADISON AVE

E 129TH ST

E 127TH ST

ROBERT F KENNEDY BRIDGE
(TRIBOROUGH BRIDGE)

3

Ⓜ 4,5,6

E 123RD ST

Marcus
Garvey
Park

LEXINGTON AVE

E 121ST ST

E 119TH ST

FIFTH AVE

MADISON AVE

PARK AVE

Ⓜ 6

THIRD AVE

SECOND AVE

FIRST AVE

E 117TH ST

E 115TH ST

㊺

4

E 113TH ST

Jefferson
Park

E 111TH ST

FRANKLIN D ROOSEVELT DR

Ⓜ 6

E 109TH ST

E 107TH ST

harles A Dana
iscovery Center

SPANISH
HARLEM

E 105TH ST

ervatory
arden

⑤ El Museo
del Barrio

5

⑥ Museum of the
City of New York

Ⓜ 6

E 103RD ST

See
p139

Time Out Shortlist | New York 2010 **141**

Wollman Rink (midpark at 62nd Street, 1-212 439 6900, www. wollmanskatingrink.com). A short stroll to about 64th Street brings you to the Friedsam Memorial Carousel (closed weekdays in winter), a bargain at $2 a ride. Come summer, kites, Frisbees and soccer balls seem to fly every which way across Sheep Meadow, the designated quiet zone that begins at 66th Street. Sheep did indeed graze here until 1934, but they've since been replaced by sunbathers. The hungry and affluent can repair to the glitzy Tavern on the Green (Central Park West, at 67th Street, 1-212 873 3200), which sets up a grand outdoor café in the summer. However, picnicking alfresco, or snacking on a hot dog from one of the park's food vendors, is a more popular option. East of Sheep Meadow, between 66th and 72nd Streets, is the elm-lined promenade,

the Mall, where in-line skaters congregate. And just east of the Mall's Naumburg Bandshell is Rumsey Playfield – site of the annual Central Park SummerStage series (p43), an eclectic roster of free and benefit concerts.

One of the most popular meeting places in the park is north of here: the grand Bethesda Fountain & Terrace, near the midpoint of the 72nd Street Transverse Road. The ornate passageway that connects the Mall to the plaza around the fountain boasts a stunning Minton tile ceiling, which was restored in 2007. *Angel of the Waters*, the sculpture in the centre of the fountain, was created by Emma Stebbins, the first woman to be granted a major public art commission in New York. To the east, the small pond called Conservatory Water is a mecca for model-yacht racers.

Neue Gallerie p146

To the west of the fountain, near the W 72nd Street entrance, sits Strawberry Fields, a section of the park that memorialises John Lennon, who lived in the nearby Dakota Building. It features a mosaic of the word 'imagine', donated by the Italian city of Naples, and more than 160 species of flowers and plants from all over the world. Just north of the Bethesda Fountain is the Loeb Boathouse (midpark, at 75th Street). From here, you can take a rowboat or gondola out on the lake, which is crossed by the elegant Bow Bridge. The Loeb houses the Central Park Boathouse Restaurant (midpark, at 75th Street, 1-212 517 2233, www.thecentralpark boathouse.com) which commands a great view of the lake, and has a popular outdoor bar.

Further north is Belvedere Castle, a restored Victorian

structure that sits atop the park's second-highest peak. Besides offering excellent views, it also houses the Henry Luce Nature Observatory. The nearby Delacorte Theater hosts Shakespeare in the Park (p44). And further north still sits the Great Lawn (midpark, between 79th & 85th Streets), a sprawling stretch of grass that serves as a rallying point for political protests, sports fields and a concert spot; the Metropolitan Opera and the New York Philharmonic perform here during the summer.

In the mid-1990s, the Jacqueline Kennedy Onassis Reservoir (midpark, between 85th & 96th Streets) was renamed in honour of the late first lady, who used to jog around it. Whether you prefer a running or walking pace, the path affords great views of the surrounding skyscrapers, especially at the northern end, looking south.

Next to the Harlem Meer, in the northern reaches of the park, is the Charles A Dana Discovery Center, which lends out fishing rods in the warmer months and has a roster of activities.

Upper East Side

Although many of Manhattan's super-rich have migrated downtown, there's still an air of old money on the Upper East Side. Along Fifth, Madison and Park Avenues, from 61st to 81st Streets, you'll see the great old mansions, many of which are now foreign consulates. Philanthropic gestures made by the moneyed classes over the past 130-odd years have helped create an impressive cluster of art collections, museums and cultural institutions. Indeed, Fifth Avenue from 82nd to 104th Streets is known as Museum Mile as it's lined with half a dozen esteemed institutions.

Cooper-Hewitt, National Design Museum

2 E 91st Street, at Fifth Avenue (1-212 849 8400/www.cooperhewitt.org). Subway 4, 5, 6 to 86th Street. **Open** 10am-5pm Mon-Fri; 10am-6pm Sat; noon-6pm Sun. **Admission** $15; free-$10 reductions. **Map** p139 D2 ❶
Founded in 1897 by the Hewitt sisters, granddaughters of industrialist Peter Cooper, the only museum in the US solely dedicated to design (both historic and modern) has been part of the Smithsonian since the 1960s. In 1976 it took up residence in the former home of steel magnate Andrew Carnegie; it's worth a look as much for the impressive mansion as for the roster of temporary exhibitions, which include an always-interesting series in which works are selected from the permanent collection by a prominent artist or designer. An extensive renovation is planned over the next few years to expand the gallery space and create a new library, but the museum will remain open throughout 2010.
Event highlights 'Design for a Living World' (until 4 Jan 2010); 'Design USA: Contemporay Innovation' (16 Oct 2009-Apr 2010).

Frick Collection

1 E 70th Street, between Fifth & Madison Avenues (1-212 288 0700/ www.frick.org). Subway 6 to 68th Street-Hunter College. **Open** 10am-6pm Tue-Sat; 11am-5pm Sun. **Admission** $15; $5-$10 reductions. Pay what you wish 11am-1pm Sun. **Map** p139 D4 ❷
Industrialist and collector Henry Clay Frick commissioned this opulent mansion with a view to leaving his legacy to the public. Designed by Carrère & Hastings (the firm behind the New York Public Library) and built in 1914, the building was inspired by 18th-century British and French architecture. In an effort to preserve the feel of a private residence, labelling is minimal,

but you can opt for a free audio guide or pay $1 for a booklet. Works spanning the 14th to 19th centuries include masterpieces by Rembrandt, Vermeer, Gainsborough and Bellini, exquisite period furniture, porcelain and other decorative objects.

Jewish Museum

1109 Fifth Avenue, at 92nd Street (1-212 423 3200/www.thejewish museum.org). Subway 4, 5 to 86th Street; 6 to 96th Street. **Open** 11am-5.45pm Mon-Wed, Sat, Sun; 11am-8pm Thur. Closed on Jewish holidays. **Admission** $12; free-$10 reductions; free Sat. **Map** p139 D2 ❸
The former home of financier, collector and Jewish leader Felix Warburg, the Jewish Museum's magnificent French Gothic-style mansion was given an exterior spruce-up for its 100th birthday in 2008. Inside, those with an interest in Jewish culture will find a far-reaching collection of more than 28,000 works of art, artefacts and media installations that are arranged thematically in a two-floor permanent exhibit. Entitled 'Culture and Continuity: The Jewish Journey', it traces the evolution of Judaism from antiquity to the present day. The excellent temporary shows appeal to a broad audience.
Event highlights 'Reinventing Ritual: Contemporary Art & Design for Jewish Life' (13 Sept 2009-31 Jan 2010); 'Alias Man Ray: The Art of Reinvention' (15 Nov 2009-14 Mar 2010).

Metropolitan Museum of Art

1000 Fifth Avenue, at 82nd Street (1-212 535 7710/www.metmuseum.org). Subway 4, 5, 6 to 86th Street. **Open** 9.30am-5.30pm Tue-Thur, Sun; 9.30am-9pm Fri, Sat. **Admission** suggested donation (incl same-day admission to the Cloisters) $20; free-$15 reductions. **Map** p139 D3 ❹
Occupying 13 acres of Central Park, the Metropolitan Museum of Art, which opened in 1880, is impressive in terms

both of quality and scale. Added in 1895 by McKim Mead and White, the neoclassical façade is daunting, but the museum is surprisingly easy to negotiate, particularly if you come early on a weekday and avoid the crowds.

In the ground floor's north wing sit the collection of Egyptian art and the glass-walled atrium housing the Temple of Dendur, moved en masse from its original Nile-side setting and now overlooking a reflective pool. Antiquity is also well represented on the southern wing of the ground floor by the halls housing Greek and Roman art, which reopened in 2007 after receiving an elegant makeover. Turning west brings you to the Arts of Africa, Oceania and the Americas collection; it was donated by Nelson Rockefeller as a memorial to his son Michael, who disappeared while visiting New Guinea in 1961. A wider-ranging bequest, the two-storey Robert Lehman Wing, can be found at the western end of the floor. This eclectic collection is housed in a re-creation of his townhouse and features Bellini's masterful *Madonna and Child*.

Rounding out the ground-floor highlights is the American Wing on the north-west corner. Its lovely Engelhard Court reopened in 2009 as part of the wing's current revamp (see box right). Upstairs are the galleries devoted to European paintings and sculpture, including an amazing reserve of old masters. The Dutch section boasts five Vermeers, the largest collection of this artist in the world. The 19th-century galleries contain some of the Met's most popular works – particularly the two-room Monet holdings and a colony of Van Goghs that includes his oft-reproduced Irises. The museum's nearby cache of modern art includes works by Pollock, de Kooning and Rothko.

At the northern wing of the floor, you'll find the sprawling collection of Asian art; be sure to check out the ceiling of the Jain Meeting Hall in the South-east Asian gallery. If you're still on your feet, give them a deserved rest

American beauties

Visitors to the **Metropolitan Museum of Art** (p144) over the past few years might have wondered 'Where is the American art?' Much of the American Wing has been closed, in stages, for a huge renovation; the entire project won't be completed until early 2011, but the new Charles Engelhard Court has just been unveiled. The overhaul included an installation of monumental sculpture on a new main floor level (near the stunning loggia designed by Louis Comfort Tiffany for the entrance of Laurelton Hall, his Long Island residence) as well as on a lower level in front of the façade of Martin E Thompson's Branch Bank of the United States (1822-24), transplanted from 15½ Wall Street.

A balcony gallery features the Met's collections of American ceramics, glass, silver and pewter. New period rooms – one from a 1750s Dutch farmhouse from Albany County upstate – complete with state-of-the-art touchscreen terminals let you zero in on details.

To help celebrate its new digs, the American Wing is mounting two big exhibitions. 'American Stories: Paintings of Everyday Life, 1765-1915' (13 Oct-24 Jan) features more than 100 works by many of America's most revered artists. 'Augustus Saint-Gauden in the Metropolitan Museum of Art' (ends 15 Nov) surveys America's most important 19th-century sculptor.

in the Astor Court, a tranquil re-creation of a Ming Dynasty garden, or head up to the Iris & B Gerald Cantor Roof Garden (late May-late Oct). For the Cloisters, which houses the Met's medieval art collection, see p158.

Event highlights 'Afghanistan: Hidden Treasures from the National Museum, Kabul' (until 20 Sept 2009); 'Robert Frank: The Americans' (22 Sept-27 Dec 2009); 'Watteau, Music & Theatre' (22 Sept-29 Nov 2009); 'American Stories: Paintings of Everyday Life, 1765-1915' (6 Oct 2009-24 Jan 2010); 'Arts of the Samurai: Japanese Armor from the Late Heian through the Edo Period' (c1156-1868) (20 Oct 2009-10 Jan 2010).

El Museo del Barrio

1230 Fifth Avenue, between 104th & 105th Streets (1-212 831 7272/ www.elmuseo.org). Subway 6 to 103rd Street. **Open** 11am-5pm Wed-Sun. **Admission** suggested $6; free-$4 reductions. **Map** p141 D5 ⑤
Located at the top of Museum Mile in Spanish Harlem (aka El Barrio), El Museo del Barrio is dedicated to the work of Latino artists who reside in the US, as well as Latin American masters. Most of the museum has been closed for a major revamp, but at press time it was set to reopen in autumn 2009 with a redesigned courtyard, a new pan-Latin café and renovated galleries to display its 8,000-piece collection, ranging from pre-Columbian artefacts to contemporary works.

Museum of the City of New York

1220 Fifth Avenue, between 103rd & 104th Streets (1-212 534 1672/ www.mcny.org). Subway 6 to 103rd Street. **Open** 10am-5pm Tue-Sun. **Admission** suggested donation $9; $5 reductions; $20 family; free 10am-noon Sun. **Map** p141 D5 ⑥
Located at the northern end of Museum Mile, this institution contains a wealth of information on the city's history,

organised into contemporary themed displays. As well as temporary shows, there are permanent exhibits devoted to the city's maritime heritage, architecture and even interiors: six rooms chart New York living spaces from 1680 to 1906. Elsewhere, 'Perform' explores the evolution and quirks of the theatre industry through artefacts, photographs and video – sit in old seats salvaged from the demolished 1918 Henry Miller's Theatre and watch actors talk about the scene.

The museum's extensive toy collection comprises playthings from the Colonial era to the present: toy trains, lead soldiers and battered teddy bears share shelf space with Kewpie dolls (created by a local artist); Brooklyn-born photographer Arthur Leipzig's shots of the city's children at play in the 1940s are also on display. Lavishly appointed dolls' houses include the amazing Stettheimer Dollhouse: it was created in the 1920s by Carrie Stettheimer, whose artist friends reinterpreted their masterpieces in miniature to hang on the walls. Don't miss the museum's 'Timescapes', a 25-minute multimedia film that tells NYC's story from 1624 to the present, shown every 30 minutes.

Neue Galerie

1048 Fifth Avenue, at 86th Street (1-212 628 6200/www.neuegalerie.org). Subway 4, 5, 6 to 86th Street. **Open** 11am-6pm Mon, Thur, Sat, Sun; 11am-9pm Fri. **Admission** $15; $10 reductions. Under-16s must be accompanied by an adult; under-12s not admitted. **Map** p139 D2 ⑦
The elegant Neue Galerie is devoted entirely to late 19th- and early 20th-century German and Austrian fine and decorative arts. The creation of the late art dealer Serge Sabarsky and cosmetics mogul Ronald S Lauder, it has the largest concentration of works by Gustav Klimt and Egon Schiele outside Vienna. The civilised Café Sabarsky serves updated Austrian cuisine and ravishing Viennese pastries.

NEW YORK BY AREA

Solomon R Guggenheim Museum

1071 Fifth Avenue, at 89th Street (1-212 423 3500/www.guggenheim.org). Subway 4, 5, 6 to 86th Street. **Open** 10am-5.45pm Mon-Wed, Sat, Sun; 10am-7.45pm Fri. **Admission** $18; free-$15 reductions; pay what you wish 5.45-7.15pm Fri. **Map** p139 D2 ❽

The Guggenheim is as famous for its landmark building – designed by Frank Lloyd Wright and restored for its 50th birthday in 2009 – as it is for its impressive collection and daring temporary shows. The museum owns Peggy Guggenheim's trove of Cubist, Surrealist and Abstract Expressionist works, along with the Panza di Biumo Collection of American Minimalist and Conceptual art from the 1960s and '70s. As well as works by Manet, Picasso, Chagall and Bourgeois, it includes the largest collection of Kandinskys in the US. In 1992 the addition of a ten-storey tower provided space for a sculpture gallery (with park views), an auditorium and a café.

Event highlights Kandinsky (18 Sept 2009-10 Jan 2010); 'Anish Kapoor: Memory' (9 Oct 2009-21 Mar 2010).

Whitney Museum of American Art

945 Madison Avenue, at 75th Street (1-212 570 3600/www.whitney.org). Subway 6 to 77th Street. **Open** 11am-6pm Wed, Thur, Sat, Sun; 1-9pm Fri. **Admission** $15; free-$10 reductions; pay what you wish 6-9pm Fri. **Map** p139 D3 ❾

Like the Guggenheim, the Whitney is set apart by its unique architecture: a Marcel Breuer-designed granite cube with an all-seeing upper-storey 'eye' window. When sculptor and art patron Gertrude Vanderbilt Whitney opened the museum in 1931, she dedicated it to living American artists. Today, the Whitney holds 18,000 pieces by around 2,700 artists, including Alexander Calder, Willem de Kooning, Edward Hopper (the museum owns his entire collection), Jasper Johns, Louise Nevelson, Georgia O'Keeffe and Claes Oldenburg. Still, the museum's reputation rests mainly on its temporary shows – particularly the Whitney Biennial, the exhibition everyone loves to hate. Held in spring-summer in even-numbered years, the Biennial is the most prestigious and controversial assessment of contemporary art in America. In 2008 Renzo Piano released initial designs for a satellite Whitney along the new High Line park.

Event highlights 'Georgia O'Keeffe: Abstraction' (17 Sept 2009-17 Jan 2010); 'Roni Horn aka Roni Horn' (6 Nov 2009-24 Jan 2010); Whitney Biennial (p43).

Eating & drinking

Bemelmans Bar

The Carlyle, 35 E 76th Street, at Madison Avenue (1-212 744 1600/www.thecarlyle.com). Subway 6 to 77th Street. **Open** noon-1am Mon-Thur, Sun; noon-2am Fri, Sat. **Bar**. **Map** p139 D3 ❿

The Plaza may have Eloise, but the Carlyle has its own children's book connection – the wonderful 1947 murals of Central Park by *Madeline* creator Ludwig Bemelmans in this, the quintessential classy New York bar. Live music adds to the atmosphere most nights (a cover charge of $20-$25 applies from 9pm).

Daniel

60 E 65th Street, between Madison & Park Avenues (1-212 288 0033/www.danielnyc.com). Subway F to Lexington Avenue-63rd Street; 6 to 68th Street-Hunter College. **Open** 5.45-11pm Mon-Thur; 5.30-11pm Fri, Sat. **$$$$**. **French**. **Map** p139 D5 ⓫

The revolving door off Park Avenue and the elegant, Adam Tihany-designed interior announce it: this is fine dining. The cuisine at Daniel Boulud's flagship is rooted in French technique with au courant flourishes like fusion elements and an emphasis on local produce. Though the seasonally changing menu always includes a few signature dishes – Boulud's black truffle and scallops in puff pastry, introduced in 1987, remains a classic – it's the chef's new creations that keep the food as fresh as the decor. **Other locations** Café Boulud, 20 E 76th Street, between Fifth & Madison Avenues (1-212 772 2600).

Etats-Unis
242 E 81st Street, between Second & Third Avenues (1-212 517 8826/ www.etatsunisrestaurant.com). Subway 6 to 77th Street. **Open** 6-10.30pm daily. **$$$**. **American creative**. **Map** p139 E3 ⑫
With simple wood floors and an open kitchen, this spot evokes a cosy neighbourhood bistro – albeit one with Michelin-star-quality food and prices to match. A daily-changing menu makes the most of the finest in-season produce and free-range meats (in summer, for example, this can be anything from roasted artichoke hearts with plump day-boat scallops to pork chops topped by peach chutney) and the execution is impeccable.

Lexington Candy Shop
1226 Lexington Avenue, at 83rd Street (1-212 288 0057/www.lexingtoncandy shop.net). Subway 4, 5, 6 to 86th Street. **Open** 7am-7pm Mon-Sat; 9am-6pm Sun. **$**. **American**. **Map** p139 D3 ⑬
You won't see much candy for sale at Lexington Candy Shop. Instead, you'll find a wonderfully preserved retro diner (it was founded in 1925), its long counter lined with chatty locals on their lunch hours, tucking into burgers and chocolate malts. If you come for breakfast, order the doorstop slabs of french toast.

Shopping

Madison Avenue, between 57th and 86th Streets, is packed with international designer names: Gucci, Prada, Chloé, Donna Karan, Tom Ford, multiple Ralph Lauren outposts and many more.

Barneys New York
660 Madison Avenue, at 61st Street (1-212 826 8900/www.barneys.com). Subway N, R, W to Fifth Avenue-59th Street; 4, 5, 6 to 59th Street. **Open** 10am-8pm Mon-Fri; 10am-7pm Sat; 11am-6pm Sun. **Map** p139 D5 ⑭
Barneys has a reputation for spotlighting less-ubiquitous designer labels than other upmarket department stores, and has its own quirky-classic line. Its Co-op boutiques (see website for locations) carry threads by up-and-comers and the latest hot denim lines. Every February and August, the Chelsea Co-op hosts the Barneys Warehouse Sale, when prices are slashed by 50-80%.

Bloomingdale's
1000 Third Avenue, at 59th Street (1-212 705 2000/www.bloomingdales. com). Subway N, R, W to Lexington Avenue-59th Street; 4, 5, 6 to 59th Street. **Open** 10am-8.30pm Mon-Fri; 10am-7pm Sat; 11am-7pm Sun. **Map** p139 D5/E5 ⑮
Ranking among the city's top tourist attractions, Bloomies is a gigantic, glitzy department store stocked with everything from bags to beauty products, home furnishings to designer duds. The hipper, compact Soho outpost offers mainly young fashion, denim and cosmetics.

Conran Shop
407 E 59th Street, at First Avenue (1-212 755 9079/www.conranusa.com). Subway N, R, W to Lexington Avenue-59th Street; 4, 5, 6 to 59th Street. **Open** 11am-7pm Mon-Fri; 10am-7pm Sat; 11am-6pm Sun. **Map** p139 E5 ⑯
Nestled under the Queensboro Bridge, Terence Conran's shop stocks a vast selection of well-designed goods for every room of the house. Large pieces

are at ground level; head downstairs for the array of cool kitchen gadgets, funky radios, niche-line bath products and unusual vases.

Edit

1368 Lexington Avenue, between 90th & 91st Streets (1-212 876 1368/ www.editfashion.com). Subway 4, 5, 6 to 86th Street. **Open** 10.30am-8pm Mon-Fri; 10.30am-6.30pm Sat; noon-6pm Sun. **Map** p139 D2 ⊕

Scanning the racks at this handsome bi-level townhouse, a short detour from Museum Mile, is akin to peeking into a socialite's closet. Luxe labels like Derek Lam and Marchesa mix with less expensive ones such as J Brand, Velvet and Nili Lotan.

Upper West Side

The gateway to the Upper West Side is Columbus Circle, where Broadway meets 59th Street,

Lexington Candy Shop

Eighth Avenue, Central Park South and Central Park West – a rare roundabout in a city that is largely made up of right angles. The cosmopolitan neighbourhood's seat of culture is **Lincoln Center**, a complex of concert halls and auditoriums built in the 1960s that's home to the New York Philharmonic, the New York City Ballet, the Metropolitan Opera and a host of other notable arts organisations.

Further uptown, Morningside Heights, between 110th and 125th Streets, from Morningside park to the Hudson, is dominated by Columbia University. The sinuous Riverside Park, designed by Central Park's Frederick Law Olmsted, starts at 72nd Street and ends at 158th Street, between Riverside Drive and the Hudson River; in the 1990s, work began to develop the abandoned Penn Central Railyard between 59th and 72nd Streets into Riverside Park South, now a peaceful city retreat with a pier and undulating waterside paths.

Sights & museums

American Museum of Natural History/Rose Center for Earth & Space

Central Park West, at 79th Street (1-212 769 5100/www.amnh.org). Subway B, C to 81st Street-Museum of Natural History. **Open** 10am-5.45pm daily. **Admission** suggested donation $15; free-$11 reductions. **Map** p138 C3 ⊕

Home to the largest and arguably most fabulous collection of dinosaur fossils in the world, the American Museum of Natural History's fourth-floor dino halls have been blowing minds for decades. Roughly 80% of the bones on display were dug out of the ground by Indiana Jones types. But during the museum's mid-1990s renovation, several specimens were

Harlem p157

remodelled to incorporate discoveries made during the intervening years.

The rest of the museum is equally dramatic. The Hall of Human Origins, which opened in 2007, boasts a fine display of our cousins the Neanderthals. The Hall of Biodiversity examines world ecosystems and environmental preservation, and a life-size model of a blue whale hangs from the cavernous ceiling of the Hall of Ocean Life. The impressive Hall of Meteorites was brushed up and reorganised in 2003. The space's focal point is Ahnighito, the largest iron meteor on display anywhere in the world, weighing in at 34 tons (more than 30,000kg).

The spectacular $210 million Rose Center for Earth & Space – dazzling to come upon at night – is a giant silvery globe where you can discover the universe via 3-D shows in the Hayden Planetarium and light shows in the Big Bang Theater. An IMAX theatre screens larger-than-life nature films.

Cathedral Church of St John the Divine

1047 Amsterdam Avenue, at 112th Street (1-212 316 7540/www.stjohn divine.org). Subway B, C, 1 to 110th Street-Cathedral Parkway. **Open**
7.30am-6pm daily. **Admission** suggested donation $5; $4 reductions. Map p140 B4 ⑲
Construction on 'St John the Unfinished' began in 1892 in Romanesque style, was put on hold for a Gothic Revival redesign in 1911, then ground to a halt in 1941, when the US entered World War II. It resumed in earnest in 1979, but a fire in 2001 destroyed the church's gift shop, further delaying completion. The cathedral hosts concerts and bills itself as a place for all people – and it means it. Annual events include the Blessing of the Bicycles in April, when more than 100 cyclists assemble.

Museum of Arts & Design

2 Columbus Circle, at Broadway (1-212 299 7777/www.madmuseum. org). Subway A, B, C, D, 1 to 59th Street-Columbus Circle. **Open** 11am-6pm Wed, Fri-Sun; 11am-9pm Thur. **Admission** $15; free-$12 reductions; pay what you wish 6-9pm Thur. Map p138 C5 ⑳
Founded in 1956 as the Museum of Contemporary Crafts, this institution brings together contemporary objects created in a wide range of media – including clay, glass, wood, metal and

NEW YORK BY AREA

cloth – with a strong focus on materials and process. And the museum recently crafted a new home. Originally designed in 1964 by Radio City Music Hall architect Edward Durell Stone to house the Gallery of Modern Art, 2 Columbus Circle was a windowless monolith that had sat empty since 1998. After an 18-month overhaul (with a price tag topping $90 million), the ten-storey building now has four floors of exhibition galleries, including the Tiffany & Co Foundation Jewelry Gallery. Curators are now able to display more of the 2,000-piece permanent collection, including porcelain by Cindy Sherman, stained glass by Judith Schaechter, black-basalt ceramics by James Turrell and Robert Arneson's mural *Alice House Wall*, on view for the first time in two decades. Visitors can also watch resident artists create works in studios on the sixth floor. A restaurant opens in autumn 2009.

Event highlights 'GlassWear' (until 20 Sept 2009); 'Slash: Paper Under the Knife' (7 Oct 2009-10 Jan 2010); 'Bigger, Better, More: The Art of Viola Frey' (3 Feb-20 May 2010); 'Craft Revolution: The American Studio Movement, 1945-1970' (23 June-19 Sept 2010).

New-York Historical Society

170 Central Park West, between 76th & 77th Streets (1-212 873 3400/ www.nyhistory.org). Subway B, C to 81st Street-Museum of Natural History. **Open** 10am-6pm Tue-Sat; 11am-5.45pm Sun. **Admission** $10; free-$7 reductions; free 6-8pm Fri. **Map** p138 C3 ㉑
Founded in 1804, New York's oldest museum was one of America's first cultural and educational institutions. Highlights in the vast Henry Luce III Center for the Study of American Culture include George Washington's Valley Forge camp cot, a complete series of the extant watercolours from Audubon's *Birds of America* and the world's largest single collection of Tiffany lamps.

Event highlights 'New York Painting Begins: Eighteenth-Century Portraits' (ends 1 Jan 2010).

Eating & drinking

Alice's Tea Cup

102 W 73rd Street, at Columbus Avenue (1-212 799 3006/www.alices teacup.com). Subway B, C, 1, 2, 3 to 72nd Street. **Open** 8am-8pm daily.
$. Café. **Map** p138 B4 ㉒
Wander into this sequestered basement and you'll be transported to a story land inspired by Lewis Carroll. First, pass through the quirky gift-boutique-cum-bakeshop, where you can browse Wonderland-themed knickknacks along with dense, delicious scones and muffins. Proceed further in (not easy on weekends) and you'll discover a sweet room serving big brunch plates and the full teatime monty. It's a fairytale indeed, except for the service, which can be slow.

Bouchon Bakery

3rd Floor, Time Warner Center, 10 Columbus Circle, at Broadway (1-212 823 9366/www.bouchonbakery.com). Subway A, B, C, D, 1 to 59th Street-Columbus Circle. **Open** 11.30am-9pm Mon-Sat; 11.30am-7pm Sun. **$-$$.**
French. **Map** p138 C5 ㉓
The appeal is obvious: sample Thomas Keller's food for far less than it costs at his first-rate fine-dining establishment, Per Se, in the same complex (1-212 823 9335, www.perseny.com), where the tasting menu is now a whopping $275 per person. However, you'll have to eat in an open café setting in a mall, under a giant Samsung sign, and choose from a limited selection of sandwiches, salads, quiches and spreadable dishes (pâté, foie gras and so on). That said, this is a great place for lunch and the pastries – French classics and Keller's takes on American ones like Oreo cookies, are real finds.

Café Luxembourg

200 W 70th Street, between Amsterdam & West End Avenues (1-212 873 7411/

www.cafeluxembourg.com). Subway B, C, 1, 2, 3 to 72nd Street. **Open** 8am-11pm Mon-Thur; 8am-midnight Fri; 9am-midnight Sat; 9am-10pm Sun. **$$. French. Map** p138 B4 🐷

Café Luxembourg isn't trying to be anything other than what it is – a classy neighbourhood bistro successfully executing traditional French-American fare. Seasonal starters and desserts punctuate a short menu of steak frites, grilled fish and crème brûlée. Uncomplicated food expertly prepared, attentive, unfussy service and an atmosphere of relaxed elegance keep the regulars (celebrities and ordinary Joes alike) coming back.

Ding Dong Lounge

929 Columbus Avenue, between 105th & 106th Street (Duke Ellington Boulevard) (1-212 663 2600/www.dingdonglounge.com). Subway B, C to 103rd Street. **Open** 4pm-4am daily. **Bar. Map** p140 B5 🐷

Goth chandeliers and kick-ass music mark this dark dive as punk – with broadened horizons. The taps, dispensing Stella Artois, Guinness and Bass, are sawn-off guitar necks, and the walls are covered with vintage concert posters (from Dylan to the Damned). The affable local clientele and mood-lit conversation nooks make it surprisingly accessible (even without a working knowledge of Dee Dee Ramone).

Fatty Crab

NEW *2170 Broadway, at 77th Street (1-212 496 2722/www.fattycrab.com). Subway 1 to 79th Street.* **Open** 5pm-midnight daily. **$$. Malaysian. Map** p138 B3 🐷

The Upper West Side's ongoing gastronomic upgrade is further evidenced by the arrival in spring 2009 of a sister location of Zak Pelaccio's Meatpacking District restaurant, named after his favourite joint in Kuala Lumpur. This larger, 74-seat space features a cocktail lounge pouring Far East-inspired tipples. The kitchen serves all the dishes

from the original location (chilli-spiked Dungeness crab, 'fatty duck' boiled and fried, and then dusted with sugar), as well as some new ones, including 'fatty sliders' (mini pork-and-beef burgers).

Good Enough to Eat

483 Amsterdam Avenue, between 83rd & 84th Streets (1-212 496-0163/www.goodenoughtoeat.com). Subway 1 to 86th Street. **Open** 8am-10.30pm Mon-Thur; 8am-11pm Fri; 9am-11pm Sat; 9am-10.30pm Sun. **$-$$. American. Map** p138 B3 🐷

Brunchers crowd this neighbourhood comfort-food specialist for the fluffy eggs, fruit-packed apple pancakes and pumpkin french toast. Everything – even the salads – is aimed at hearty appetites and served in grizzly-bear portions. If home cooking were really this good, we'd still be living there.

Shopping

Allan & Suzi

416 Amsterdam Avenue, at 80th Street (1-212 724 7445/www.allanandsuzi.net). Subway 1 to 79th Street. **Open** 12.30-7pm Mon-Sat; noon-6pm Sun. **Map** p138 B3 🐷

Models and celebs drop off worn-once Gaultiers, Muglers, Pradas and Manolos here. The platform shoe collection is flashback-inducing and incomparable, as is the selection of vintage jewellery.

H&H Bagels

2239 Broadway, at 80th Street (1-212 595 8003/www.hhbagels.com). Subway 1 to 79th Street. **Open** 24hrs daily. **Map** p138 B3 🐷

For a taste of the real, old-fashioned (boiled and baked) thing, head straight to H&H, which lays claim to being the city's largest bagel purveyor.

Shops at Columbus Circle

Time Warner Center, 10 Columbus Circle, at 59th Street (1-212 823 6300/www.shopsatcolumbuscircle.com). Subway A, B, C, D, 1 to 59th Street-

Changing of the (old) guard

There's new blood in classical music's institutions.

Peter Gelb

For several seasons after Peter Gelb arrived to take over at the **Metropolitan Opera** (p156), it seemed as if that old bastion of conservative values, moneyed privilege and secrecy had been mysteriously replaced by an exact duplicate that behaved in the opposite manner. Gelb miraculously returned the Met to the epicentre of NYC's cultural life.

And now, change has come to the Met's Lincoln Center (p155) neighbours, **New York City Opera** and the **New York Philharmonic**. In City Opera's case, the arrival of new general director George Steel followed a year of darkness while awaiting the arrival of Belgian maverick Gerard Mortier. (The financial shortfall caused Mortier to reject the post.)

Steel, credited for working wonders at Columbia University's Miller Theatre, had only recently taken over at the Dallas Opera. But the appeal of returning to New York – and perhaps the potential of becoming City Opera's saviour –

was enough to lure him back. A schedule of only five productions for 2009/10, including a new *Don Giovanni* by Christopher Alden, has been announced, bringing City Opera back to life as it lays the groundwork for a bold new future.

When the New York Philharmonic announced its first season under the artistic leadership of Alan Gilbert, the mantra cited was 'evolution, not revolution'. The classical repertoire was in no danger of being replaced. But Gilbert's dedication to blazing new trails has been proved by his appointment of a composer-in-residence (Finnish modernist Magnus Lindberg) and an artist-in-residence (baritone Thomas Hampson), both starting in the 2009/10 season, as well as the revelation that the orchestra would be launching its own new-music ensemble. Those steps ought to see the New York Philharmonic hit a new stride without leaving longtime supporters panting for breath.

The Cloisters p158

Columbus Circle. **Open** 10am-9pm Mon-Sat; 11am-7pm Sun (hrs vary for some shops, bars and restaurants). **Map** p138 C5 ③⓪

Classier than your average mall, the retail contingent of the 2.8 million-sq-ft Time Warner Center features upscale stores such as Coach and Cole Haan for accessories and shoes, Bose home entertainment, the fancy kitchenware purveyor Williams-Sonoma and True Religion jeans, as well as national shopping centre staples J Crew, Crabtree & Evelyn, Borders and excellent organic grocer Whole Foods. Some of the city's top restaurants have made it a dining destination that transcends the stigma of eating at the mall.

Zabar's

2245 Broadway, at 80th Street (1-212 787 2000/www.zabars.com). Subway 1 to 79th Street. **Open** 8am-7.30pm Mon-Fri; 8am-8pm Sat; 9am-6pm Sun. **Map** p138 B3 ③①

Zabar's is more than just a market – it's a New York City landmark. It began in 1934 as a tiny storefront specialising in Jewish 'appetising' delicacies and has gradually expanded to take over half a block of prime Upper West Side real estate. What never ceases to surprise, however, is its reasonable prices, even for high-end foods. Besides the famous smoked fish and rafts of delicacies, Zabar's has fabulous bread, cheese, olives and coffee and an entire floor dedicated to homewares.

Nightlife

Beacon Theatre

2124 Broadway, at 74th Street (1-212 465 6500/www.beacontheatrenyc.com). Subway 1, 2, 3 to 72nd Street. **Map** p138 B3 ③②

Resplendently restored, this spacious, former vaudeville theatre hosts a variety of popular acts, from Emmylou Harris to ZZ Top; once a year, the Allman Brothers take over for a lengthy residency. While the vastness can be daunting to performers and audience alike, the baroque, gilded interior makes you feel as though you're having a real night out on the town.

Built in the 1960s, this massive complex is the nexus of Manhattan's performing arts scene. It's currently in the midst of a major rebuilding project, which will include a new visitors' space (see box p127), restaurant and film centre and is slated for completion in early 2011. Also situated here are the Juilliard School and the Fiorello H LaGuardia High School of Music & Art and Performing Arts, which frequently host professional performances. The main entry point for Lincoln Center is at Columbus Avenue, at 65th Street, but the venues that follow are spread out across the square of blocks from 62nd to 66th Streets, between Amsterdam and Columbus Avenues. Centercharge (1-212 721 6500) sells tickets for events at Alice Tully Hall, Avery Fisher Hall and the Juilliard School, as well as for the Lincoln Center Out of Doors Festival.

Jazz at Lincoln Center

Broadway, at 60th Street (1-212 258 9800/www.jalc.org). Subway A, B, C, D, 1 to 59th Street-Columbus Circle. **Map** p138 C5 ㉝

The jazz arm of Lincoln Center is several blocks away from the main campus (below), situated high atop the Time Warner Center. It features three separate rooms: the Rose Theater is a traditional mid-size space, but the crown jewels are the Allen Room and the smaller Dizzy's Club Coca-Cola, which feel like a Hollywood cinematographer's vision of a Manhattan jazz club. Some of the best players in the business regularly grace the spot, among them Wynton Marsalis, who is also Jazz at Lincoln Center's famed artistic director.

Arts & leisure

Lincoln Center

Columbus Avenue, at 65th Street (1-212 546 2656/www.lincolncenter.org). Subway 1 to 66th Street-Lincoln Center. **Map** p138 B5 ㉞

Alice Tully Hall 1-212 875 5050.

Home to the Chamber Music Society of Lincoln Center (1-212 875 5788, www.chambermusicsociety.org), Alice Tully Hall somehow feels cosy despite a capacity of 1,096 seats. Following extensive remodelling in the first phase of Lincoln Center's reinvention, the hall reopened in February 2009 with greatly improved acoustics and a soaring, glass-enclosed lobby.

Avery Fisher Hall 1-212 875 5030.

This handsome, comfortable 2,700-seat hall is the headquarters of the New York Philharmonic (1-212 875 5656, www.nyphilharmonic.org), the country's oldest symphony orchestra (founded in 1842) and one of its finest. The sound, which ranges from good to atrocious depending on who you ask, stands to be improved (although the timing of this hasn't been confirmed). Inexpensive early-evening 'rush hour' concerts and weekday-morning open rehearsals are presented several times per season. The Great Performers series features top international soloists and ensembles.

NEW YORK BY AREA

David H Koch Theater
1-212 870 5570.

Formerly the New York State Theater, the David H Koch Theater is home to both the New York City Ballet (www.nycballet.com) and the New York City Opera (www.nycopera.com). The NYCO has long tried to overcome its second-best reputation by being both ambitious and defiantly populist: rising young American singers often take their first bows here. The theatre – which architect Philip Johnson designed to resemble a jewellery box – has been closed for renovation during much of 2009, thanks to a $100 million gift from the eponymous donor, with a grand re-opening no doubt in store for the autumn. The winter ballet season begins in November, just before Thanksgiving, and features more than a month of performances of *The Nutcracker*; it then continues until the end of February with repertory performances. The nine-week spring ballet season begins in late April.

Lincoln Center Theater 1-212 239 6200/www.lct.org.

The majestic and prestigious Lincoln Center Theater complex has a pair of amphitheatre-style drama venues. The Broadway house, the 1,138-seat Vivian Beaumont Theater, is home to star-studded and elegant major productions. (When the Beaumont is tied up in long runs, LCT presents its larger works at available Times Square theatres.) Downstairs from the Beaumont is the 338-seat Mitzi E Newhouse Theater, an Off Broadway space devoted to new work by the upper layer of American playwrights. In an effort to shake off its reputation for stodginess, Lincoln Center launched LCT3 in autumn 2008, which presents the work of emerging playwrights and directors at other theatres (see LCT website for details). Ultimately, there are plans for a devoted space.

Metropolitan Opera House 1-212 362 6000/www.metopera.org.

The grandest of the Lincoln Center buildings, the Met is a spectacular

Apollo Theater p159

place to see and hear opera. It hosts the Metropolitan Opera from September to May, and major visiting companies in summer. Audiences are knowledgeable and fiercely devoted, with subscriptions remaining in families for generations. The Met had already started becoming more inclusive before Peter Gelb took the reins in 2006. Now, the company is placing a priority on creating novel theatrical experiences while assembling a new company of physically graceful, telegenic stars (Anna Netrebko, Rolando Villazón, Juan Diego Flórez) for a programme of high-definition cinema broadcasts. A range of international dance companies, from the Paris Opera Ballet to the Kirov, also performs at the Met. In spring, the space is home to American Ballet Theatre, which presents full-length traditional story ballets, contemporary classics, and the occasional world première by the likes of Twyla Tharp.

Walter Reade Theater 1-212 875 5601/www.filmlinc.com.

The complex's cinema is the home of the Film Society of Lincoln Center, founded in 1969 to promote contemporary film. The FSLC now also hosts the prestigious New York Film Festival (p39) and other festivals throughout the year. Programmes are usually thematic with an international perspective. Until early 2011, when Lincoln Center's state-of-the-art Elinor Bunin-Munroe Film Center opens with two screens, a gallery and café, all of your filmgoing needs will be met here.

Symphony Space
2537 Broadway, at 95th Street (1-212 864 5400/www.symphonyspace.org). Subway 1, 2, 3 to 96th Street. **Map** p138 B1 ㉟
Despite its name, programming at this multi-disciplinary performing-arts centre is anything but orchestra-centric: recent seasons have featured sax quartets, Indian classical music and a cappella ensembles. The annual Wall to Wall marathons in spring serve up 12 hours of free music, all focused on a particular composer. The venue is also home to the famed Thalia art house cinema, featured in *Annie Hall* (when it was screening *The Sorrow and the Pity*), and stages works by contemporary choreographers.

Harlem & beyond

Extending north from the top of Central Park at 110th Street as far as 155th Street, Harlem is the cultural capital of black America – the legacy of the Harlem Renaissance. By the 1920s, it had become the country's most populous African-American community, attracting some of black America's greatest artists: writers such as Langston Hughes and musicians like Duke Ellington and Louis Armstrong. West Harlem, between Fifth and St Nicholas Avenues, is the Harlem of popular imagination, and 125th Street is its lifeline. The area around the landmarked Mount Morris Historic District (from

119th to 124th Streets, between Malcolm X Boulevard/Lenox Avenue & Mount Morris Park West) continues to gentrify, and new boutiques, restaurants and cafés dot the double-wide Malcolm X Boulevard. Further uptown, Strivers' Row, also known as the St Nicholas Historic District, from 138th to 139th Streets, between Adam Clayton Powell Jr Boulevard (Seventh Avenue) and Frederick Douglass Boulevard (Eighth Avenue), was developed in 1891. East of Fifth Avenue is East Harlem, better known to its primarily Puerto Rican residents as El Barrio.

From 155th Street to Dyckman (200th) Street is Washington Heights, which contains a handful of attractions and, at the tip of Manhattan, pretty Fort Tryon Park.

Sights & museums

For **El Museo del Barrio**, see p146.

Abyssinian Baptist Church
132 Odell Clark Place (138th Street), between Malcolm X Boulevard (Lenox Avenue) & Adam Clayton Powell Jr Boulevard (Seventh Avenue) (1-212 862 7474/www.abyssinian.org). Subway 2, 3 to 135th Street. **Map** p140 C1 ㊱
From the staid gingerbread Gothic exterior, you'd never suspect the energy that charges the Abyssinian when the gospel choir rocks the church every Sunday (9am and 11am – get there early, and don't wear shorts or flip-flops). A cauldron of community activism since its Ethiopian elders moved it uptown in the 1920s, the church was under the leadership of legendary civil rights crusader Adam Clayton Powell Jr in the 1930s (there's a modest exhibit about him inside). Today, the pulpit belongs to Reverend Calvin Butts, who continues in the same vein.

The Cloisters

Fort Tryon Park, Fort Washington Avenue, at Margaret Corbin Plaza (1-212 923 3700/www.metmuseum.org). Subway A to 190th Street, then M4 bus or follow Margaret Corbin Drive north to the museum. **Open** Mar-Oct 9.30am-5.15pm Tue-Sun. Nov-Feb 9.30am-4.45pm Tue-Sun. **Admission** suggested donation (incl same-day admission to Metropolitan Museum of Art) $20; free-$15 reductions.

Set in a lovely park overlooking the Hudson River, the Cloisters houses the Met's medieval art and architecture collections. A path winds through the peaceful grounds to a castle that was built a mere 71 years ago using pieces of five medieval French cloisters. The collection itself is a trove of Romanesque, Gothic and Baroque treasures brought from Europe and then assembled together in a manner that manages not to clash. Be sure to check out the Unicorn Tapestries, the 12th-century Fuentidueña Chapel and the Annunciation Triptych by Robert Campin.

Studio Museum in Harlem

144 W 125th Street, between Malcolm X Boulevard (Lenox Avenue) & Adam Clayton Powell Jr Boulevard (Seventh Avenue) (1-212 864 4500/www.studiomuseum.org). Subway 2, 3 to 125th Street. **Open** noon-6pm Wed-Fri, Sun; 10am-6pm Sat. **Admission** suggested donation $7; free-$3 reductions; free Sun. No credit cards. **Map** p140 C3 ③⑦

The first black fine arts museum in the country when it opened in 1968, the Studio Museum has become one of the jewels in the crown of the art scene of the African diaspora. Under the leadership of director Lowery Stokes Sims (formerly of the Met) and chief curator Thelma Golden (formerly of the Whitney), this vibrant institution presents shows in a variety of media by black artists from around the world.

Amy Ruth's

113 W 116th Street, between Malcolm X Boulevard (Lenox Avenue) & Adam Clayton Powell Jr Boulevard (Seventh Avenue) (1-212 280 8779/www.amyruthsharlem.com). Subway 2, 3 to 116th Street. **Open** 11.30am-11pm Mon; 8.30am-11pm Tue-Thur; 8.30am-5.30am; 24hrs Fri, Sat; 7.30am-11pm Sun. **$**. **American regional**. **Map** p140 C4 ③⑧

Portraits of jazz giants hang on the walls of this perpetually packed two-storey Harlem fave. A bottle of Frank's RedHot dresses every table, and the richly battered catfish or the fried chicken and waffles platters go down peppery-sweet with a splash of the hot stuff. Titanic helpings of cinnamon-crusted peach cobbler and thickly iced red velvet cake lend the menu a grandmotherly touch.

Camaradas El Barrio

2241 First Avenue, at 115th Street (1-212 348 2703/www.camaradaselbarrio.com). Subway 6 to 116th Street. **Open** 4pm-1am Mon-Wed, Sun; 4pm-4am Thur-Sat (hrs may vary). **Bar**. **Map** p141 E4 ③⑨

At this Puerto Rican self-styled 'workers' public house', tapas bar and music venue, wooden benches, exposed brick and modest gallery create a casual hang for kicking back over a pitcher of sangria or taking in a salsa show.

Nectar Wine Bar

NEW *2235 Frederick Douglass Boulevard (Eighth Avenue), between 120th and 121st Streets (1-212 961 9622). Subway A, B, C, D to 125th Street.* **Open** 5pm-1am daily. **Wine bar**. **Map** p140 C3 ④⓪

The offspring of the beloved adjoining wineshop Harlem Vintage, sleek Nectar continues the store's legacy with hands-on service and a well-curated wine list. Europe- and California-heavy selections (36 by the glass) are mercifully priced at around $10. Servers ably match the wines to charcuterie and cheese.

Shopping

Hue-Man Bookstore & Café

2319 Frederick Douglass Boulevard (Eighth Avenue), between 124th & 125th Streets (1-212 665 7400/www. huemanbookstore.com). Subway A, B, C, D to 125th Street. **Open** 10am-8pm Mon-Sat; 11am-7pm Sun. **Map** p140 C3 ④①

Focusing on African-American non-fiction and fiction, this superstore-size Harlem independent also stocks best-sellers and general interest books.

Malcolm Shabazz Harlem Market

52 W 116th Street, at Malcolm X Boulevard (Lenox Avenue) (1-212 987 8131). **Open** 10am-8pm daily. **Map** p140 C4 ④②

In one of New York's most culturally diverse areas, this open-air market sells magnificent African crafts, textiles, hand-carved arts, ornate masks and clothing for men, women and children.

N

114 W 116th Street, between Malcolm X Boulevard (Lenox Avenue) & Adam Clayton Powell Jr Boulevard (Seventh Avenue) (1-212 961 1036/www. nharlemnewyork.com). Subway 2, 3 to 116th Street; A, C, E to 116th Street. **Open** 2-8pm Tue-Thur; noon-8pm Fri, Sat; noon-6pm Sun. **Map** p140 C4 ④③

Reflecting West Harlem's gentrification, this upscale boutique sells contemporary clothing, accessories and grooming products by a mix of emerging local talent and established designers. Good for unusual denim lines.

Nightlife

Apollo Theater

253 W 125th Street, between Adam Clayton Powell Jr Boulevard (Seventh Avenue) & Frederick Douglass Boulevard (Eighth Avenue) (1-212 531 5300/ www.apollotheater.org). Subway A, B, C, D, 1 to 125th Street. **Map** p140 C3 ④④

Visitors may think they know this venerable theatre from TV's *Showtime at the Apollo*. But as the saying goes, the small screen adds ten pounds: the city's home of R&B and soul is actually quite cosy. Known for launching the careers of Ella Fitzgerald and D'Angelo, the Apollo continues to mix veteran talents like Dianne Reeves with younger artists such as the Roots and Duffy.

Lenox Lounge

288 Malcolm X Boulevard (Lenox Avenue), between 124th & 125th Streets (1-212 427 0253/www.lenox lounge.com). Subway 2, 3 to 125th Street. **Open** noon-4am daily. **Map** p140 C3 ④⑤

This is where a street hustler named Malcolm worked before he found religion and added an X to his name. Now the famous Harlem lounge and jazz club welcomes a mix of old-school cats, unobtrusive booze hounds and tourists. Settle into the restored art deco bar at the front, or retire to the back, where Billie Holiday and John Coltrane once graced the stage.

Uptown Jazz Lounge at Minton's Playhouse

20 W 118th Street, between St Nicholas Avenue & Adam Clayton Powell Jr Boulevard (Seventh Avenue) (1-212 864 8346/www.uptownatmintons.com). Subway B, C to 116th Street. **Map** p140 C4 ④⑥

Few clubs in the city can boast as rich a history as Minton's, which Miles Davis once dubbed 'the black jazz capital of the world'. After being boarded up for more than 30 years, the club reopened in 2006 and now presents five house bands from Sunday to Thursday. On Saturdays, when it's more crowded, you can see guest acts, which have included the likes of percussionist Joe Chambers. A DJ is in the house on Friday nights.

NEW YORK BY AREA

Brooklyn

The Outer Boroughs

The Bronx

Sights & museums

Bronx Zoo/Wildlife Conservation Society

Bronx River Parkway, at Fordham Road (1-718 367 1010/www.bronx zoo.org). Subway 2, 5 to West Farms Square-East Tremont Avenue. **Open** *Apr-Oct* 10am-5pm Mon-Fri; 10am-5.30pm Sat, Sun. *Nov-Mar* 10am-4.30pm daily. **Admission** $15; $11-$13 reductions; pay what you wish Wed.

Home to more than 16,000 creatures, the zoo shuns cages in favour of indoor and outdoor environments that mimic the natural habitats of its mammals, birds and reptiles. Nearly 100 species, including monkeys, leopards and tapirs, live in the lush, steamy Jungle World, a re-creation of an Asian rainforest inside a 37,000sq ft building. The super-popular Congo Gorilla Forest has turned 6.5 acres into a dramatic Central African rainforest habitat. A glass-enclosed tunnel allows visitors to get close to the dozens of primate families here, including 26 majestic western lowland gorillas. For those who prefer felines, Tiger Mountain has six adult Siberian tigers, while the African Plains habitat is home to lions, giraffes and African wild dogs. In 2008 the zoo's Lion House was transformed into Madagascar!, devoted to exotic animals from the lush island nation. Lemurs, giant crocodiles, lovebirds, radiated tortoises and hissing cockroaches all live here.

New York Botanical Garden

Bronx River Parkway, at Fordham Road (1-718 817 8700/www.nybg. org). Subway B, D to Bedford Park Boulevard, then Bx26 bus to Garden gate; or Metro-North (Harlem Line local) from Grand Central Terminal to Botanical Garden. **Open** 10am-6pm Tue-Sun (see website for early closings

Brooklyn buzz: art

If the Manhattan art scene is starting to look too tame, there's a newer, grittier place to go: Bushwick. The majority of galleries here – almost all of them artist-run, and many dedicated at least in part to performance art – are near the Morgan Avenue stop on the L train. Many are open weekends only.

Bushwick's wealth of industrial buildings has attracted artists priced out of Williamsburg. As you emerge from the station, you notice the abundance of street art on the exterior of warehouses. So it's no surprise that many galleries here are devoted to street art. **Factory Fresh** (1053 Flushing Avenue, between Knickerbocker & Morgan Avenues, 1-917 682 6753, www.factoryfresh.net), run by artists Ali Ha and Ad Deville, formerly of the Orchard Street Art Gallery on the Lower East Side, displays their work and that of other artists. **Ad Hoc Art** (49 Bogart Street, between Moore & Seigel Streets, 1-718 366 2466, www.adhocart.org) features graffiti old-schoolers like Crash and Daze, and a younger generation of artists inspired by them. And the scene goes beyond storefront galleries to multi-purpose spaces. **Pocket Utopia** (1037 Flushing Avenue, between Morgan Avenue & Vandervoort Place, www.pocket utopia.com), run by collage artist Austin Thomas, is described as a 'relational exhibition, salon and social space'.

and exceptions). **Admission** $20; free-$18 reductions. *Grounds only* $6; free-$3 reductions; grounds free Wed, 10am-noon Sat.

The serene 250 acres of the New York Botanical Garden comprise 50 gardens and plant collections, including the Rockefeller Rose Garden, the Everett Children's Adventure Garden and the last 50 original acres of a forest that once covered all of New York City. In spring, the gardens are frothy with pastel blossoms, while autumn brings vivid foliage in the oak and maple groves. The Enid A Haupt Conservatory – the nation's largest greenhouse, built in 1902 – contains the World of Plants, a series of environ-mental galleries that takes you on an eco-tour through tropical rainforests, deserts and a palm-tree oasis.

Brooklyn

Sights & museums

Brooklyn Botanic Garden
1000 Washington Avenue, at Eastern Parkway, Prospect Heights (1-718 623 7200/www.bbg.org). Subway B, Q,

Brooklyn buzz: food

Brooklyn has a thriving eating out scene characterised by a dedication to local artisanal foods. One of the best areas in which to sample the community-oriented wares is BoCoCa – a real-estate agents' contraction for the three blurry-boundaried 'hoods of Boerum Hill, Cobble Hill and Carroll Gardens.

Hip Italian spot **Frankies 457 Spuntino** (457 Court Street, between Lucquer Street & 4th Place, Carroll Gardens, 1-718 403 0033) has a local focus that helped pave the way for like-minded restaurants when it opened in 2004.

Winner of *Time Out New York*'s Eat Out Readers' Choice award for best new Brooklyn restaurant in 2009, **Buttermilk Channel** (524 Court Street, at Huntington Street, Carroll Gardens, 1-718 852 8490) features many local foods. The seasonal American bistro has quickly become a go-to spot for comfort food innovations like duck meat loaf and one of the best sundaes around: pecan pie layered with organic butter-pecan ice-cream from nearby **Blue Marble** (420 Atlantic Avenue, between Bond & Nevins Streets, Boerum Hill, 1-718 858 1100).

There's also new life in Brooklyn's cocktail scene. Cobble Hill's **Clover Club** (210 Smith Street, between Baltic & Butler Streets, 1-718 855 7939) is a Victorian-style drinks parlour from Julie Reiner of the Flatiron Lounge (p116).

Franklin Avenue S to Prospect Park; 2, 3 to Eastern Parkway-Brooklyn Museum. **Open** *Mar-Oct* 8am-6pm Tue-Fri; 10am-6pm Sat, Sun. *Nov-Feb* 8am-4.30pm Tue-Fri; 10am-4.30pm Sat, Sun. **Admission** $8; free-$4 reductions; free Tue, 10am-noon Sat (except during special events).

This 52-acre haven of luscious greenery was founded in 1910. In April, when Sakura Matsuri, the annual Cherry Blossom Festival, takes place, prize buds and Japanese culture are in full bloom. The restored Eastern Parkway entrance and the Osborne Garden – an Italian-style formal garden – are also well worth a peek.

Brooklyn Bridge
Subway A, C to High Street; J, M, Z to Chambers Street; 4, 5, 6 to Brooklyn Bridge-City Hall.
Even if your trip to New York doesn't include a romp in the boroughs, it's worth walking to the centre of the Brooklyn Bridge along its wide, wood-planked promenade. Designed by German-born civil engineer John

Augustus Roebling, who died before it was completed, the bridge was constructed in response to the harsh winter of 1867 when the East River froze over, severing connection between Manhattan and what was then the nation's third most populous city. When it opened in 1883, the 5,989ft-long structure was the world's longest bridge, and the first in the world to use steel suspension cables. From it, you'll enjoy striking views of the Statue of Liberty and New York Harbor.

Brooklyn Museum

200 Eastern Parkway, at Washington Avenue, Prospect Heights (1-718 638 5000/www.brooklynmuseum.org). Subway 2, 3 to Eastern Parkway-Brooklyn Museum. **Open** 10am-5pm Wed-Fri; 11am-6pm Sat, Sun; 11am-11pm 1st Sat of mth (except Sept). **Admission** $8; free-$4 reductions; free 5-11pm 1st Sat of mth (except Sept).
Brooklyn's premier institution is a less crowded alternative to the bigger-name spaces in Manhattan. Among the museum's many assets is a rich,

4,000-piece Egyptian collection, which includes a gilded-ebony statue of Amenhotep III and, on the ceiling, a large-scale rendering of an ancient map of the cosmos, as well as a mummy preserved in its original coffin. Masterworks by Cézanne, Monet and Degas, part of an impressive European art collection, are displayed in the museum's recently renovated Beaux Arts Court. On the fifth floor, American paintings and sculptures include native son Thomas Cole's *The Pic-Nic* and Louis Rémy Mignot's *Niagara*. Don't miss the renowned Pacific Island and African galleries (this was the first American museum to display African objects as art).

Green-Wood Cemetery

Fifth Avenue, at 25th Street, Sunset Park (1-718 768 7300/www.green-wood.com). Subway M, R to 25th Street. **Open** 8am-5pm daily (call or check website for summer hours). **Admission** free.
A century ago, this site vied with Niagara Falls as New York State's

New York Botanical Garden p160

greatest tourist attraction. Filled with Victorian mausoleums, cherubs and gargoyles, Green-Wood is the resting place of some half-million New Yorkers, among them Jean-Michel Basquiat, Leonard Bernstein and Mae West. The spectacular, soaring arches of the main gate are carved from New Jersey brownstone, and the 1911 chapel was designed by Warren & Wetmore, the firm behind Grand Central Terminal. Battle Hill, the single highest point in Brooklyn offering prime Manhattan skyline views, is on cemetery grounds.

Queens

Sights & museums

Isamu Noguchi Garden Museum

9-01 33rd Road, between Vernon Boulevard & 10th Street, Astoria (1-718 204 7088/www.noguchi.org). Subway N, W to Broadway, then bus Q104 to 11th Street; 7 to Vernon Boulevard-Jackson Avenue, then Q103 bus to 10th Street. **Open** 10am-5pm Wed-Fri; 11am-6pm Sat, Sun. **Admission** $10; free-$5 reductions; pay what you wish 1st Fri of mth. No baby strollers. No credit cards.

The former studio of Japanese-American sculptor Isamu Noguchi (1904-88), who moved to Queens to be closer to the quarries that supplied the granite and marble for his works, this museum is a monument to the artist's exquisitely harmonious sensibility. Its 13 indoor galleries showcase his organic, undulating work in granite, marble, bronze and wood and move seamlessly into the adjoining gardens with fountains and small footpaths. Particularly intriguing is the room devoted to his akari works (light fixtures encased by inventive paper shades). A shuttle service from Manhattan ($5 each way) is available on weekends; call or see the website for more details.

P.S.1 Contemporary Art Center

22-25 Jackson Avenue, at 46th Avenue, Long Island City (1-718 784 2084/www.ps1.org). Subway E, V (V weekdays only) to 23rd Street-Ely Avenue; G to 21st Street-Jackson Avenue; 7 to 45th Road-Court House Square. **Open** noon-6pm

Isamu Noguchi Garden Museum

Brooklyn buzz: music

Pete's Candy Store

Both celebrated and mocked for its saturation of tattooed, guitar-case-carrying youth, Williamsburg has emerged as the city's rock mecca. The clearest indication of the scene's arrival was the debut of Northsix, a laid-back club that opened in 2001 on what was then a sleepy side street. Five years later, the block was swarming with bars. The club was bought by Bowery Presents, which turned it into **Music Hall of Williamsburg** (66 N 6th Street, between Kent & Wythe Avenues, 1-718 486 5400, www.williamsburgmusichall.com) – a carbon copy of its Manhattan namesake, Bowery Ballroom (p84). Its bookings mirror the original club too: touring rock bands (Of Montreal, King Khan & the Shrines) as well as local big shots (Crystal Stilts, Bishop Allen).

Smaller clubs such as **Union Pool** (484 Union Avenue, at Meeker Avenue, 1-718 609 0484) better capture the 'hood's vibe, however. This performance space is modest in size yet decorated in mock grandeur. Bookings are

consistently impressive, featuring talented local underdogs (Jeffrey Lewis, Larkin Grimm) and touring indies (Celebration, Noah and the Whale), and admission generally costs less than a night at the movies. Even so, it's more expensive than **Pete's Candy Store** (709 Lorimer Street, between Frost & Richardson Streets, 1-718 302 3770, www.petescandystore.com), a tiny bar that's always free. Bands are spotty – the room works best with eccentric acts and singer-songwriters – yet the space itself, in an old candy shop, is charming.

One notable venue – **Knitting Factory** (361 Metropolitan Avenue, at Havemeyer Street, 1-212 219 3006, www.knittingfactory.com) – had, at the time of writing, yet to open its doors. In its Downtown locations, the club presented a forum for edgy rock and jazz. That its new owners have chosen Williamsburg for its new space seems logical; whether they have arrived late to an ever-shifting party, though, remains to be seen.

Ballpark figures

What are the odds? In 2009 New York acquired not one, but two new baseball stadiums for its major league baseball teams. The plans date back to the Giuliani administration. In December 2001 the outgoing mayor disagreed with detractors who thought the money would be better spent elsewhere. However, the projects came up against unforeseen difficulties.

Already the most expensive stadium built in the US, the new **Yankee Stadium** (River Avenue, at 161st Street, Bronx, 1-718 293 6000, www.yankees.com) surpassed its estimated $1 billion budget by 50 per cent. As well as increased leg room, amenities have been bumped up considerably: there's a martini bar and a white-tablecloth steak house, and people in premium seats (costing up to $2,500) are treated to fare created by guest chefs from the likes of Le Cirque and the Spotted Pig. Yet in its first few weeks, these seats were noticeably empty (one night, only 64 of the 146 top-priced seats were occupied in the bottom of the second inning) – embarrassing given that both teams sacrificed affordable seating for more luxury boxes. Coming in at $800 million, the **Mets' Citi Field** (Flushing, Queens, 1-718 507 8499, www.mets.com) is designed to command a good view from any angle; upmarket fare includes 'A Taste of New York', a food-court sampler from restaurateur Danny Meyer.

Mon-Thur, Sun. **Admission** suggested donation $5; $2 reductions.
Housed in a distinctive Romanesque Revival building (a former public school), P.S.1 mounts cutting-edge shows and hosts an acclaimed international studio programme. Artwork crops up in every corner, from the stairwells to the roof. P.S.1 became an affiliate of MoMA in 1999, and sometimes stages collaborative exhibitions. Reflecting the museum's global outlook, it has focused in recent years on such luminaries as Janet Cardiff and Olafur Eliasson. It also hosts a popular Saturday-afternoon party, Warm Up, from July to mid September.

Queens Museum of Art

New York City Building, park entrance on 49th Avenue, at 111th Street, Flushing Meadows-Corona Park (1-718 592 9700/www.queens museum.org). Subway 7 to 111th Street, then walk south on 111th Street, turning left on to 49th Avenue; continue into the park & over Grand Central Parkway Bridge. **Open** *Sept-June* 10am-5pm Wed-Fri; noon-5pm Sat, Sun. *July, Aug* noon-6pm Wed, Thur, Sat, Sun; noon-8pm Fri. **Admission** suggested donation $5; $2.50 reductions. No credit cards.
In the grounds of the 1939 and 1964-5 World's Fairs, the QMA holds one of the city's most curious sights: the Panorama of the City of New York, a 9,335sq-ft scale model (one inch equals 100 feet) of all five boroughs, featuring 895,000 buildings. A modern lighting system mimics the arc of the sun as it passes over NYC, yet despite periodic updates of the early 1960s model, one part of the panorama remains decidedly untouched – the Twin Towers still stand proudly (albeit at one twelve-hundredth of their actual size). Elsewhere in the museum, contemporary and visiting exhibits have grown more bold and inventive in recent years, garnering increasing acclaim.

Essentials

Harlem Flophouse p182

Hotels

In April 2009 the *New York Times* reported that the average occupancy rate in the city's hotels – a buoyant market for more than a decade – had dropped to just 61.8 per cent in the first two months of the year. The good news: the average room rate had also dropped, from $232.25 to $196.30.

The situation stands to get worse for hoteliers – and better for bargain-hunting travellers – as 10,000 new hotel rooms are in the pipeline for 2009 and 2010 (although, of course, plans are subject to delays and cancellations). A recent surge in development hasn't just hit the expected neighbourhoods (Tribeca, Midtown), but also previously under-served areas like the Lower East Side and Brooklyn. Reflecting the second borough's growing attractions for visitors, it recently acquired its first boutique properties, **Hotel Le**

Bleu in Park Slope (www.hotelle bleu.com) and **Nu Hotel** (www. nuhotelbrooklyn.com) in downtown Brooklyn. The latter boasts eco-friendly features such as cork floors and organic sheets, and the coming year should see more green hotels, including the **NoMad** (www.the nomadhotel.com) in Midtown.

Luxury chains continue to branch out. Following the opening of **Thompson Lower East Side**, Thompson is further boosting its empire with **Smyth Tribeca** in winter 2009. The formerly Midtown-focused stable of Vikram Chatwal (Dream, p178, Night, Time and Stay) is cutting loose in the coming year. Not only is he converting a Stanford White-designed landmark building in his usual patch into the glamorous Chatwal, he's migrating south to the Meatpacking District with **Dream Downtown**. The area around Ground Zero is set to become a boom district as the World Trade Center site redevelopment nears completion. Stylish brands **W Hotels** (www.whotels.com) and Hyatt's **Andaz** are both set to open outposts here by early 2010.

Andaz isn't the only out-of-towner moving into Manhattan. Hip small chains the **Standard** (p175) and **Ace** (p177) have just opened New York properties. The latter has colonised an area that could emerge as the next hotel hotspot: the Flatiron District. And **Hotel Gansevoort** (p175) is opening an outpost on Park Avenue South in summer 2010.

Price wise

While there's no doubt that visitors are currently getting more bang for their buck (check hotel websites or call to ask about special deals), rates in the city are higher than in other parts of the country; reflecting this, $ in the listings represents rack rates of $150 or less. Locally based discount agency Quikbook (www.quikbook.com) has a good selection of the properties listed in this chapter, and more, on its website. When budgeting, don't forget to factor in the hefty 14.25 per cent tax, which includes city, state and hotel-room occupancy tax.

Downtown

Tribeca & Soho

Cosmopolitan

95 West Broadway, at Chambers Street (1-212 566 1900/1-888 895 9400/ www.cosmohotel.com). Subway A, C, 1, 2, 3 to Chambers Street. **$$**.
Despite the name, you won't find froufrou cocktails at this well-maintained hotel in two adjacent 1850s buildings – or even a bar in which to drink them. The Cosmopolitan is geared towards travellers with little

---

SHORTLIST

Best new
- Ace Hotel (p177)
- The Jane (p175)
- The Standard (p175)

Most luxurious
- Four Seasons (p181)
- Greenwich Hotel (p171)
- The Plaza (p180)

Hottest restaurants
- Hotel Elysée (p181)
- London NYC (p178)
- On the Ave Hotel (p182)
- 60 Thompson (p171)

Best spas
- Dream Hotel (p178)
- Waldorf-Astoria (p181)

Most historical
- Algonquin Hotel (p180)
- Hotel Chelsea (p176)
- Washington Square Hotel (p175)

Cheap and chic inns
- Chelsea Lodge (p175)
- East Village Bed & Coffee (p173)
- Harlem Flophouse (p182)

Best bargains for the location
- Abingdon Guest House (p175)
- Hotel Edison (p180)
- Off Soho Suites Hotel (p172)
- SoHotel (p171)

Best art
- Carlton Arms Hotel (p177)
- Gershwin Hotel (p177)
- Gramercy Park Hotel (p177)

Most glamorous scene
- Hotel Gansevoort (p175)
- Hotel on Rivington (p172)

ESSENTIALS

© 2004 Private

WHEREVER CRIMES AGAINST HUMANITY ARE PERPETRATED.

Across borders and above politics.
Against the most heinous abuses
and the most dangerous oppressors.
From conduct in wartime
to economic, social, and cultural rights.
Everywhere we go,
we build an unimpeachable case
for change and advocate action
at the highest levels.

HUMAN RIGHTS WATCH TYRANNY HAS A WITNESS

WWW.HRW.ORG

HUMA
RIGH
WATC

need for extras. Open continuously since the mid-19th century, it remains a tourist favourite for its address, clean rooms and reasonable rates.

Duane Street Hotel

130 Duane Street, at Church Street (1-212 964 4600/www.duanestreet hotel.com). Subway A, C, 1, 2, 3 to Chambers Street. **$$$**.

This boutique hotel opened in 2007 and, after a somewhat rocky start, seems to have got back on track with improved customer service and better soundproofing. The small, understated rooms are accented with a warm colour palette and dark mahogany floors, and feature plasma-screen TVs and slate-and-marble bathrooms with glass-enclosed, rain-style showers.

Greenwich Hotel

377 Greenwich Street, between Franklin & North Moore Streets (1-212 941 8900/www.thegreenwichhotel.com). Subway 1 to Franklin Street. **$$$$**.

Well-heeled travellers love Robert De Niro's lavish Tribeca bolthole, which opened to much fanfare in April 2008. It's so exclusive, there's no sign at the entrance. Even the more modest courtyard rooms have hardwood floors, plush sofas, walk-in showers and French doors that open on to the private patio. In the secluded subterranean Shibui Spa, lumber from a 250-year-old Kyoto farmhouse shelters the low-lit swimming pool.

Mercer

147 Mercer Street, at Prince Street (1-212 966 6060/1-888 918 6060/ www.mercerhotel.com). Subway N, R, W to Prince Street. **$$$$**.

Opened in 2001 by red-hot hotelier André Balazs, Soho's first luxury boutique hotel still has ample flourishes to keep it a notch above nearby competitors, which may be why celebs like Marc Jacobs and Mischa Barton favour it. The lobby, appointed with oversized white couches and bookshelves, acts as a bar,

library and lounge – exclusive to hotel guests. The loft-like rooms are large by New York standards and feature furniture by Christian Liagre and huge washrooms. The restaurant, Mercer Kitchen, serves Jean-Georges Vongerichten's stylish version of American cuisine.

60 Thompson

60 Thompson Street, between Broome & Spring Streets (1-212 431 0400/1-877 431 0400/www.60thompson.com). Subway C, E to Spring Street. **$$$$**.

The first of a growing luxury chain (see website for further NYC properties) has been luring chic jetsetters since it opened in 2001. A60, the exclusive guests-only rooftop bar, offers commanding city views. The modern rooms are dotted with pampering details like pure down duvets and pillows, and the acclaimed restaurant Kittichai serves a sumptuous spread of creative Thai cuisine beside a pool filled with floating orchids.

Chinatown, Little Italy & Nolita

SoHotel

341 Broome Street, between Bowery & Elizabeth Street (1-212 226 1482/ www.sohotel-ny.com). Subway J, M, Z to Bowery; 6 to Spring Street. **$$**.

In previous incarnations, this modest hotel at the nexus of Chinatown, Little Italy and Nolita hosted financier William Waldorf Astor and boxing legend Gentleman Jim Corbett, among other colourful guests. Today, the rooms are basic, but charming touches like large paintings, hardwood floors and vaulted ceilings place SoHotel a rung above similar establishments.

Lower East Side

Blue Moon

100 Orchard Street, between Broome & Delancey Streets (1-212 533 9080/ www.bluemoon-nyc.com). Subway F to Delancey Street. **$$**.

New York, London-style

The new, British-owned Crosby Street Hotel.

The city's boutique hoteliers had better prepare for a British invasion. Husband-and-wife team Tim and Kit Kemp are bringing their super-successful formula across the Atlantic. Due to open in September 2009, the 11-storey, warehouse-style **Crosby Street Hotel** (79 Crosby Street, between Prince & Spring Streets, 1-212 226 6400, www.crosbystreethotel.com) is rising in a former parking lot in Soho, presenting formidable competition to the Mercer (p171) around the corner. The couple's luxury group, Firmdale Hotels, comprises six properties in the English capital, the most high-profile of which are the Covent Garden Hotel, the Charlotte Street Hotel, the Soho Hotel and, the latest opening, the Haymarket Hotel. As design director, Kit Kemp masterminds all the interiors and, although each hotel has a different vibe, her signature style – a fresh take on classic English decor – is instantly recognisable.

Like its British cousins, Crosby Street will have a carefully selected art collection. It will also import the amenities that have made Firmdale a favourite with celebrities such as Kate Winslet, Daniel Day-Lewis and Scarlett Johansson: a guests-only drawing room as well as a public restaurant and bar, a slick, 100-seat screening room and a verdant garden.

This eight-storey, 22-room hotel housed in a former 19th-century tenement eschews chic modernism in favour of old-world charm. Owner Randy Settenbrino incorporated historic newspaper clippings, ads and photos he discovered during renovation into the decor, complementing original wood mouldings, art nouveau fixtures and wrought-iron beds. Some rooms offer views of the nearby Williamsburg Bridge.

Bowery Hotel
335 Bowery, at 3rd Street (1-212 505 9100/www.theboweryhotel.com). Subway B, D, F, V to Broadway-Lafayette Street; 6 to Bleecker Street. **$$$$**.
This fanciful boutique hotel, opened in 2007 by Eric Goode and Sean MacPherson (the team behind the Maritime and the Jane), is the capstone in the gentrification of the Bowery. Shunning minimalism, the duo created plush rooms that pair old-world touches (oriental rugs, wood-beamed ceilings, marble washstands) with floor-to-ceiling windows and modern amenities.

Hotel on Rivington
107 Rivington Street, between Essex & Ludlow Streets (1-212 475 2600/ www.hotelonrivington.com). Subway F to Delancey Street; J, M, Z to Delancey-Essex Streets. **$$$$**.
Floor-to-ceiling windows are a theme throughout this 20-storey palace: the second-floor lobby overlooks the storefronts of Rivington Street, and every chic but simple room has an unobstructed view. Even Thor, the eclectic restaurant now run by Stanton Social executive chef Jesi Solomon, has a 21ft glass ceiling. To make the most of the potential for exhibitionism, get your tresses tamed at the on-site Ricardo Rojas Salon before slipping into a banquette at 105 Riv, the street-level bar.

Off Soho Suites Hotel
11 Rivington Street, between Bowery & Chrystie Street (1-212 979 9808/1-800

Duane Street Hotel p171

633 7646/www.offsoho.com). Subway B, D to Grand Street; F, V to Lower East Side-Second Avenue; J, M, Z to Bowery. **$$**.
These no-frills suites have become a great deal more popular since the Lower East Side emerged as a dining and nightlife hotspot. The rates are decent value for the now-thriving location, and the spartan but spacious rooms can accommodate either two or four guests (the latter have an added sleeper sofa). Rooms have kitchenettes and there's a coin-operated laundry room.

East Village

East Village Bed & Coffee
110 Avenue C, between 7th & 8th Streets (1-212 533 4175/www.bed andcoffee.com). Subway F, V to Lower East Side-Second Avenue; L to First Avenue. **$**.
Each of the nine guest rooms has a unique theme – for example, the 'Black & White Room' or the 'Treehouse' (not as outlandish as it sounds, with an ivory and olive colour scheme and animal-print linens). Owner Anne Edris encourages guests to mingle in the communal areas, which include

fully equipped kitchens, three loft-like living rooms and a private garden (bathrooms are also shared).

Hotel 17
225 E 17th Street, between Second & Third Avenues (1-212 475 2845/ www.hotel17ny.com). Subway L to Third Avenue; N, Q, R, W, 4, 5, 6 to 14th Street-Union Square. **$-$$**.
Shabby chic is the best way to describe this hotel a few blocks from Union Square. Rooms are a study in contrast: antique dressers are paired with paisley bedspreads and vintage wallpaper. In most cases, bathrooms are shared among two to four rooms, but they're kept immaculately clean. Over the years, the building has been featured in numerous films – including Woody Allen's *Manhattan Murder Mystery* – and has put up Madonna and, more recently, transgender Downtown diva Amanda Lepore.

St Marks Hotel
2 St Marks Place, at Third Avenue (1-212 674 0100/www.stmarkshotel. net). Subway 6 to Astor Place. **$**.
Nestled among the tattoo parlours and cheap eateries of St Marks Place, this

small hotel received a much-needed facelift in 2007; its modest rooms, which have double beds and private baths, are now bright, clean and understated and offer Wi-Fi and flatscreen TVs. Note: there is no elevator.

Greenwich Village

Washington Square Hotel

103 Waverly Place, between MacDougal Street & Sixth Avenue (1-212 777 9515/ 1-800 222 0418/www.washington squarehotel.com). Subway A, B, C, D, E, F, V to W 4th Street. **$$**.
Occupying an enviable spot, this hotel has lodged writers and artists for more than a century. Bob Dylan and Joan Baez lived here back when they sang for change in nearby Washington Square Park. The deluxe rooms come with art deco furnishings and leather headboards, and the cosy bar-lounge serves afternoon tea and light fare.

West Village & Meatpacking District

Abingdon Guest House

21 Eighth Avenue, between Jane & W 12th Streets (1-212 243 5384/ www.abingdonguesthouse.com). Subway A, C, E to 14th Street; L to Eighth Avenue. **$$**.
A charming option for those who want to be close to the Meatpacking District but can't afford the Gansevoort (below). Rooms in the converted townhouse are done up in plush fabrics and antique furnishings (many with four-posters) and have private baths.

Hotel Gansevoort

18 Ninth Avenue, at 13th Street (1-212 206 6700/1-877 426 7386/www.hotel gansevoort.com). Subway A, C, E to 14th Street; L to Eighth Avenue. **$$$$**.
This six-year-old contemporary luxury property still gets high marks for style. Enter through the world's tallest revolving door into a lobby featuring four 18ft light boxes that change hue throughout

the evening. The sleek rooms offer a more muted colour scheme, but are fitted with plush beds, photography by local artists and roomy marble bathrooms. Perks include the rooftop pool (with underwater music) and bar, Jeffrey Chodorow's glossy Japanese eaterie Ono and a basement spa.

The Jane

NEW *113 Jane Street, at West Street (1-212 924 6700/www.thejanenyc.com). Subway A, C, E to 14th Street; L to Eighth Avenue.* **$-$$**.
See box p179.

The Standard

NEW *848 Washington Street, at 13th Street (1-212 645 4646/www.standard hotel.com). Subway A, C, E to 14th Street; L to Eighth Avenue.* **$$$**.
André Balazs's lauded West Coast mini-chain has arrived in New York. Straddling the High Line (see box p121), the retro 18-storey structure has been configured to give each of the 337 rooms an exhilarating view. Quarters are compact (from 230sq ft), but floor-to-ceiling windows, curving tambour wood panelling (think old-fashioned roll-top desks) and 'peekaboo' bathrooms with Japanese-style tubs or huge showerheads give a sense of space. Eating and drinking options (due to open by publication of this guide) include a chop house, beer garden and a top-floor bar with jacuzzi and 180-degree views.

Midtown

Chelsea

Chelsea Lodge

318 W 20th Street, between Eighth & Ninth Avenues (1-212 243 4499/ www.chelsealodge.com). Subway C, E to 23rd Street. **$**.
If Martha Stewart decorated a log cabin, it would probably end up looking something like this inn, housed in a landmark brownstone just blocks

ESSENTIALS

The Standard p175

from the Chelsea gallery district. All of the rooms (including the four suites down the block at 334 West 20th Street) come with TVs, showers and air-conditioning. Although most are fairly small, the accommodation is so charming that it books up quickly. Note: there's no sign outside.

Hotel Chelsea (aka Chelsea Hotel)

222 W 23rd Street, between Seventh & Eighth Avenues (1-212 243 3700/ www.hotelchelsea.com). Subway C, E, 1 to 23rd Street. **$$**.

Built in 1884, the Chelsea has an infamous past: writer (and noted sot) Dylan Thomas slipped into a fatal coma here after imbibing at the White Horse Tavern in 1953, *Lost Weekend* author Charles R Jackson committed suicide in his room in 1968, and Nancy Spungen was allegedly murdered in Room 100 by her Sex Pistol boyfriend Sid Vicious a decade later. Rooms are generally large with high ceilings, but certain amenities, such as flatscreen TVs and marble fireplaces, vary. Make no mistake, you're paying for the hotel's past – the rooms aren't exactly gleaming.

Inn on 23rd Street

131 W 23rd Street, between Sixth & Seventh Avenues (1-212 463 0330/ www.innon23rd.com). Subway F, V, 1 to 23rd Street. **$$**.

This Chelsea gem, a renovated 19th-century townhouse, offers the charm of a traditional bed and breakfast with enhanced amenities (a lift, private bathrooms, white-noise machines). Owners and innkeepers Annette and Barry Fisherman have styled each of the 14 bedrooms with a unique theme, such as Maritime or 1940s.

Maritime Hotel

363 W 16th Street, between Eighth & Ninth Avenues (1-212 242 4300/ www.themaritimehotel.com). Subway A, C, E to 14th Street; L to Eighth Avenue. **$$$**.

Taking inspiration from the building's former life as the headquarters of the Maritime Union, in 2002 owners Eric Goode and Sean MacPherson created the Maritime Hotel by blending the look of a luxury yacht with a chic 1960s aesthetic. Each of the teak-panelled rooms, modelled after ship's cabins, has one large porthole window.

Numerous on-site eating and drinking options incude a Japanese restaurant, an Italian trattoria and a rooftop bar.

Flatiron District & Union Square

Ace Hotel

`NEW` *1185 Broadway, between 28th & 29th Streets (1-212 679 2222/ www.acehotel.com/newyork). Subway N, R, W to 28th Street.* **$$-$$$$**.
At the New York outpost of the Seattle-born hip-hotel chain, choose from six room types based on size: Cheap or Bunk if you're on a budget; moderately priced Standard or Deluxe; and Super Deluxe or Loft if you want more space and perks. The laid-back comfort factor is high in all rooms with nice details like Pendleton blankets and hoodie robes. The buzzed-about restaurant is from the team behind the Spotted Pig (p99). See also box p179.

Gershwin Hotel

7 E 27th Street, between Fifth & Madison Avenues (1-212 545 8000/ www.gershwinhotel.com). Subway N, R, W, 6 to 28th Street. **$**.
Works by Lichtenstein line the hallways, and an original Warhol soup can painting hangs in the lobby of this Pop Art-themed budget hotel. Rooms are less than pristine – especially the hostel-style dorms – but the rates are extremely reasonable for a location just off Fifth Avenue.

Gramercy Park & Murray Hill

Carlton Arms Hotel

160 E 25th Street, at Third Avenue (1-212 679 0680/www.carltonarms. com). Subway 6 to 23rd Street. **$**.
The Carlton Arms Art Project started in the late 1970s, when a small group of creative types brought fresh paint and new ideas to a run-down shelter. Today, the site is a bohemian backpackers' paradise and a live-in gallery: every room,

bathroom and hallway is festooned with outré artwork. Most guests share baths; tack on $15 for a private toilet.

Gramercy Park Hotel

2 Lexington Avenue, at 21st Street (1-212 475 4320/www.gramercypark hotel.com). Subway 6 to 23rd Street. **$$$$**.
Revamped by Ian Schrager in 2006, this 1924 gem has hosted everyone from Humphrey Bogart to David Bowie. The lobby retains the boho spirit with ruby-red banquettes, enormous Venetian chandelier and fireplace, and artwork from Cy Twombly, Andy Warhol and Julian Schnabel (the hotel's art director). The eclectic elegance continues in the spacious, richly hued rooms, which include tapestry-covered chairs, hand-tufted rugs and mahogany drinking cabinets. Perks abound, but the best is the key to exclusive Gramercy Park.

Marcel at Gramercy

201 E 24th Street, at Third Avenue (1-212 696 3800/www.nychotels.com). Subway 6 to 23rd Street. **$$$**.
Revamped in early 2008, this hotel has a hip aesthetic that extends from the lobby – with its marble concierge desk, sprawling leather banquette and in-house library – to the medium-size rooms in a sleek black and pewter palette, with rain-head showers and Frette linens. The hotel's new Bar Milano – run by chefs Eric Kleinman and Steve Connaughton (of 'inoteca and Lupa fame, respectively) – serves inventive takes on classic Italian fare.

Herald Square & Garment District

Americana Inn

69 W 38th Street, at Sixth Avenue (1-212 840 6700/www.newyorkhotel.com). Subway B, D, F, N, Q, R, V, W to 34th Street-Herald Square; B, D, F, V to 42nd Street. **$**.
The signage is discreet and you'll have to ring the doorbell to enter. What the

Americana might lack in ambience (with its linoleum floors and fluorescent lighting), it makes up for in location (a rhinestone's throw from the Theater District) and reasonable prices. And although all bathrooms are shared, the rooms are equipped with mini-sinks and large walk-in closets.

Hotel Pennsylvania

401 Seventh Avenue, between 32nd & 33rd Streets (1-212 736 5000/1-800 223 8585/www.hotelpenn.com). Subway A, C, E, 1, 2, 3 to 34th Street-Penn Station. **$$**.

One of the city's largest and most popular hotels, the Pennsylvania offers reasonable rates and a convenient location (directly opposite Penn Station, and mere blocks from Macy's and the Empire State Building). After a $7 million renovation in 2008, the rooms are still fairly modest, but offer pleasant respite from the hubbub outside. The host hotel for the annual Westminster Kennel Club Dog Show, the Penn is also happy to accommodate pets.

Theater District & Hell's Kitchen

Big Apple Hostel

119 West 45th Street, between Sixth & Seventh Avenues (1-212 302 2603/ www.bigapplehostel.com). Subway B, D, F, V to 42nd Street-Bryant Park; N, Q, R, S, W, 1, 2, 3, 7 to 42nd Street-Times Square. **$**.

It may be lacking in frills, but the Big Apple's dorms are spotless and cheap for the location, steps from the Theater District. If you want to get away from the masses, though, you can take refuge in the breezy back patio. Linens are provided, but remember to pack a towel.

Dream Hotel

210 W 55th Street, between Broadway & Seventh Avenue (1-212 247 2000/ 1-866 437 3266/www.dreamny.com). Subway N, Q, R, W to 57th Street. **$$$**.

Vikram Chatwal – the mastermind behind the nearby colour-themed Time Hotel (www.thetimeny.com), the Night Hotel (www.nighthotelny.com) and the new Stay (www.stayhotelny.com) – created this luxury lodge with a trippy slumberland theme. In the lobby, a crystal boat dangles from the ceiling, and an enormous gold statue of Catherine the Great stands guard. Rooms are more streamlined, with white walls, satin headboards and an ethereal blue backlight that glows under the bed. On-site facilities include Italian restaurant Serafina, with a Fellini-esque interior crafted by David Rockwell, rooftop bar Ava, and an Ayurvedic spa conceived by New Age guru Deepak Chopra.

414 Hotel

414 W 46th Street, between Ninth & Tenth Avenues (1-212 399 0006/ www.414hotel.com). Subway A, C, E to 42nd Street-Port Authority. **$$**.

This small hotel's highly affordable rates and off-the-beaten-track Hell's Kitchen location make it feel like a secret you've been lucky to stumble upon. The immaculate rooms are tastefully appointed with suede headboards and framed black-and-white photos of the city. There's a fireplace and shared computer in the lobby, and many rooms face the attractive central courtyard.

Hotel Edison

228 W 47th Street, at Broadway (1-212 840 5000/1-800 637 7070/ www.edisonhotelnyc.com). Subway N, R, W to 49th Street; 1 to 50th Street. **$$**.

Theatre-lovers – many of the blue-haired variety – flock to this 1931 art deco hotel for its affordable rates and proximity to the Broadway show palaces. The rooms are of a standard size but decidedly spruce. Café Edison, a classic diner just off the lobby, is a longtime favourite with Broadway actors and their fans – Neil Simon was so taken with it, he immortalised it in one of his plays.

Vintage vibe, vintage rates

Ace

In the sconce-lit lobby, a check-in clerk produces your key from the bank of cubbyholes, and a red-uniformed bellman takes you up in a manually operated elevator. But this is no relic of a bygone era. Welcome to the **Jane** (p175), the latest accommodation from hot hoteliers Eric Goode and Sean MacPherson of the Bowery and the Maritime. The difference is, they're now charging under $100 a night.

Opened in 1907 as the American Seaman's Friend Society Sailors Home, the 14-storey landmark was a residential hotel when the duo took it over (some long-term residents remain). Panelled, 50-square-foot single rooms were inspired by old train compartments – with iPod docks and flatscreen TVs. Doubles are also available.

Inspiration came from various celluloid sources, including *Barton Fink*'s Hotel Earle for the lobby. The 'ballroom', decorated with mismatched chairs, oriental rugs and a fireplace topped with a stuffed ram, evokes an eccentric mansion. 'I want it to feel intensely residential and slightly

quirky, not like a typical corporate hotel,' says Sean MacPherson. Although he ackowledges an element of escapism in the decor, the main goal was to be true to the building's past.

The owners of the **Ace** (p177), formerly the 1904 Hotel Breslin, wanted to create the feel of staying with plugged-in friends. They enlisted designers Stephen Alesch and Robin Standefer of Roman & Williams, who have combined custom-made furnishings with pieces from different periods to interesting effect. Double rooms start from $169; some feature old-school turntables, retro Smeg fridges, even Epiphone guitars. In the lobby, where 1970s seating mingles with industrial salvage, the bar is housed in a panelled library salvaged from a Madison Avenue apartment, and there's a collection of New York-centric books. 'We wanted there to be a real sense of comfort,' says Standefer. 'I hope people do put their legs on the furniture and grab a book from the library and hang out.'

London NYC

151 W 54th Street, between Sixth & Seventh Avenues (1-866 690 2029/ www.thelondonnyc.com). Subway B, D, E to Seventh Avenue. **$$$**.

Formerly the Rihga Royal Hotel, this 54-storey high-rise was completely overhauled in a contemporary English style (by David Collins, the designer behind some of London's most fashionable bars and restaurants) and re-opened as the London NYC in early 2007. Space is the biggest luxury here: the 500sq ft London Suites offer living quarters and bedrooms divided by mirrored French doors. Appropriately, the London houses two eateries from Britain's favourite foul-mouthed chef: Gordon Ramsay at the London and the less formal (and less expensive) Maze.

Fifth Avenue & around

Algonquin Hotel

59 W 44th Street, between Fifth & Sixth Avenues (1-212 840 6800/ www.thealgonquin.net). Subway B, D, F, V to 42nd Street-Bryant Park; 7 to Fifth Avenue. **$$$**.

This 1902 landmark hotel has a strong literary legacy; Alexander Woollcott and Dorothy Parker swapped bon mots in the famous Round Table Room). Drinks are served in the eclectic lobby, decked out with upholstered chairs, antique lamps and paintings of Jazz Age greats. Although modern amenities like flatscreen TVs and free Wi-Fi are standard, there's a strong sense of old New York in the rooms furnished with dark mahogany dressers and intricately patterned carpets and bedspreads.

The Plaza

768 Fifth Avenue, at Central Park South (1-212 759 3000/1-800 759 3000/www.fairmont.com/theplaza). Subway N, R, W to Fifth Avenue-59th Street. **$$$$**.

This 1907 French Renaissance-style landmark building re-opened in spring 2008 following a two-year, $400 million renovation. Although 152 rooms were converted into private condo units, guests can still check into one of 282 quarters complete with Louis XV-inspired furnishings and white-glove butler service. The opulent vibe extends into the bathrooms, which feature 24-carat gold-plated sinks. The public spaces – the Palm Court restaurant, the restored Oak Room and Oak Bar, and

Library Hotel

Grand Ballroom (the setting of Truman Capote's famed Black and White Ball in 1966) – have been designated as landmarks and preserved for the public.

Midtown East

Four Seasons

57 E 57th Street, between Madison & Park Avenues (1-212 758 5700/1-800 332 3442/www.fourseasons.com/newyorkfs). Subway N, R, W to Lexington Avenue-59th Street; 4, 5, 6 to 59th Street. **$$$$**.
One of New York's most opulent hotels, the Four Seasons hasn't slipped a notch in its two decades in business. Everybody who's anybody, from music-industry executives to politicians, continues to stay here. Renowned architect IM Pei came out of retirement to craft its sharp geometric look (in neutral cream and honey tones), and the rooms – which include deep-soak tubs and terraces – are among the largest in the city. At 52 storeys, the Four Seasons is New York's tallest hotel, and from the higher floors the views are superb.

Hotel Elysée

60 E 54th Street, between Madison & Park Avenues (1-212 753 1066/www.elyseehotel.com). Subway E, V to Lexington Avenue-53rd Street; 6 to 51st Street. **$$$**.
The Elysée is a well-preserved piece of New York's Jazz Age: quarters are appointed with a touch of romance (period fabrics, antique furniture), and some rooms have coloured-glass conservatories and terraces. It's popular with publishers and literary types, and its landmark Monkey Bar has renewed cachet since it was taken over by *Vanity Fair* editor Graydon Carter.

Library Hotel

299 Madison Avenue, at 41st Street (1-212 983 4500/www.libraryhotel.com). Subway S, 4, 5, 6, 7 to 42nd Street-Grand Central; 7 to Fifth Avenue. **$$$**.
Even before you enter this literary-themed boutique hotel, you'll see quotations from famous authors inscribed in the pavement. The books, and the rooms they occupy, are organised according to the Dewey decimal system: each of the hotel's ten floors is allocated one of the ten categories of the DDC (Literature, Philosophy, The Arts, etc), and each room contains a collection of books and artwork pertaining to a subject within its category (Botany, Fairy Tales and Political Science, to name a few). The hotel has some lovely public spaces, including Bookmarks Rooftop Lounge & Terrace (p136).

Pod Hotel

230 E 51st Street, at Third Avenue (1-212 355 0300/www.thepodhotel.com). Subway E to Lexington Avenue-53rd; 6 to 51st Street. **$$**.
As its name suggests, the rooms in this minimalist bolthole, opened in 2007 by the Mercer's owners, are small-scale. IKEA-style rooms are equipped with iPod stations, LCD-screen TVs and free Wi-Fi. A third of them have shared bathrooms. The outdoor Pod Café serves treats from Balthazar Bakery.

Waldorf-Astoria

301 Park Avenue, at 50th Street (1-212 355 3000/1-800 925 3673/www.waldorf.com). Subway E, V to Lexington Avenue-53rd; 6 to 51st Street. **$$$**.
First built in 1893, the original Waldorf-Astoria was the city's largest hotel before it was demolished to make way for the Empire State Building. The current art deco Waldorf opened in 1931 and now has protected status; past guests include a long list of US presidents. The rooms, with wingback chairs, rich colours and layered fabrics, feel as if they were decorated by Upper East Side socialites of yore. Those socialites would feel right at home at the exclusive new Guerlain Spa. Note that you won't be allowed in if you're wearing a baseball cap or ripped jeans.

Upper East Side

Wales Hotel

*1295 Madison Avenue, at 92nd Street
(1-212 876 6000/www.waleshotel.com).
Subway 4, 5, 6 to 86th Street; 6 to 96th
Street.* **$$$**.

Purpose-built as a hotel in the early
1900s, the ten-storey Wales is a comfort-
able choice for a culture jaunt or a posh
shopping spree. Standard double rooms
are small, but high ceilings, large win-
dows and an unfussy contemporary-
classic style prevent them from seeming
cramped. At the time of writing, the
hotel was undergoing a rolling renova-
tion; most quarters had already been
redecorated with designer wallpaper,
sleek new bathrooms and HD TVs. The
roof terrace offers Central Park views.

Upper West Side

Hotel Belleclaire

*250 W 77th Street, at Broadway
(1-212 362 7700/www.hotelbelleclaire.
com). Subway 1 to 79th Street.* **$$**.

Housed in a landmark building, the
sleek Belleclaire is a steal for savvy travellers. The recently renovated rooms
feature goose-down comforters, padded
headboards and mod lighting fixtures.
Each room is equipped with a fridge –
perfect for chilling your protein shake
while hitting the modern fitness centre.

Jazz on the Park Hostel

*36 W 106th Street, between Central
Park West & Manhattan Avenue (1-
212 932 1600/www.jazzhostels.com).
Subway B, C to 103rd Street.* **$**.

One of the city's trendiest hostels, with
a lounge kitted out like a space-age
techno club, with a piano and pool table.
But some visitors have been known to
complain about the service, so be sure to
double-check your room type and check-
in date before you arrive. In summer, the
back patio hosts a weekly barbecue for
guests. Linens, towels and continental

breakfast are complimentary. Visit the
website for the hostel's other locations.

Marrakech

*2688 Broadway, at 103rd Street
(1-212 222 2954/www.marrakechhotel
nyc.com). Subway 1 to 103rd Street.* **$**.

Nightclub and restaurant designer
Lionel Ohayon (Crobar, Koi) was
enlisted to turn this Upper West Side
accommodation into a Manhattan take
on Morocco. Rooms are warm-toned,
with diffused lighting and North African
decorative touches such as colourful
embroidered cushions. However, frills
are limited and there's no elevator.

On the Ave Hotel

*222 W 77th Street, between Broadway
& Amsterdam Avenue (1-212 362 1100/
1-800 497 6028/www.ontheave-nyc.
com). Subway 1 to 79th Street.* **$$$**.

Given the affluent area, it's hardly sur-
prising that On the Ave's rooms are
stylish (industrial-style bathroom sinks,
ergonomic Herman Miller chairs).
Penthouse suites have fantastic views
of Central Park, and all guests have
access to the verdant Adirondack bal-
cony on the 16th floor. The hotel has two
new eateries worth checking out: Fatty
Crab (p152) and West Branch, the latest
outing from celebrity chef Tom Valenti.

Harlem

Harlem Flophouse

*242 W 123rd Street, between Adam
Clayton Powell Jr Boulevard (Seventh
Avenue) & Frederick Douglass
Boulevard (1-212 662 0678/www.
harlemflophouse.com). Subway A,
B, C, D to 125th Street.* **$**.

The dark-wood interior, moody light-
ing and lilting jazz make Rene Calvo's
Harlem inn feel more like a 1930s
speakeasy than a 21st-century B&B.
The airy suites, named for Harlem
Renaissance figures such as Chester
Himes and Cozy Cole, have restored
tin ceilings, chandeliers and working
sinks in antique cabinets.

Getting Around

Airports

John F Kennedy International Airport

1-718 244 4444/www.panynj.gov.

At $2.25, the bus and subway link from JFK is dirt cheap, but it can take up to two hours to get to Manhattan. At the airport, look for the yellow shuttle bus to the Howard Beach station (free), then take the A train to Manhattan. If you don't mind paying a little more, JFK's AirTrain offers faster service between all eight terminals and the A, E, J and Z subway lines, as well as the Long Island Rail Road, for $5. For more information, see www.airtrainjfk.com.

Private bus and van services are a good compromise between value and convenience. New York Airport Service (1-212 875 8200, www.ny airportservice.com) runs frequently between Manhattan and JFK (one way $15, round trip $27) from early morning to late night, with stops near Grand Central Terminal (Park Avenue, between 41st & 42nd Streets), near Penn Station (33rd Street, at Seventh Avenue), at the Port Authority Bus Terminal and outside a number of Midtown hotels (for an extra charge). Buses also run from JFK to LaGuardia (one way $13). SuperShuttle (1-212 209 7000, 1-800 258 3826, www.supershuttle.com) offers door-to-door service between NYC and the three major airports, but you'll need to allow extra time as vans will make multiple stops to pick up or drop off other passengers. Fares vary according to location, but it's around $21 one way or $40 round trip to/from Midtown.

A yellow cab from JFK to Manhattan will charge a flat $45 fare, plus toll (usually $4) and tip (around $7 if service is fine). The fare from Manhattan to JFK is metered, but it will be about the same price.

LaGuardia Airport

1-718 533 3400/www.panynj.gov.

Seasoned New Yorkers take the M60 bus ($2.25), which runs between the airport and 106th Street at Broadway. The ride takes 40-60mins (depending on traffic) from 4.30am to 1.30am daily. The route crosses Manhattan at 125th Street in Harlem. Get off at Lexington Avenue for the 4, 5 and 6 trains; at Malcolm X Boulevard (Lenox Avenue) for the 2 and 3; or at St Nicholas Avenue for the A, B, C and D trains. You can also disembark on Broadway at 116th or 110th Street for the 1 and 9 trains.

Less time-consuming options are New York Airport Service private buses (1-212 875 8200, www.nyairportservice.com), which run frequently between Manhattan and LaGuardia (one way $12, round trip $21), and SuperShuttle (see John F Kennedy International Airport). Taxis and car services charge about $30, plus toll and tip.

Newark Liberty International Airport

1-973 961 6000/
www.newarkairport.com.

Newark has good mass transit access to New York City. The best bet is a 40min, $15 trip offered by New Jersey Transit to or from Penn Station. The airport's monorail, AirTrain Newark (www.airtrainnewark.com), connects to both the NJ Transit and Amtrak train systems. Bus services operated by Coach USA (1-877 894 9155, www.coachusa.com) run between Newark and Manhattan, stopping outside Grand Central Terminal (p135), and at Port Authority (one way $15, round trip $25); buses leave every 15-30mins. SuperShuttle (see John F Kennedy International Airport) is another option. A car or taxi will run at about $60, plus toll and tip.

Arriving by bus

Port Authority Bus Terminal

625 Eighth Avenue, between 40th & 42nd Streets, Garment District (1-212 564 8484/www.panynj.gov). Subway A, C, E to 42nd Street-Port Authority.

Most out-of-town buses come and go from Port Authority. Greyhound (1-800 231 2222, www.greyhound.com) offers long-distance travel to destinations across North America. New Jersey Transit (1-800 772 2222, www.njtransit. com) runs a service to nearly everywhere in the Garden State and parts of New York State. Finally, Peter Pan (1-800 343 9999, www.peterpanbus.com) runs services to cities across the Northeast.

Arriving by train

Grand Central Terminal

From 42nd to 44th Streets, between Vanderbilt & Lexington Avenues, Midtown East. Subway S, 4, 5, 6, 7 to 42nd Street-Grand Central.

Grand Central is home to Metro-North, which runs trains to more than 100 stations in New York State and Connecticut.

Penn Station

31st to 33rd Streets, between Seventh & Eighth Avenues, Garment District. Subway A, C, E, 1, 2, 3 to 34th Street-Penn Station.

The national rail service, Amtrak (www.amtrak.com), departs from this terminal, as well as Long Island Rail Road and New Jersey Transit trains.

Public transport

Metropolitan Transportation Authority (MTA)

Travel information 1-718 330 1234/ updates 1-718 243 7777/www.mta.info.

The MTA runs the subway and bus lines, as well as services to points outside Manhattan. News of service interruptions and MTA maps are on its website.

Be warned: backpacks and handbags may be subject to random searches.

Fares & tickets

The standard fare across the subway and bus network is $2.25. Although you can pay cash on buses, you'll need a MetroCard to enter the subway system. You can buy one from booths or vending machines in the stations, from tourist information centres and many hotels. Free transfers between the subway and buses are available only with a MetroCard. Up to four people can use a pay-per-use MetroCard; the best deal is to load up a card with a dozen or more rides to capitalise on the 15 per cent discount.

However, if you're planning to use the subway or buses often, an unlimited-ride MetroCard is great value. These cards are offered in four denominations, available at station vending machines but not at booths: a single-day Fun Pass ($8.25), a seven-day pass ($27), a 14-day pass ($51.50) and a 30-day pass ($89). All are good for unlimited rides, but you can't share a card with your travel companions.

When you swipe an unlimited-ride MetroCard, if the message comes up to swipe again, make sure you do so at that turnstile, or it may not work for another 17 minutes (a safeguard to prevent card-sharing). With a pay-per-use card, if you try another turnstile, you could end up being charged twice.

Buses

White and blue MTA buses are fine if you're not in a hurry and are also useful for travelling cross-town. They have a digital destination sign on the front, along with a route number preceded by a letter (M for Manhattan). Maps are posted on

ESSENTIALS

most buses and at all subway stations; they're also available from NYC Information Center (p189). The Manhattan bus map is reprinted on the back flap of this guide. All local buses are equipped with wheelchair lifts. The $2.25 fare is payable with a MetroCard (see Fares & tickets) or exact change (coins only; no pennies). MetroCards allow for an automatic transfer from bus to bus, and between bus and subway. If you pay cash, and you're travelling uptown or downtown and want to go crosstown (or vice versa), ask the driver for a transfer when you get on – you'll be given a ticket for use on the second leg of your journey, valid for two hours. MTA's express buses usually head to the outer boroughs for a $5.50 fare.

Subway

Far cleaner and safer than it was 20 years ago, the city's subway system is one of the world's largest and cheapest, even with recent increases bringing the flat fare up to $2.25. Trains run around the clock; however, with sparse service and fewer riders at night, it's advisable to take a cab after 11pm.

The most current subway maps are reprinted on the back flap of this guide; you can also ask at MTA service booths for a free copy. Changes to schedules can occur at short notice, so pay attention to the posters on subway station walls and announcements you may hear in trains and on subway platforms.

Trains are identified by letters or numbers, colour-coded according to the line on which they run. Stations are most often named after the street on which they're located.

Entrances are marked with a green globe (open 24 hours) or a red globe (limited hours). Many stations have separate entrances for uptown and downtown platforms – look

before you pay. Local trains stop at every station on the line; express trains stop at major stations only.

Train services

The following commuter trains service NY's hinterland.
Long Island Rail Road *1-718 217 5477/www.lirr.org.* Provides rail services from Penn Station, Brooklyn and Queens.
Metro-North *1-212 532 4900/ 1-800 638 7646/www.mnr.org.* Commuter trains service towns north of Manhattan and leave from Grand Central Terminal.
New Jersey Transit *1-973 275 5555/www.njtransit.com.* Service from Penn Station reaches most of New Jersey, some points in New York State and Philadelphia.
PATH Trains *1-800 234 7284/ www.pathrail.com.* PATH (Port Authority Trans-Hudson) trains run from six stations in Manhattan to various places across the Hudson in New Jersey, including Hoboken, Jersey City and Newark. The 24-hour service is automated; entry costs $1.75 (change or bills). Manhattan PATH stations are marked on the subway map.

Taxis & car services

Yellow cabs are rarely in short supply, except at rush hour and in nasty weather. If the centre light atop the taxi is lit, the cab is available and should stop if you flag it down. Get in and then tell the driver where you're going. (New Yorkers generally give cross-streets instead of addresses.) By law, taxis cannot refuse to take you anywhere inside the five boroughs or to New York airports. Use only yellow medallion (licensed) cabs; avoid unregulated gypsy cabs.

Taxis will carry up to four passengers for the same price: $2.50 plus 40¢ per fifth of a mile, with an extra 50¢ charge from 8pm to 6am and a $1 surcharge during rush hour (4-8pm Mon-Fri). Cabbies rarely allow more than four passengers in a cab (it's illegal, unless the fifth person is a child under seven).

Not all drivers know their way around the city, so it helps if you know where you're going. If you have a problem, take down the medallion and driver's numbers, posted on the partition. Always ask for a receipt – there's a meter number on it. To complain or trace lost property, call the Taxi & Limousine Commission (1-212 227 0700, 8am-4pm Mon-Fri) or visit www.nyc.gov/taxi. It's common to tip 15-20 per cent.

Car services are also regulated by the Taxi & Limousine Commission. Unlike cabs, drivers can make only pre-arranged pickups. Don't try to hail one, and be wary of those that offer you a ride. The following companies will pick you up anywhere in the city, at any time, for a set fare.

Carmel *1-212 666 6666.*
Dial 7 *1-212 777 7777.*
Limores *1-212 777 7171.*

Driving
Car rental

Car rental is cheaper in the city's outskirts, and in New Jersey and Connecticut, than in Manhattan, although Upper West Side discount specialist **Aamcar** (1-800 722 6923, 1-212 222 8500, www.aamcar.com) offers competitive rates. Chains include **Alamo** (1-800 462 5266, www.alamo.com), **Budget** (1-800 527 0700, www.budget.com) and **Hertz** (1-800 654 3131, www.hertz.com). Rental companies in New York State are required by law to insure their own cars (the renter pays the first $100 in damage to the

vehicle). UK residents may find cheaper rental insurance on www.insurance4carhire.com.

Parking

Make sure you read parking signs and never park within 15 feet of a fire hydrant (to avoid a ticket and/or having your car towed). Parking is off-limits on most streets for at least a few hours daily. The Department of Transportation (dial 311) provides information on daily changes to regulations. If precautions fail, call 1-718 935 0096 for towing and impoundment information. **Central Parking System** (1-800 836 6666, www.centralparking.com) is the city's largest garage chain.

Cycling

Aside from the pleasurable cycling in Central Park, and along the wide bike paths around the perimeter of Manhattan (now virtually encircled by paths), biking in the city streets is not recommended for urban beginners. However, provision for cyclists is improving, thanks in part to the efforts of not-for-profit campaigning group **Transportation Alternatives** (1-212 629 8080, www.transalt.org); you can download cycling maps from a New York City Department of Transportation link on its website.

Bike rental

Bike and Roll (557 Twelfth Avenue, at 43rd Street, Midtown (1-212 260 0400, www.bikeandroll.com/newyork), conveniently located along the riverside cycle path, and **Loeb Boathouse** in Central Park (entrance on Fifth Avenue, at 72nd Street, 1-212 517 2233, www.centralparknyc.org) both rent out bikes.

ESSENTIALS

Resources A-Z

Accident & emergency

In the event of a serious accident, attack, fire or other emergency, call 911, free from any phone including pay phones, and specify whether you need the police, fire service or an ambulance. The following hospitals have emergency rooms:

Cabrini Medical Center *227 E 19th Street, between Second & Third Avenues, Gramercy Park (1-212 222 7464). Subway L to Third Avenue; N, Q, R, W, 4, 5, 6 to 14th Street-Union Square.*

New York – Presbyterian Hospital/Weill Cornell Medical Center *525 E 68th Street, at York Avenue, Upper East Side (1-212 746 5454). Subway 6 to 68th Street.*

St Luke's – Roosevelt Hospital *1,000 Tenth Avenue, at 59th Street, Upper West Side (1-212 523 6800). Subway A, B, C, D, 1 to 59th Street-Columbus Circle.*

St Vincent's Hospital *153 W 11th Street, at Seventh Avenue, West Village (1-212 604 7998). Subway F, V, 1, 2, 3 to 14th Street; L to Sixth Avenue.*

Credit card loss

American Express *1-800 528 2122.*
Diners Club *1-800 234 6377.*
Discover *1-800 347 2683.*
MasterCard/Maestro *1-800 826 2181*
Visa/Cirrus *1-800 336 8472.*

Customs

For allowances, see US Customs (www.customs.gov).

Dental emergencies

New York County Dental Society (1-212 573 8500, www. nycdentalsociety.org) can provide local referrals and operates an emergency line outside of office hours; alternatively, use the search facility on the website.

Disabled

Under New York law, all facilities constructed after 1987 must provide complete access for the disabled – restrooms, entrances and exits included. In 1990 the Americans with Disabilities Act made the same requirement federal law. In the wake of this legislation, many older buildings have added disabled-access features. There has been widespread (though imperfect) compliance with the law, but call ahead to check. *Access for All*, a guide to New York's cultural institutions published by **Hospital Audiences Inc** (1-212 575 7676, www.hospaud.org), is a useful online resource. All Broadway theatres are equipped with devices for the hearing-impaired; call **Sound Associates** (1-888 772 7686, www.soundassociates.com) for details. **Theatre Development Fund's Theater Access Project** (1-212 221 1103, www. tdf.org) arranges sign-language interpretation and captioning in American Sign Language for both Broadway and Off Broadway shows.

Electricity

The US uses 110-120V, 60-cycle alternating current rather than the 220-240V, 50-cycle AC. The transformers that power or recharge newer electronic devices such as laptops are designed to handle either current and may need nothing more than an adaptor for the wall outlet. Other appliances may also require a power converter. Adaptors and converters can be purchased at airport shops, pharmacies and branches of Radio Shack (www.radioshack.com).

Embassies & consulates

Check the phone book for a complete list of consulates and embassies.
Australia *1-212 351 6500.*
Canada *1-212 596 1628.*
Great Britain *1-212 745 0200.*
Ireland *1-212 319 2555.*
New Zealand *1-212 832 4038.*

Internet

There are dozens of hotspots in the city for free wireless access (and most parks below 59th Street are covered). Visit www.nycwireless. net for information and a map. Branches of the New York Public Library (www.nypl.org) throughout the five boroughs offer free internet access. The **Science, Industry & Business Library** (188 Madison Avenue, at 34th Street) has more than 40 workstations that you can use for up to an hour per day.

Cyber Café
250 W 49th Street, between Broadway & Eighth Avenue, Theater District (1-212 333 4109). Subway C, E, 1 to 50th Street; N, R, W to 49th Street. **Open** 8am-11pm Mon-Fri; 11am-11pm Sat, Sun.

Opening hours

The following are general guidelines.
Banks 9am-5pm Mon-Fri; sometimes also Saturday mornings.
Businesses 9am-5pm Mon-Fri.
Bars 4pm-2am Mon-Thur, Sun; noon-4am Fri, Sat (hours vary).

Shops 9am or 10am-7pm Mon-Sat (some until 9pm). Many are also open on Sunday, usually 11am-6pm.

Police

The NYPD stations below are in central, tourist-heavy areas of Manhattan. For the location of your nearest police precinct or information about police services, call 1-646 610 5000.
Midtown North Precinct *306 W 54th Street, between Eighth & Ninth Avenues, Hell's Kitchen (1-212 760 8300).*
17th Precinct *167 E 51st Street, between Third & Lexington Avenues, Midtown East (1-212 826 3211).*
Central Park Precinct *86th Street & Transverse Road, Central Park (1-212 570 4820).*

Post

Post offices are usually open from 9am to 5pm Monday to Friday (a few open as early as 7.30am and close as late as 8.30pm); sometimes also Saturday mornings. The **General Post Office** (421 Eighth Avenue, between 31st & 33rd Streets, Garment District) is open 24/7. For general enquiries, call 1-800 275 8777 or consult www.usps.com.

Smoking

The 1995 NYC Smoke-Free Air Act makes it illegal to smoke in virtually all indoor public places. Some bars and restaurants offer smoking gardens or terraces.

Telephones

As a rule, you must dial 1 + the area code before a number, even if the place you are calling is in the same area code. The area codes for Manhattan are 212 and 646;

Brooklyn, Queens, Staten Island and the Bronx are 718 and 347; 917 is reserved mostly for mobile phones and pagers. Numbers preceded by 800, 877 and 888 are free of charge when dialled from within the US.

To dial abroad from the US, dial 011 followed by the country code, then the number. For the operator dial 0.

Mobile phone users from outside the US will need a tri-band handset.

Most public payphones take coins or credit cards. The best way to make long-distance calls is with a phone card, available from the post office, chain drugstores like Duane Reade or Rite Aid and some newspaper and convenience stores.

Tickets

While it's cheaper to buy tickets for performances directly from the venue, many of them don't offer this option, especially when it comes to booking online. The main booking agencies for concerts and other events are **Ticketmaster** (1-212 307 4100, www.ticketmaster. com) and **TicketWeb** (1-866 468 7619, www.ticketweb.com), while **Telecharge** (1-212 239 6200, www.telecharge.com) specialises in Broadway and Off Broadway shows.

Time

New York is on Eastern Standard Time. This is five hours behind Greenwich Mean Time. Clocks are set forward one hour in early March for Daylight Saving Time (Eastern Daylight Time) and back one hour at the beginning of November. Going from east to west, Eastern Time is one hour ahead of Central Time, two hours ahead of Mountain Time and three hours ahead of Pacific Time.

Tipping

In the US, it's customary to tip 15-20 per cent of the tab in taxis, restaurants, bars, hotels and hairdressers. A quick way to calculate the tip on a restaurant bill is to double the tax.

Tourist information

NYC Information Center 810 *Seventh Avenue, between 52nd & 53rd Streets, Theater District (1-646 484 1200/www.nycgo.com). Subway B, D, E to Seventh Avenue.* **Open** 8.30am-6pm Mon-Fri; 9am-5pm Sat, Sun. See website for further locations.

Visas

Some 27 countries currently participate in the Visa Waiver Program (VWP). Citizens of Andorra, Australia, Austria, Belgium, Brunei, Denmark, Finland, France, Germany, Iceland, Ireland, Italy, Japan, Liechtenstein, Luxembourg, Monaco, the Netherlands, New Zealand, Norway, Portugal, San Marino, Singapore, Slovenia, Spain, Sweden, Switzerland and the UK do not need a visa for stays in the US shorter than 90 days (business or pleasure) as long as they have a machine-readable passport valid for the full 90-day period and a return ticket. If you do not qualify for entry under the VWP, you will need a visa; check before travelling.

What's on

The weekly *Time Out New York* magazine, which hits newsstands on Wednesdays, is NYC's essential arts and entertainment guide. The best sources for all things gay are *HX* and *Next*, available at bars and eateries catering to the LGBT crowd; girls should pick up *Go*.

ESSENTIALS

Index

Sights & Areas

a
Abyssinian Baptist Church p157
AIA Center for Architecture p93
American Folk Art Museum p129
American Museum of Natural History p149
Apollo Theater p159

b
Bloomingdale's p148
Bronx, The p160
Bronx Zoo p160
Brooklyn p161
Brooklyn Botanic Garden p161
Brooklyn Bridge p162
Brooklyn Museum p163

c
Carnegie Hall p128
Cathedral Church of St John the Divine p150
Central Park p137
Chelsea p104
Chinatown p75
Chrysler Building p134
Circle Line Cruises p122
City Hall p59
Cloisters, The p158
Cooper-Hewitt, National Design Museum p144

d
Downtown p58

e
East Village p85
Ellis Island Immigration Museum p67
Empire State Building p129

f
Federal Reserve Bank p59
Fifth Avenue p129
Financial District p58
Flatiron Building p115
Flatiron District p114
Fraunces Tavern Museum p59
Frick Collection p144

g
Garment District p120
Governors Island p59
Gramercy Park p118
Grand Central Terminal p135
Greenwich Village p93
Green-Wood Cemetery p163
Ground Zero p65

h
Harlem p157
Hell's Kitchen p122
Herald Square p120

i
International Center of Photography p130
Intrepid Sea-Air-Space Museum p123
Isamu Noguchi Garden Museum p164

j
Jazz at Lincoln Center p155
Jewish Museum p144

l
Lenox Lounge p159
Little Italy p75
Lower East Side p78
Lower East Side Tenement Museum p78

m
Macy's p121
Madison Square Garden p122
Madison Square Park p115
Meatpacking District p98
Metropolitan Museum of Art p144
Midtown p104
Midtown East p134
Morgan Library & Museum p118
Murray Hill p118
Museo del Barrio, El p146
Museum at Eldridge Street (Eldridge Street Synagogue) p79
Museum at FIT p104
Museum of American Finance p65
Museum of Arts & Design p150
Museum of Chinese in America p76

Museum of Modern Art (MoMA) p130
Museum of Sex p115
Museum of the City of New York p146

n
National Museum of the American Indian p65
Neue Galerie p146
New Museum of Contemporary Art p79
New York Botanical Garden p160
New-York Historical Society p151
New York Public Library p130
Nolita p75

p
Paley Center for Media p131
Performance Space 122 p92
P.S.1 Contemporary Art Center p164

q
Queens p164
Queens Museum of Art p166

r
Radio City Music Hall p134
Ripley's Believe It or Not! Odditorium p123
Rock & Roll Hall of Fame Annex NYC p69
Rockefeller Center p131
Rose Center for Earth & Space p149
Rubin Museum of Art p105

s
St Patrick's Cathedral p131
St Paul's Chapel & Trinity Church p65
Skyscraper Museum p66
Soho p68
Solomon R Guggenheim Museum p147
South Street Seaport Museum p66
Staten Island Ferry p66
Statue of Liberty p67
Studio Museum in Harlem p158

ESSENTIALS

ESSENTIALS

WWW.VISITBROOKLYN.ORG   718.802.3846

THE BROOKLYN TOURISM & VISITORS CENTER
HISTORIC BROOKLYN BOROUGH HALL, GROUND FLOOR
209 JORALEMON ST. (BTW COURT/ADAMS), BROOKLYN, NY 11201
SUBWAY - BOROUGH HALL STOP: M R 2 3 4 5 A C F
OPEN MONDAY-FRIDAY 10AM-6PM (SATURDAY SEASONAL)